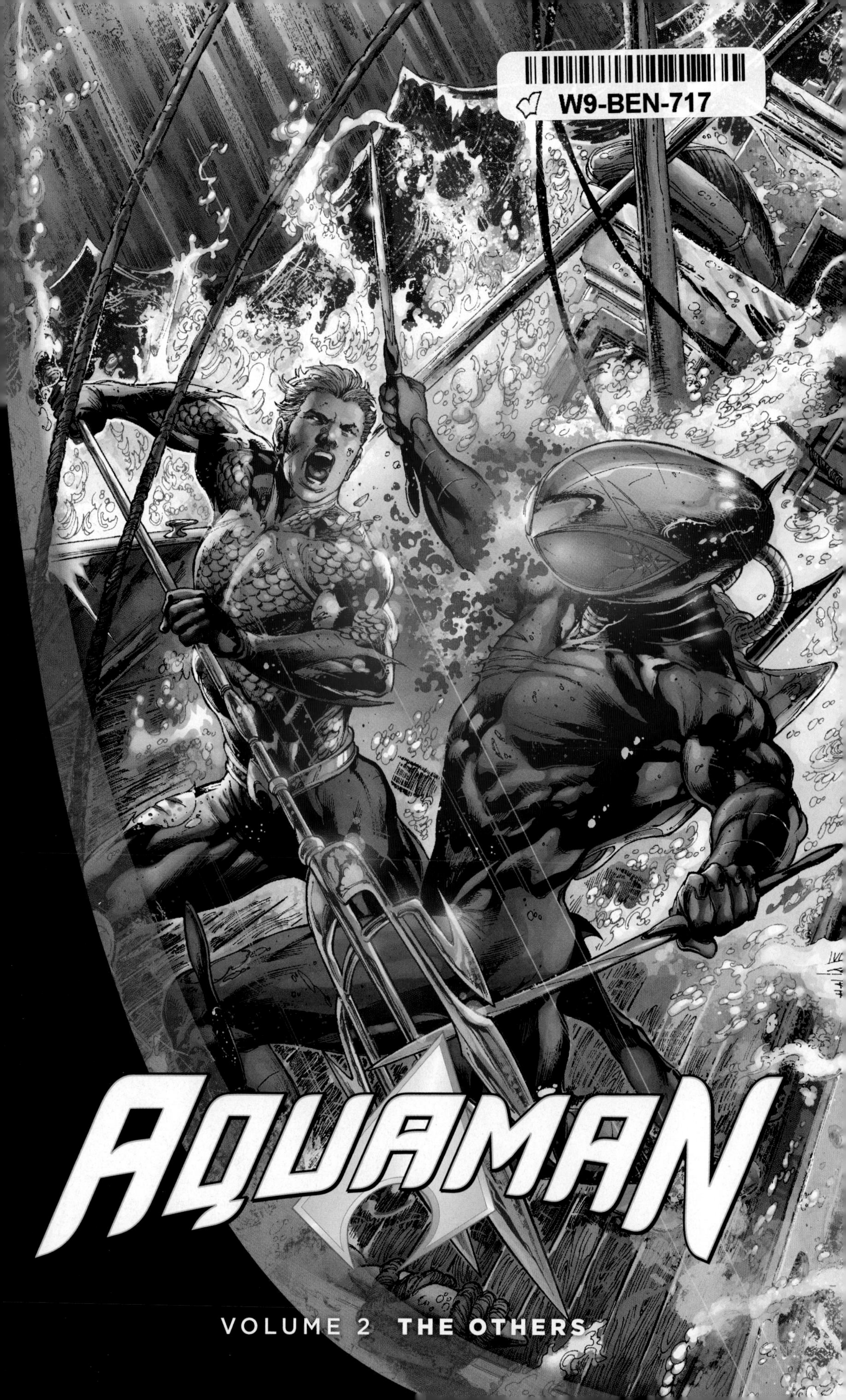

AQUAMAN

VOLUME 2 THE OTHERS

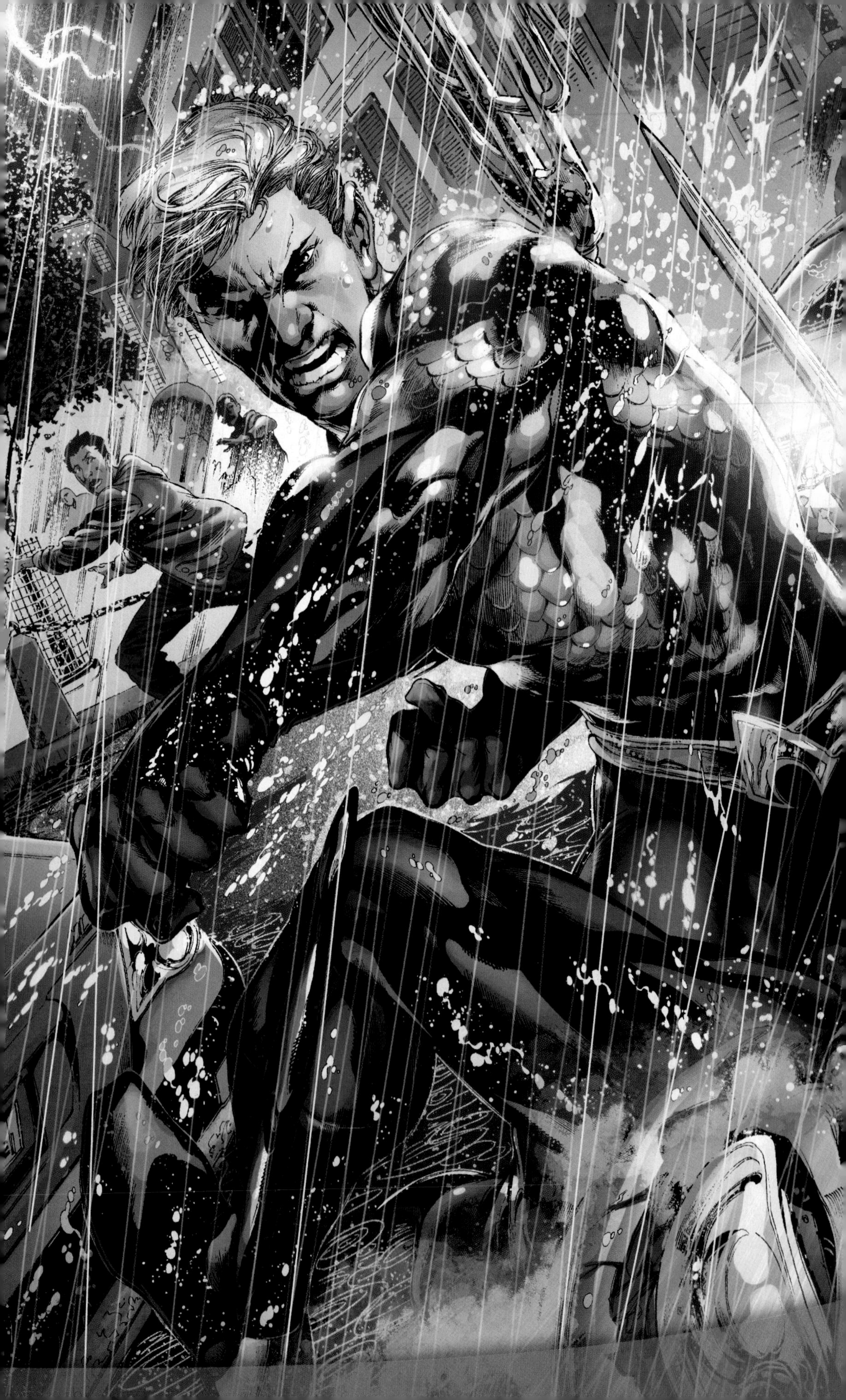

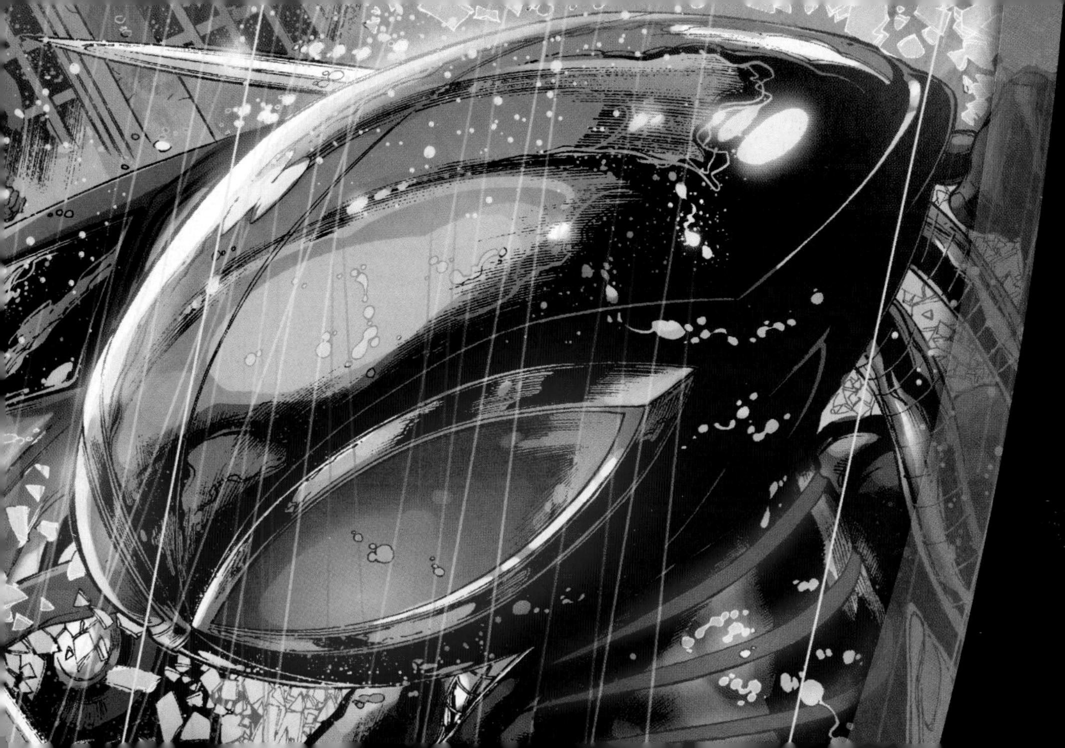

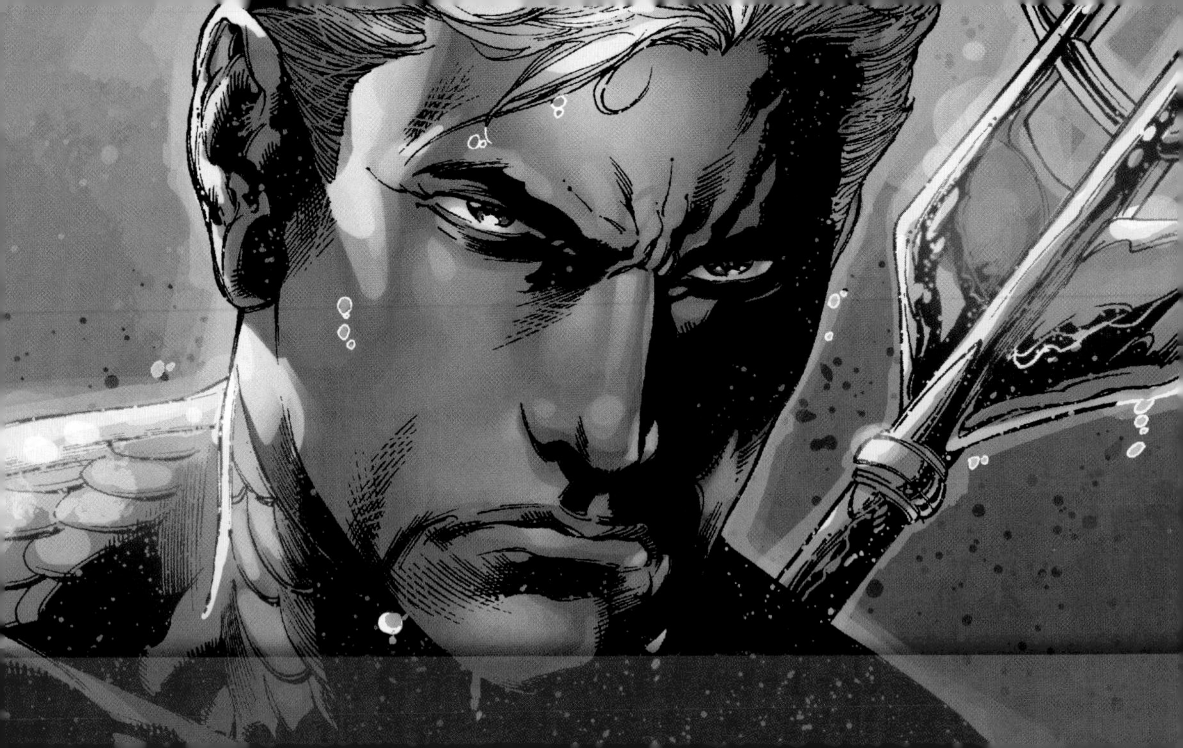

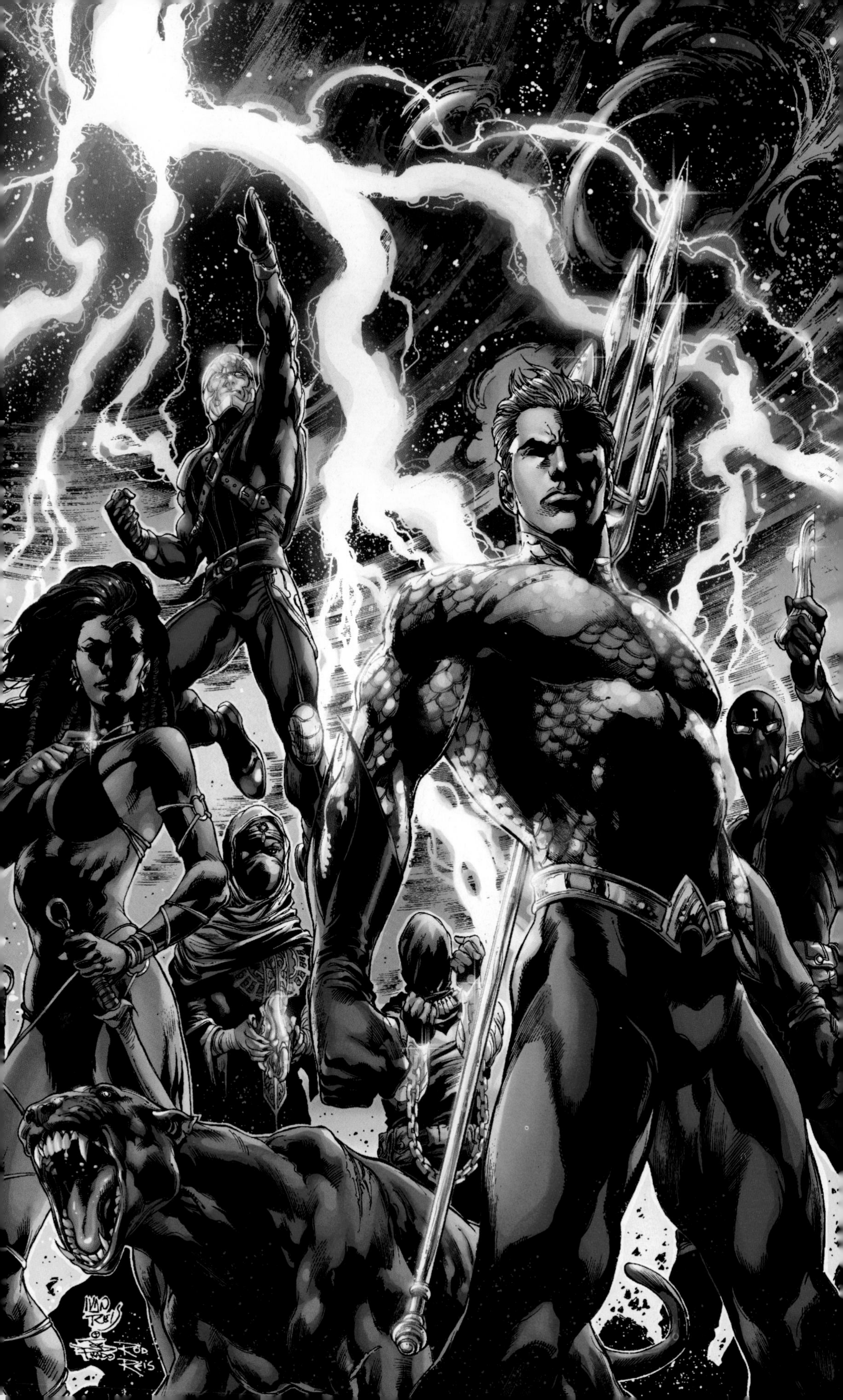
IVAN REIS
ROD REIS

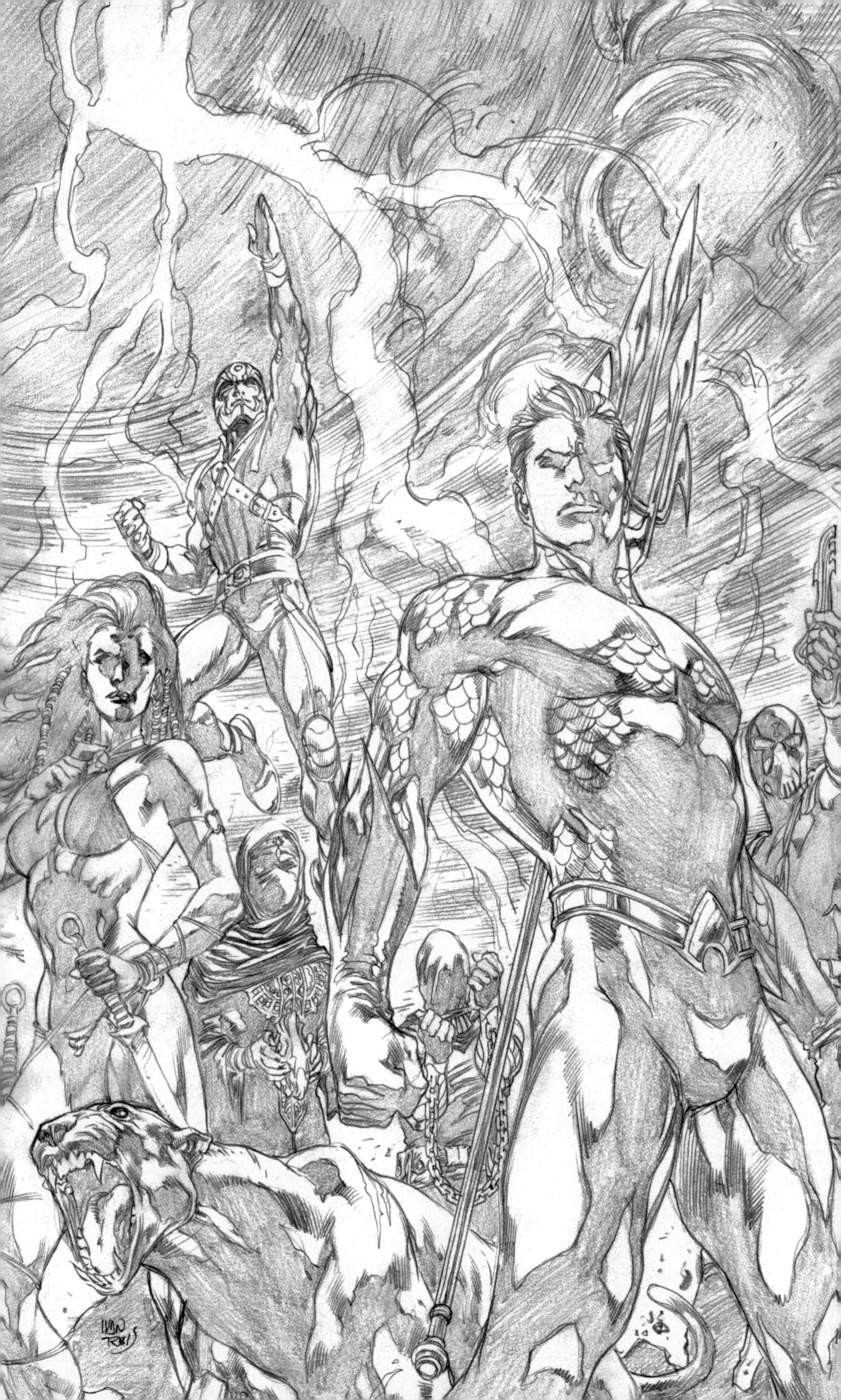

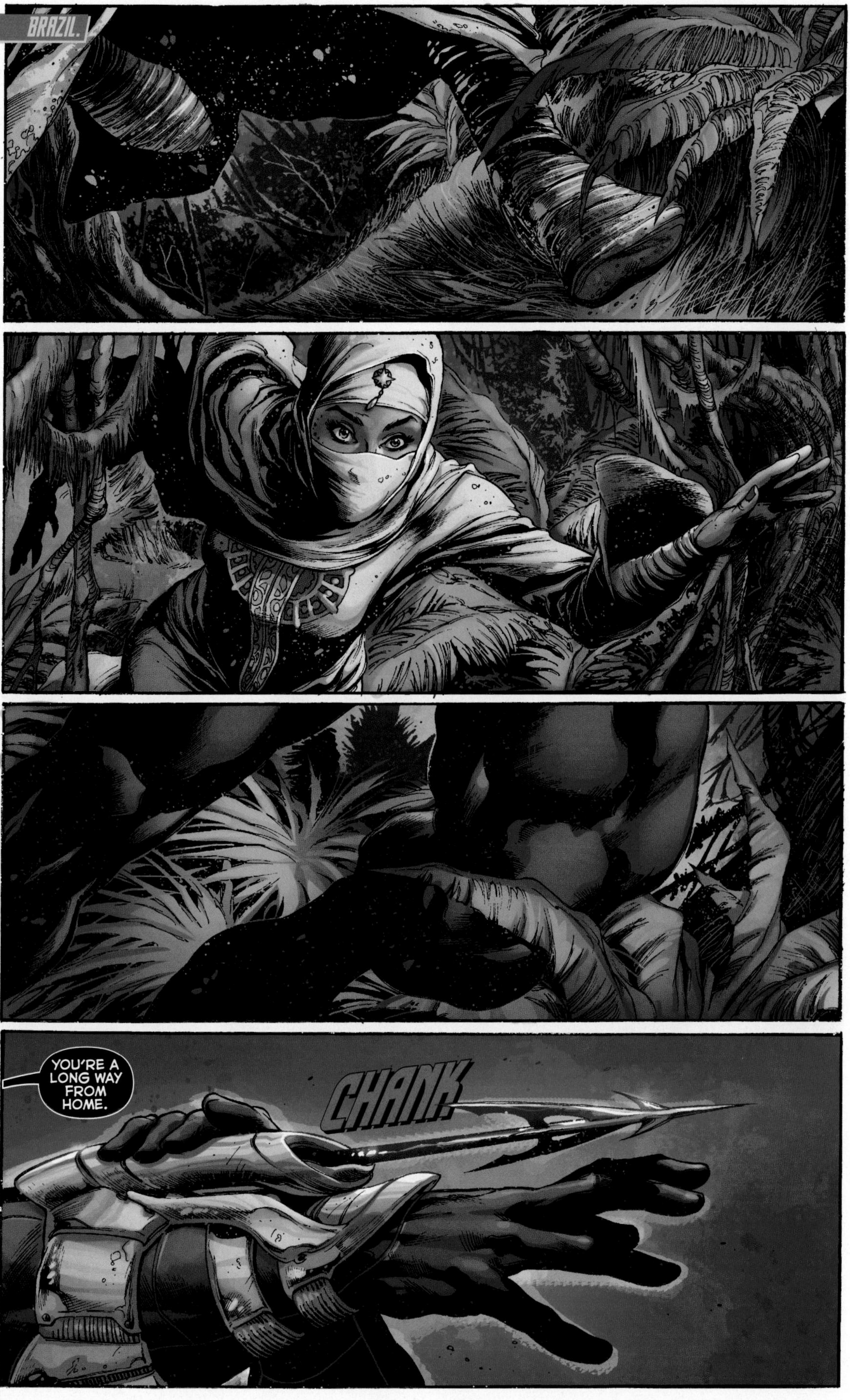
BRAZIL.
YOU'RE A LONG WAY FROM HOME.
CHANK

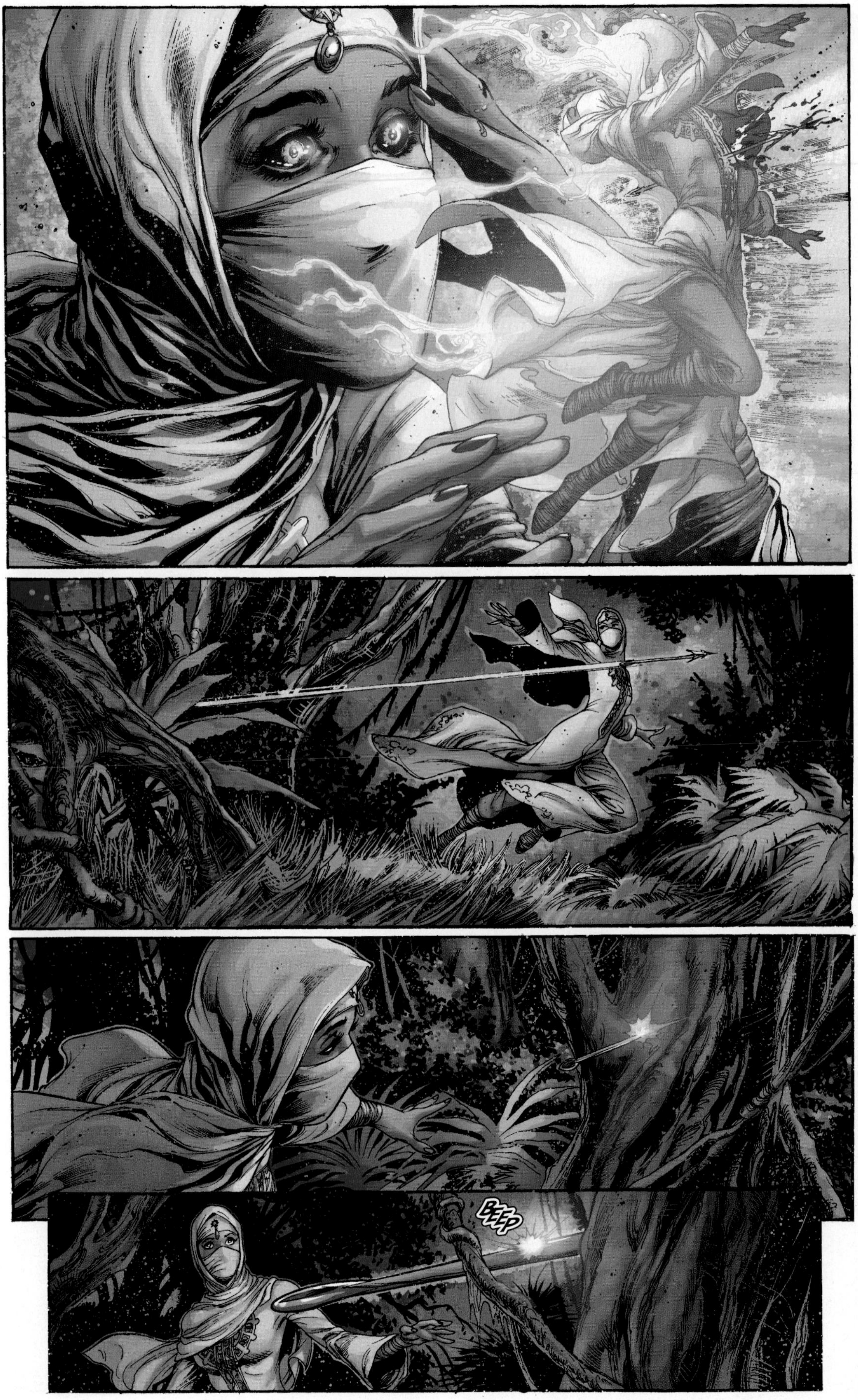
BEEP

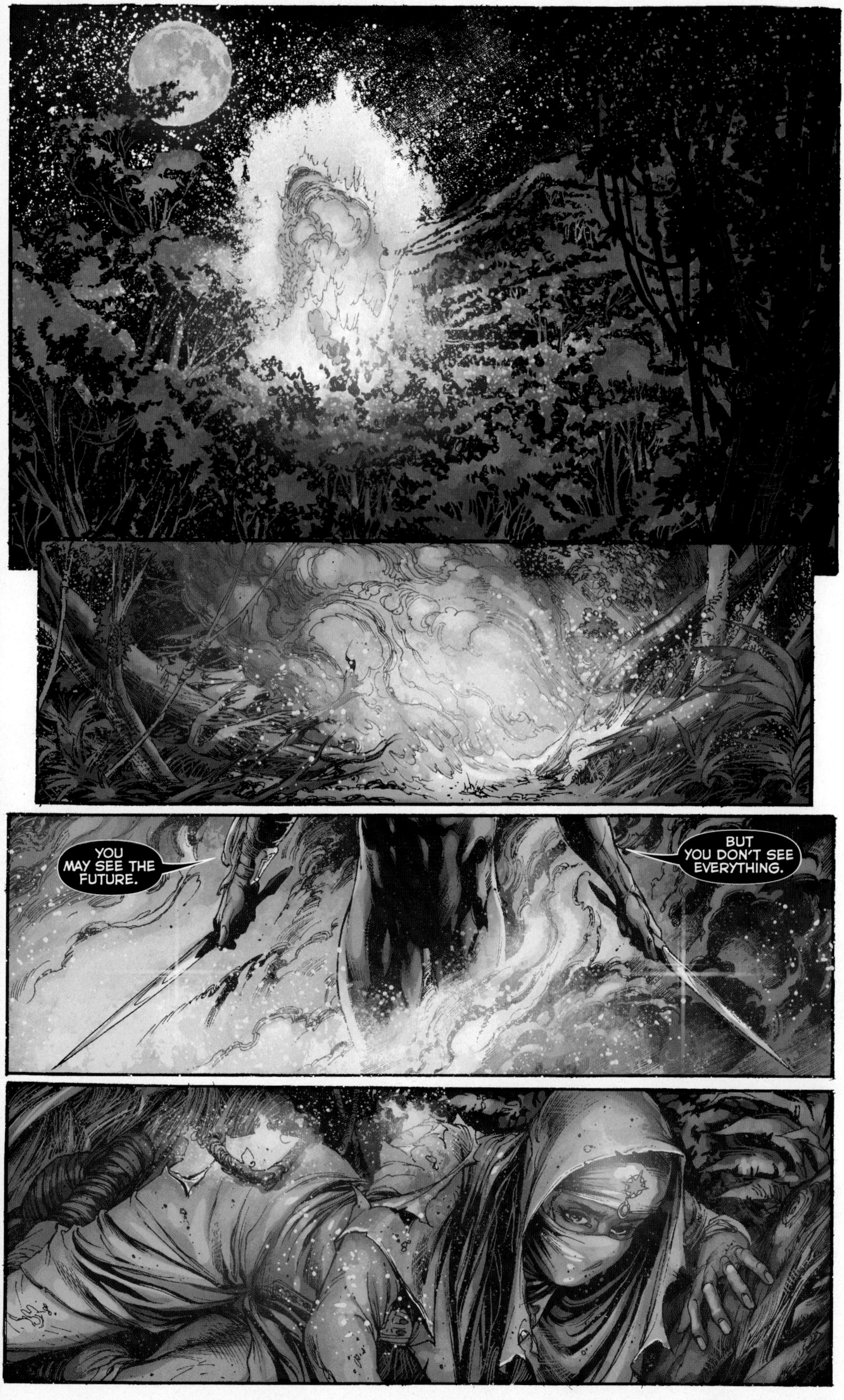
YOU MAY SEE THE FUTURE.
BUT YOU DON'T SEE EVERYTHING.

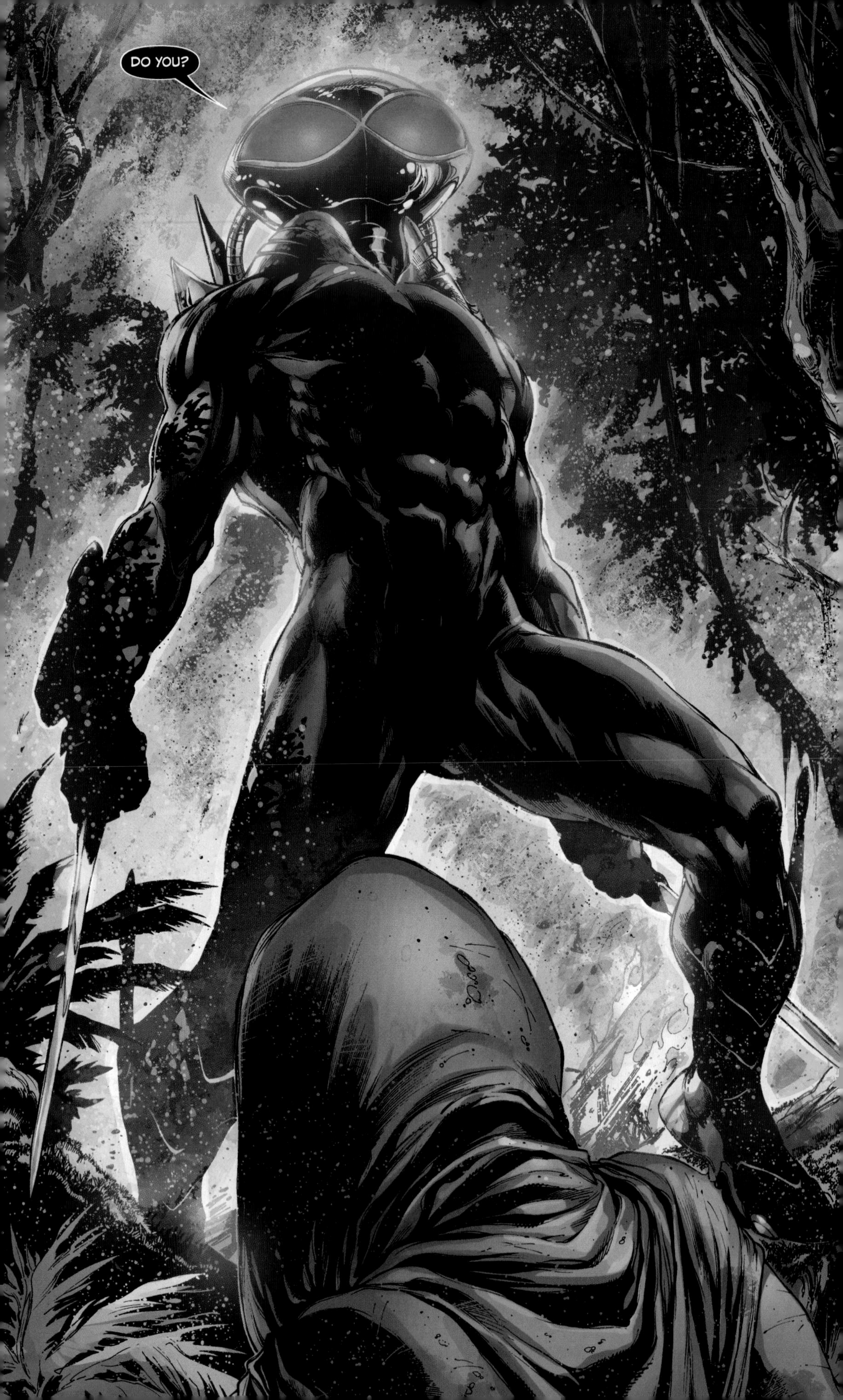
DO YOU?

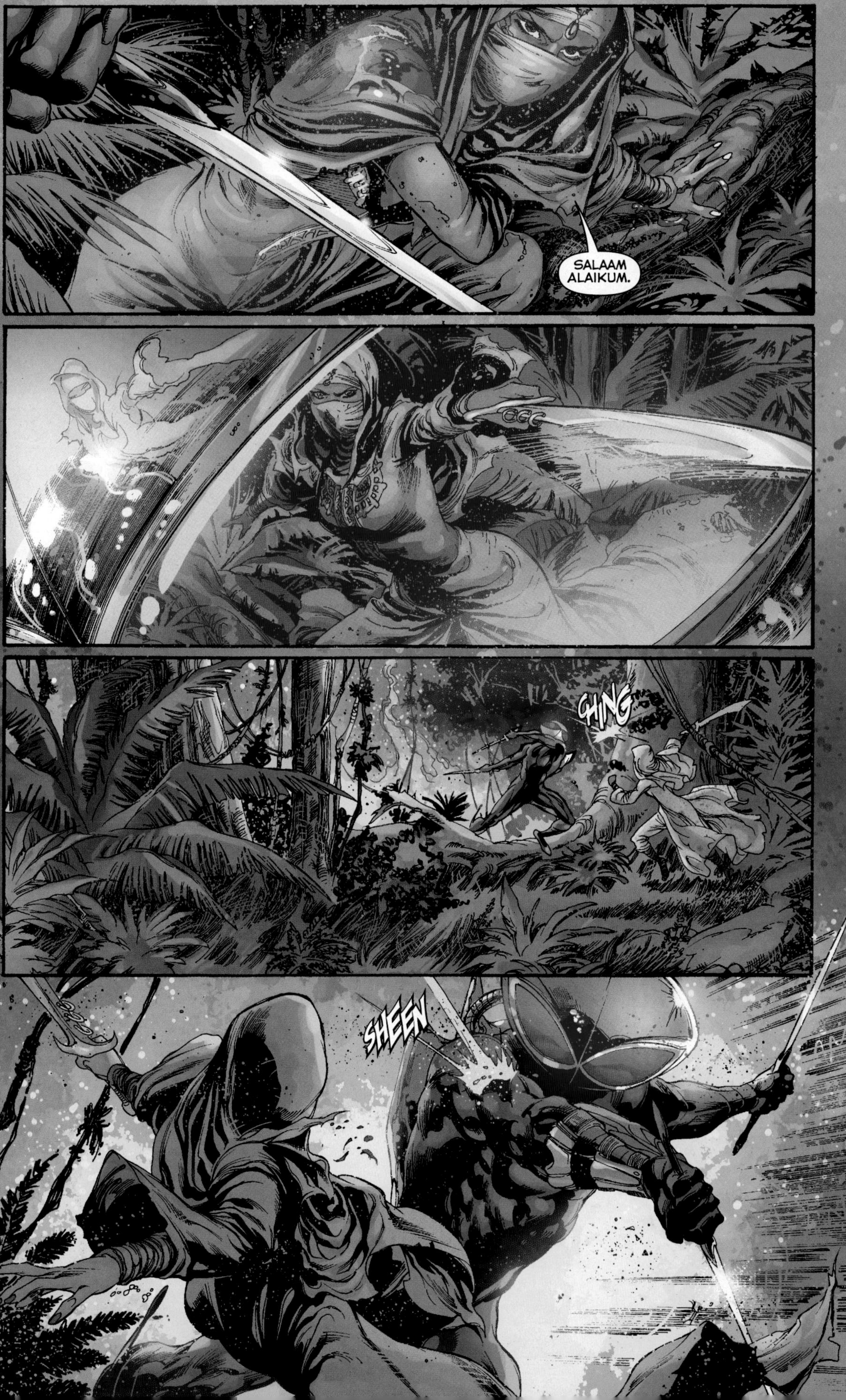
SALAAM ALAIKUM.
CHING
SHEEN

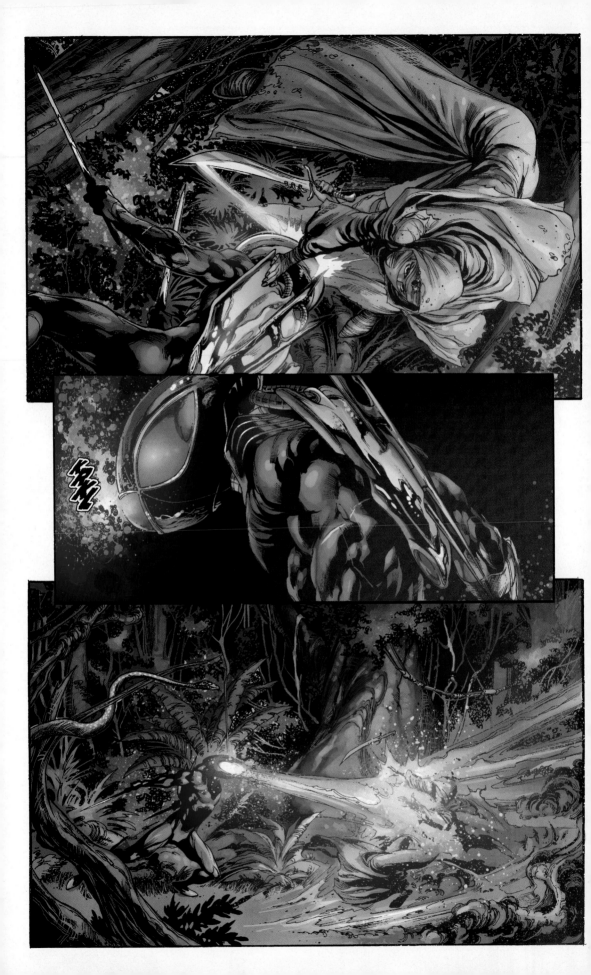

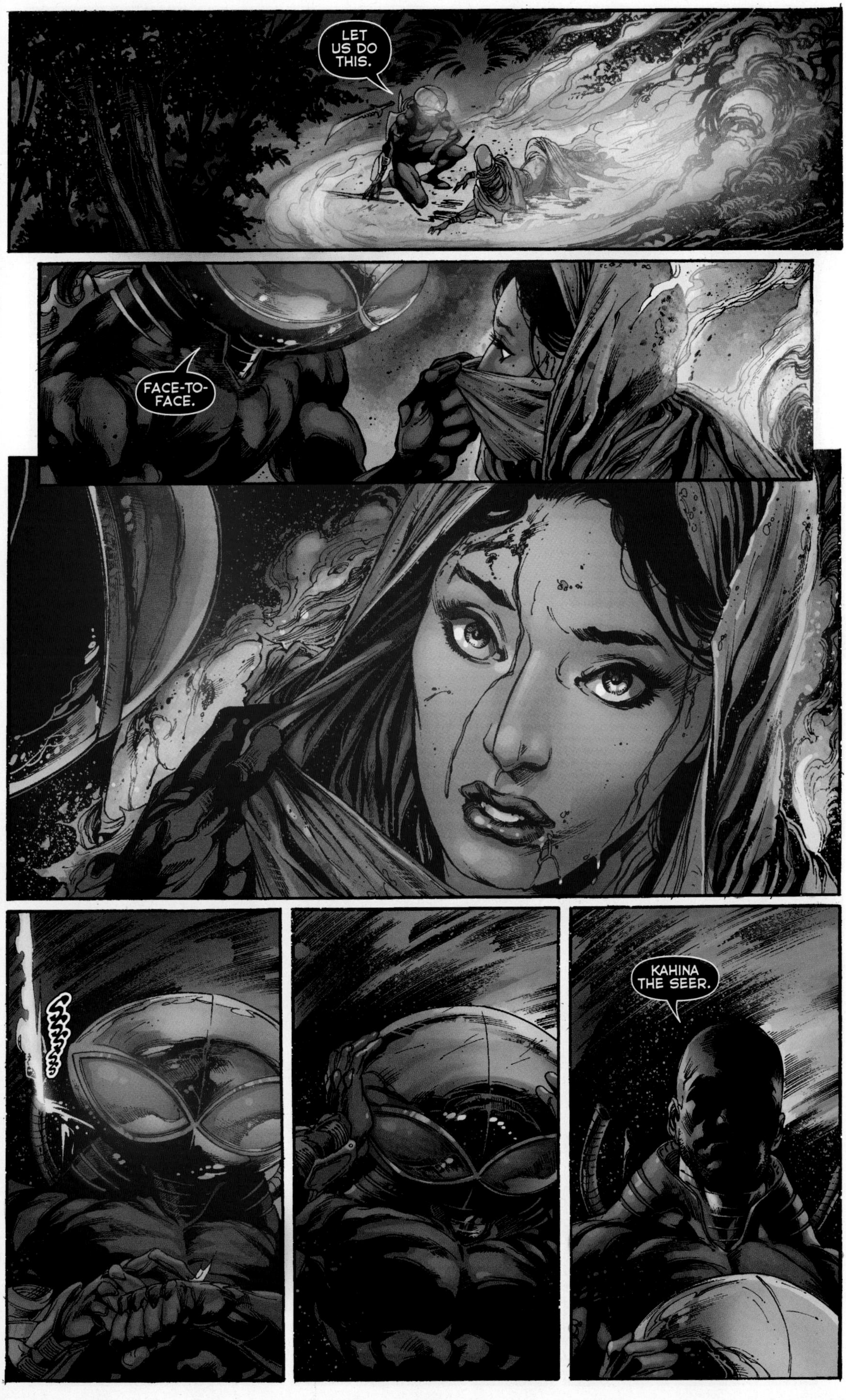
LET US DO THIS.
FACE-TO-FACE.
KAHINA THE SEER.

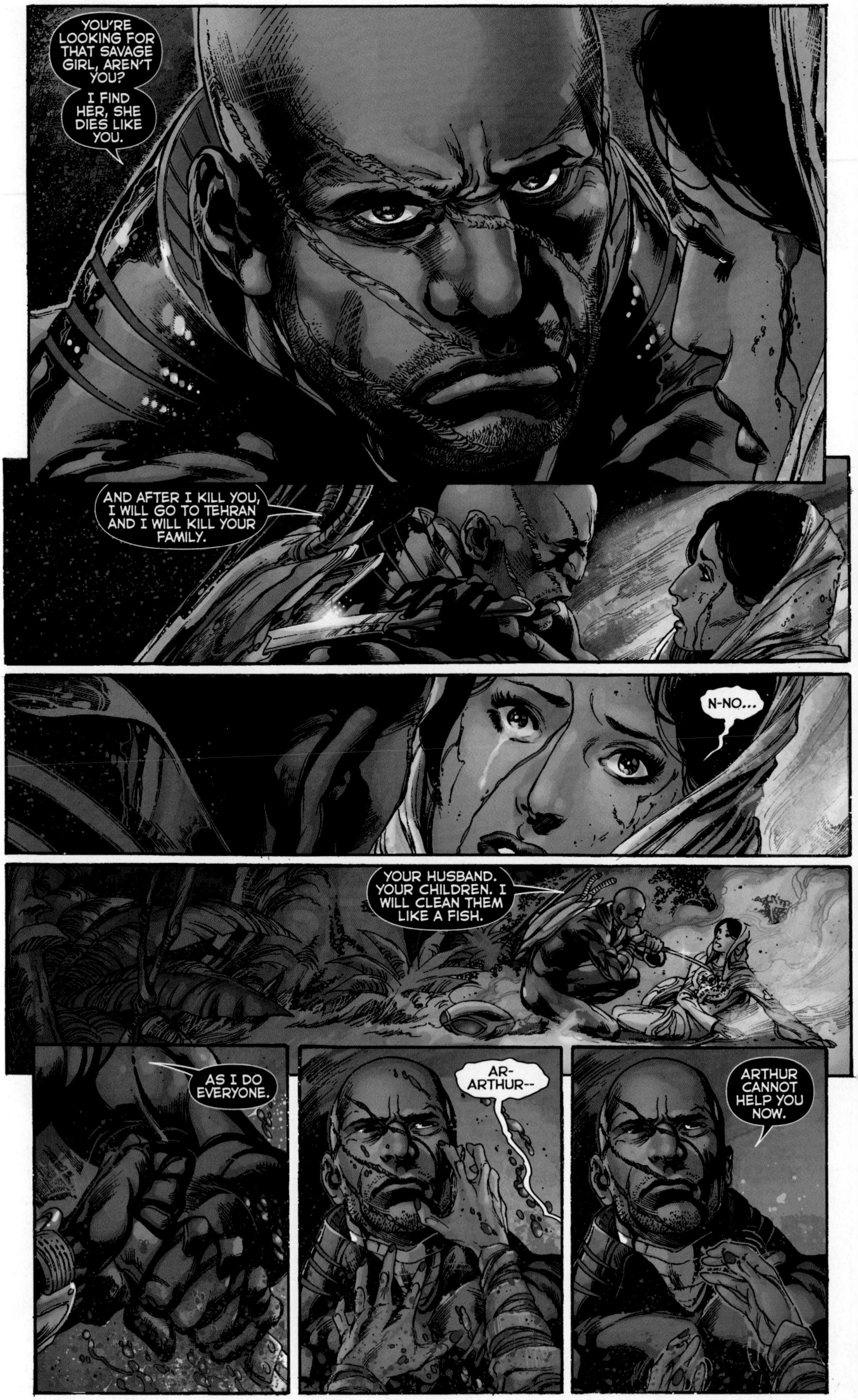
YOU'RE LOOKING FOR THAT SAVAGE GIRL, AREN'T YOU?
I FIND HER, SHE DIES LIKE YOU.
AND AFTER I KILL YOU, I WILL GO TO TEHRAN AND I WILL KILL YOUR FAMILY.
N-NO...
YOUR HUSBAND. YOUR CHILDREN. I WILL CLEAN THEM LIKE A FISH.
AS I DO EVERYONE.
AR-ARTHUR--
ARTHUR CANNOT HELP YOU NOW.

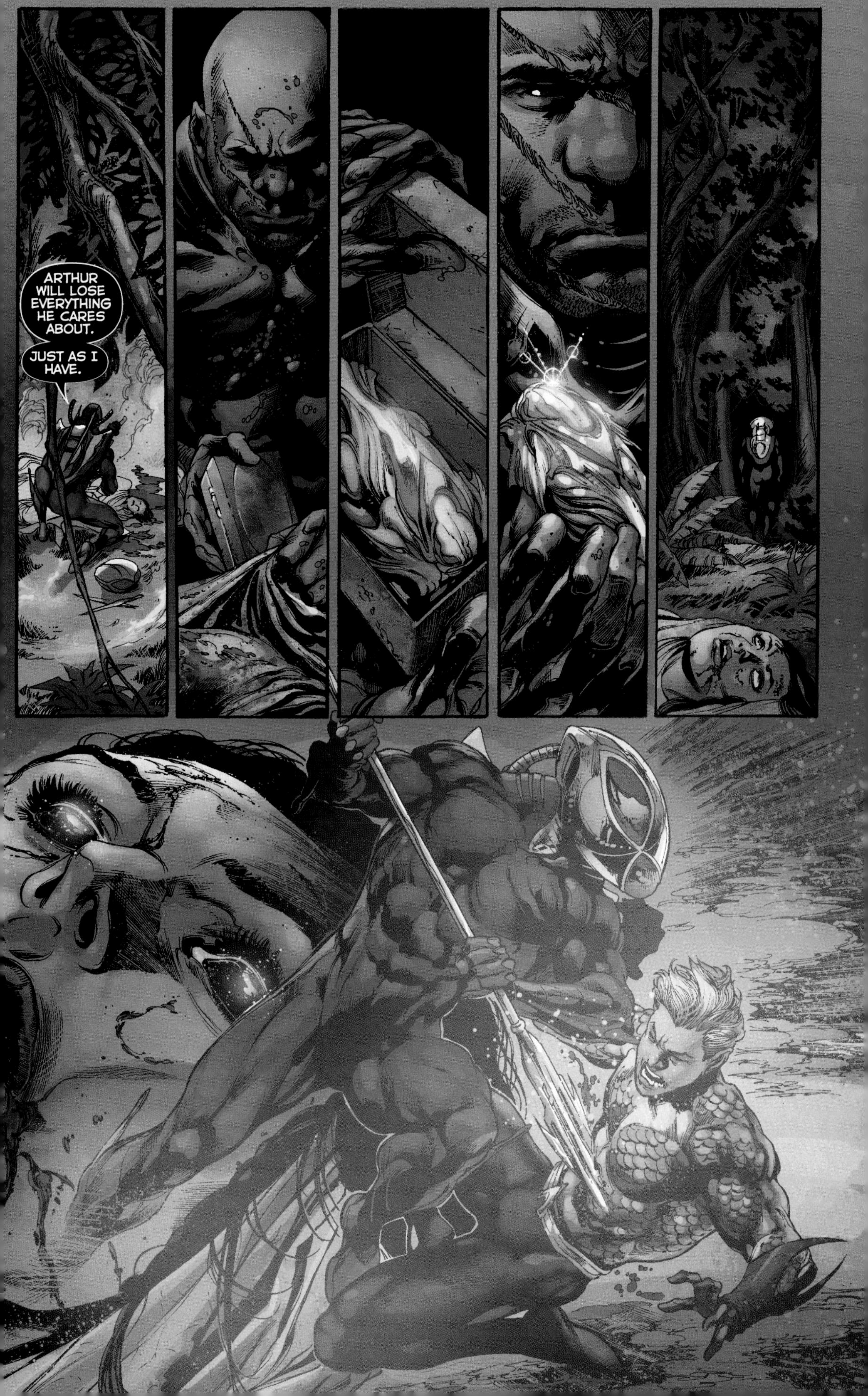
ARTHUR WILL LOSE EVERYTHING HE CARES ABOUT.
JUST AS I HAVE.

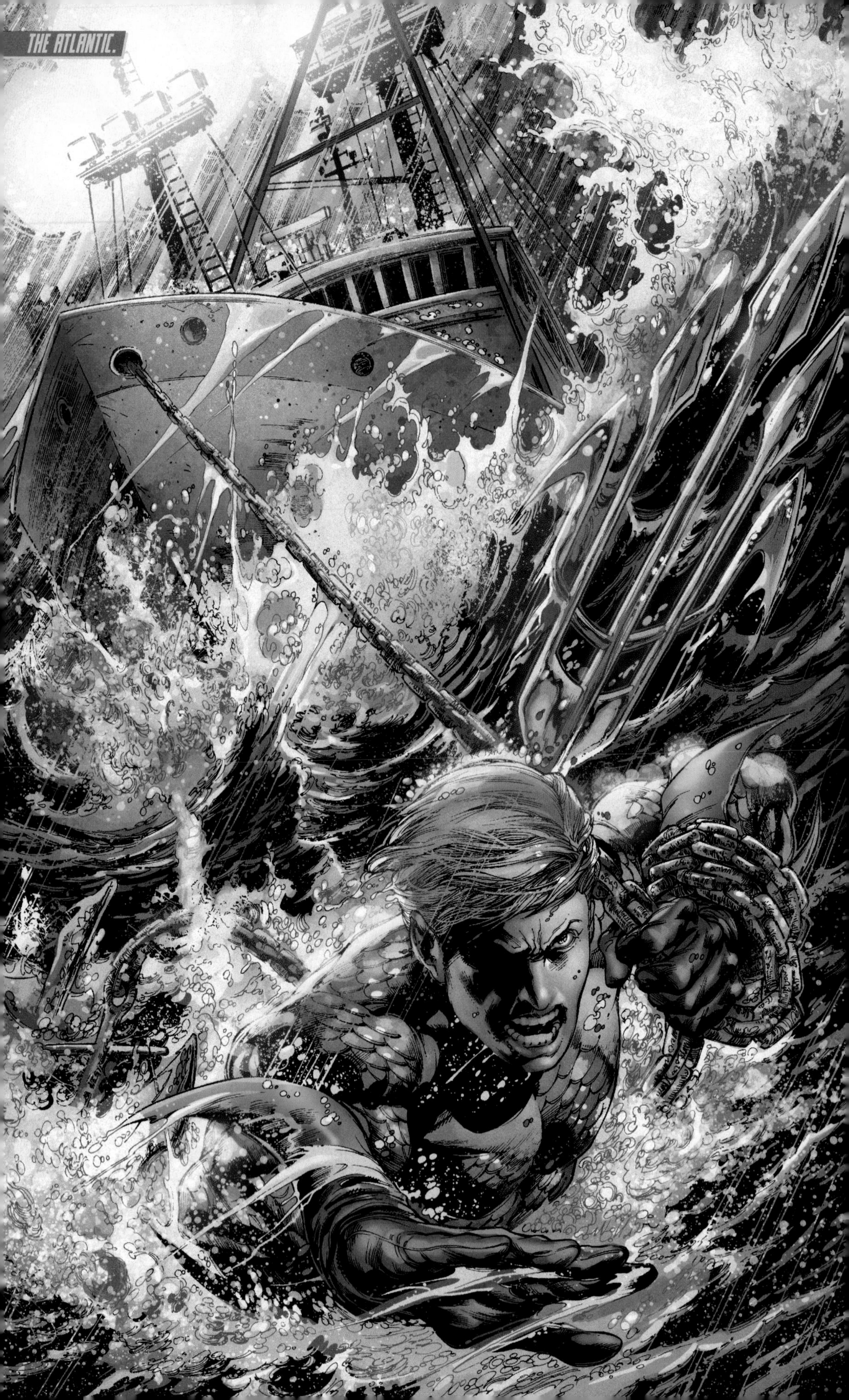
THE ATLANTIC.

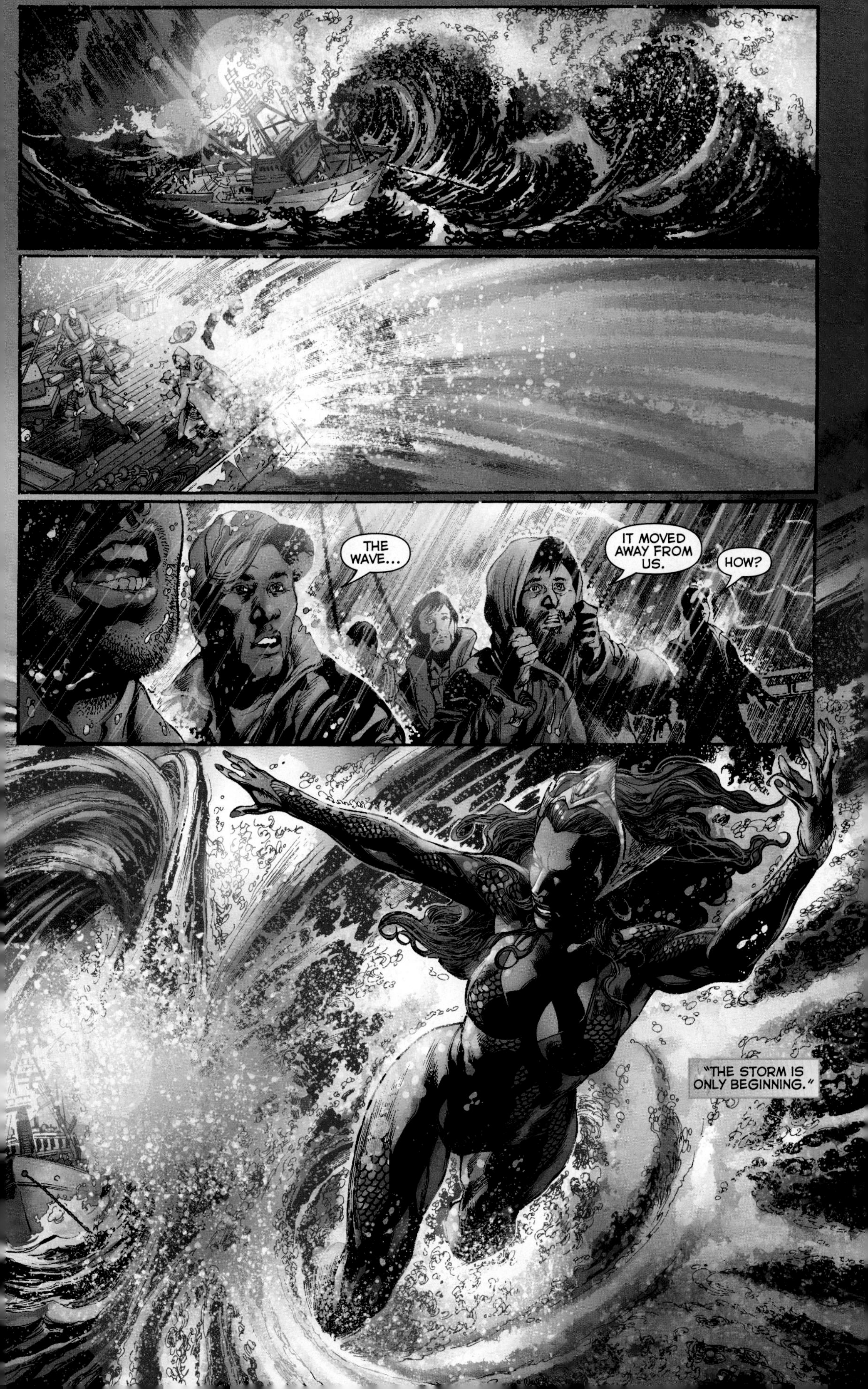
THE WAVE...
IT MOVED AWAY FROM US.
HOW?
"THE STORM IS ONLY BEGINNING."

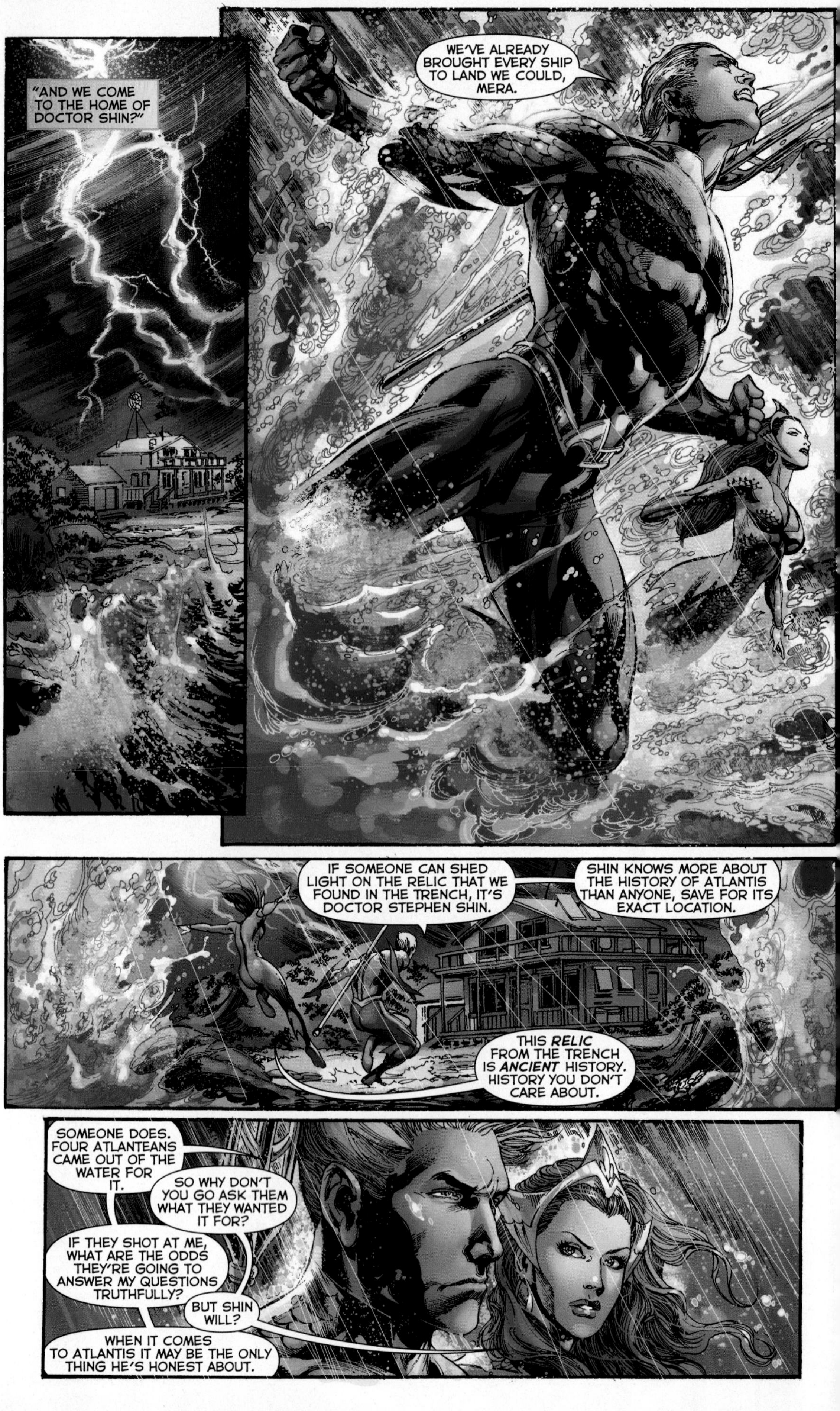
"AND WE COME TO THE HOME OF DOCTOR SHIN?"
WE'VE ALREADY BROUGHT EVERY SHIP TO LAND WE COULD, MERA.
IF SOMEONE CAN SHED LIGHT ON THE RELIC THAT WE FOUND IN THE TRENCH, IT'S DOCTOR STEPHEN SHIN.
SHIN KNOWS MORE ABOUT THE HISTORY OF ATLANTIS THAN ANYONE, SAVE FOR ITS EXACT LOCATION.
THIS RELIC FROM THE TRENCH IS ANCIENT HISTORY. HISTORY YOU DON'T CARE ABOUT.
SOMEONE DOES. FOUR ATLANTEANS CAME OUT OF THE WATER FOR IT.
SO WHY DON'T YOU GO ASK THEM WHAT THEY WANTED IT FOR?
IF THEY SHOT AT ME, WHAT ARE THE ODDS THEY'RE GOING TO ANSWER MY QUESTIONS TRUTHFULLY?
BUT SHIN WILL?
WHEN IT COMES TO ATLANTIS IT MAY BE THE ONLY THING HE'S HONEST ABOUT.

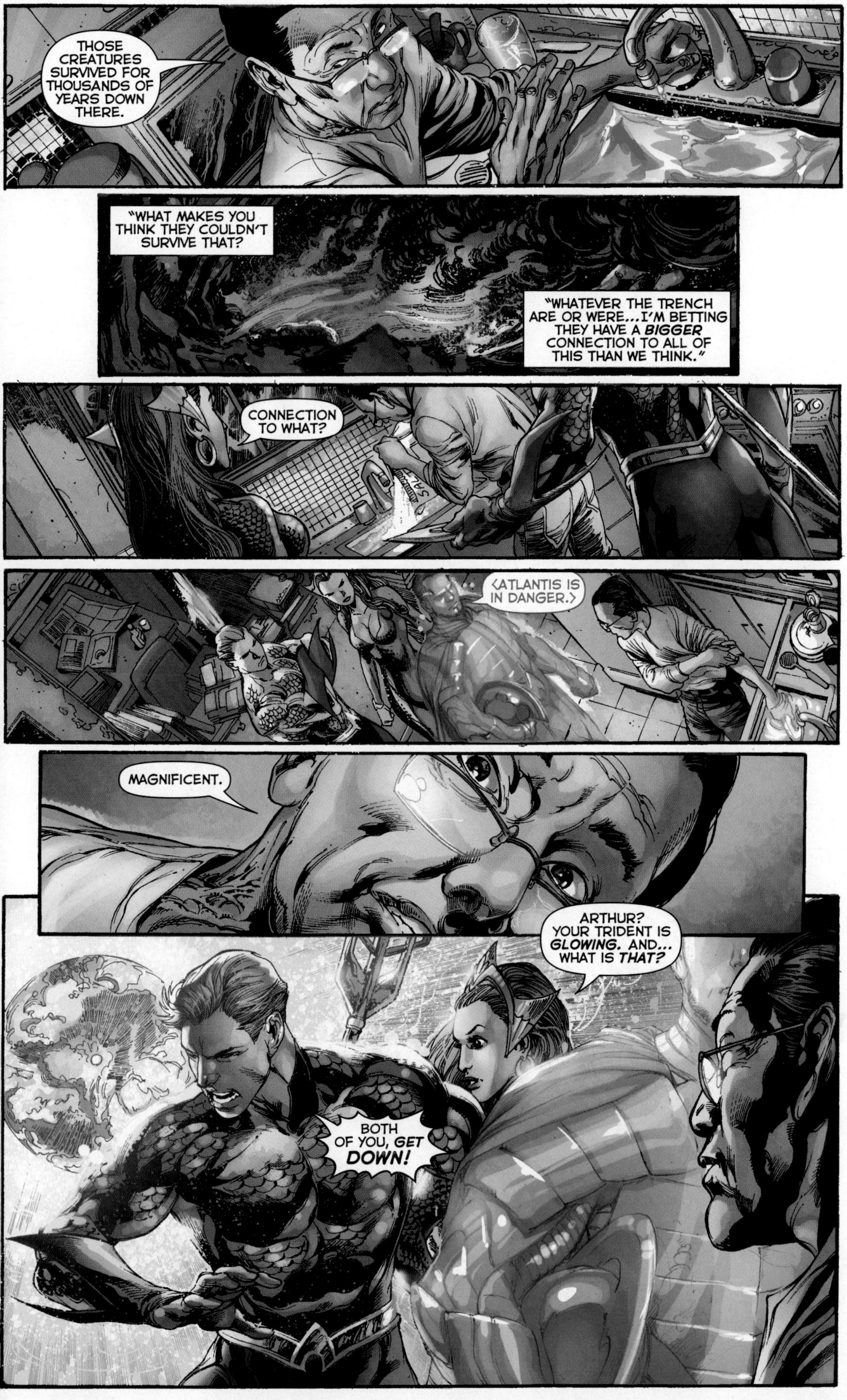
THOSE CREATURES SURVIVED FOR THOUSANDS OF YEARS DOWN THERE.
"WHAT MAKES YOU THINK THEY COULDN'T SURVIVE THAT?
"WHATEVER THE TRENCH ARE OR WERE...I'M BETTING THEY HAVE A *BIGGER* CONNECTION TO ALL OF THIS THAN WE THINK."
CONNECTION TO WHAT?
<ATLANTIS IS IN DANGER.>
MAGNIFICENT.
ARTHUR? YOUR TRIDENT IS *GLOWING.* AND... WHAT IS *THAT?*
BOTH OF YOU, *GET DOWN!*

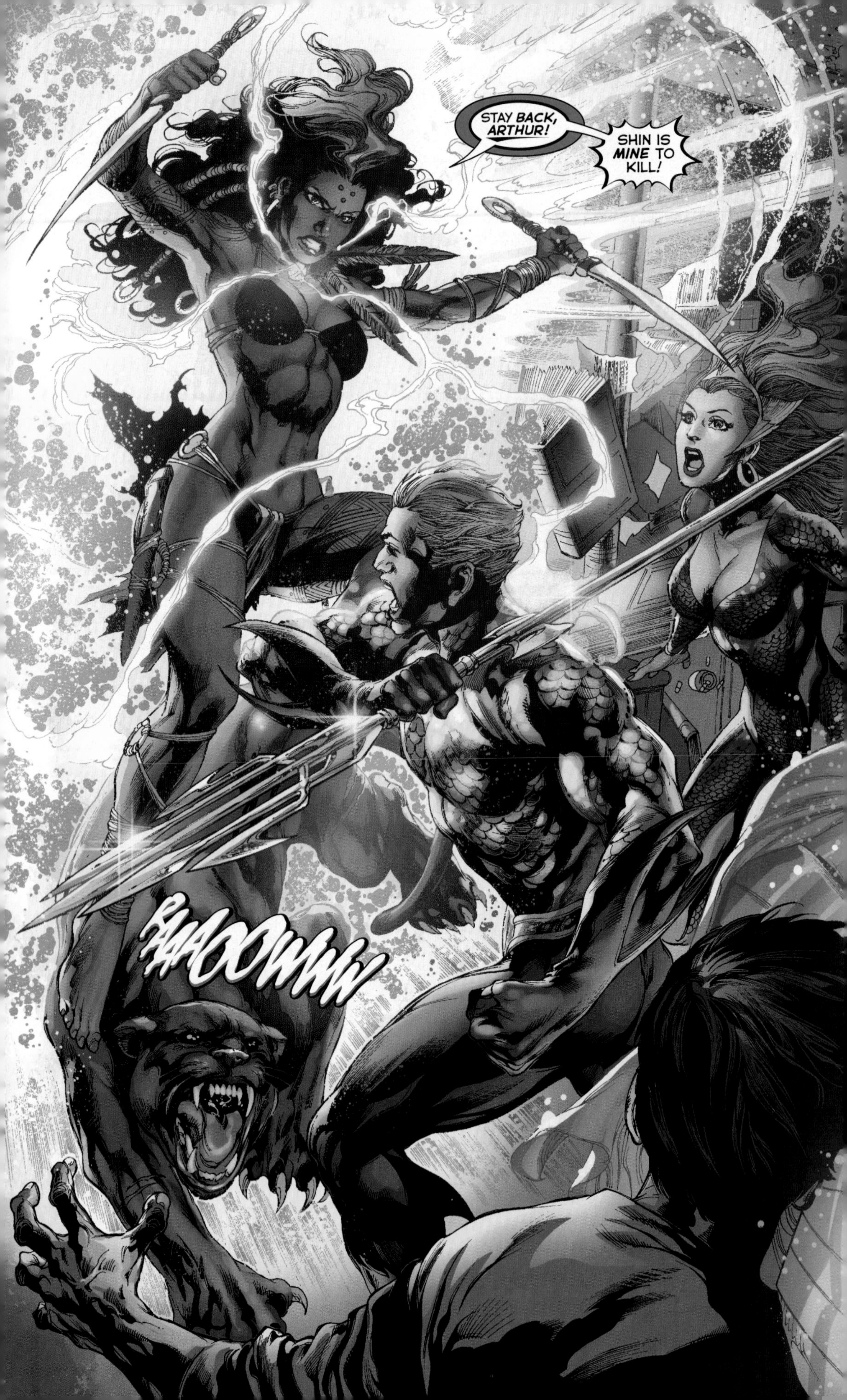
STAY BACK, ARTHUR!
SHIN IS MINE TO KILL!
RAAOOWWW

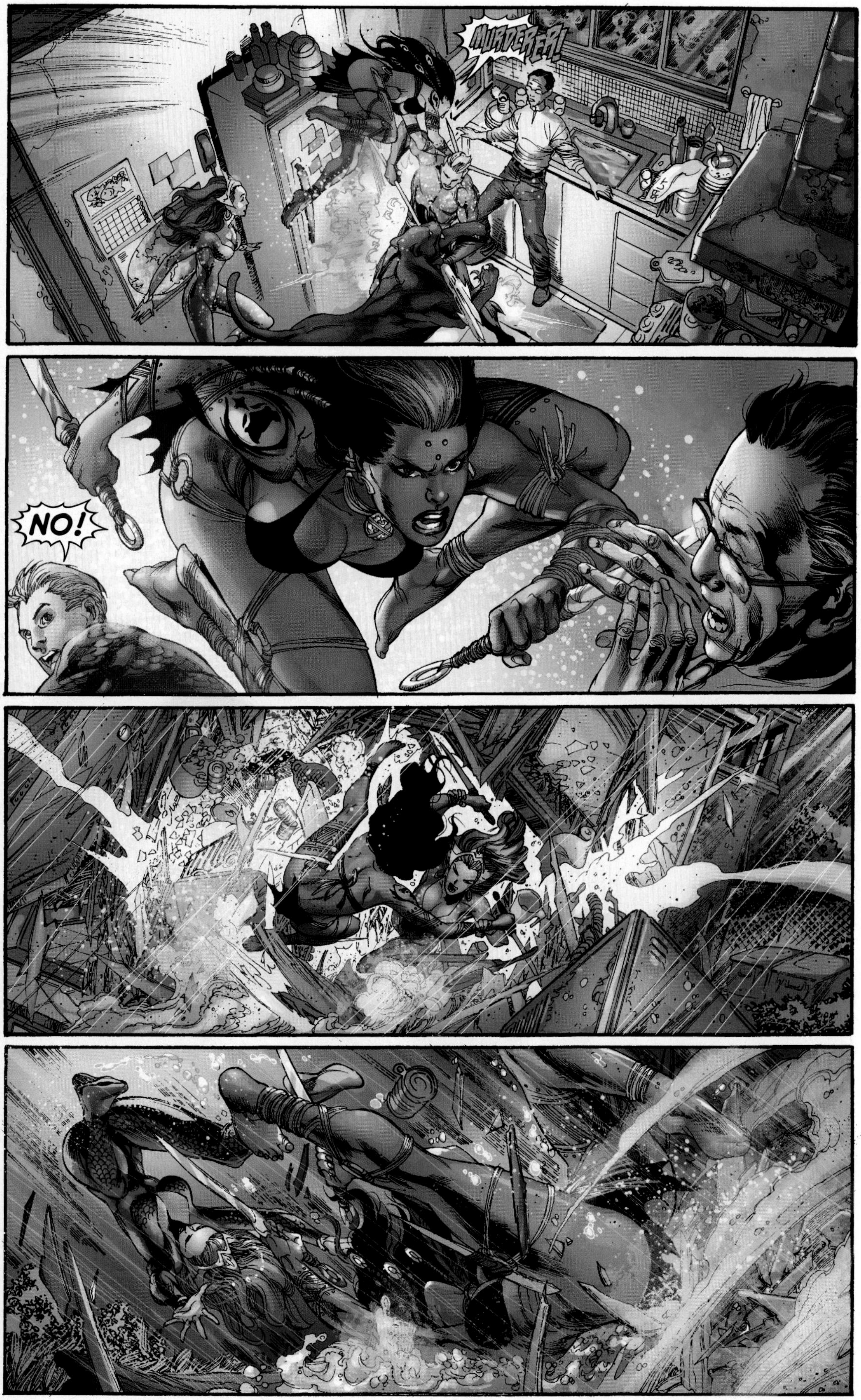
MURDERER!
NO!

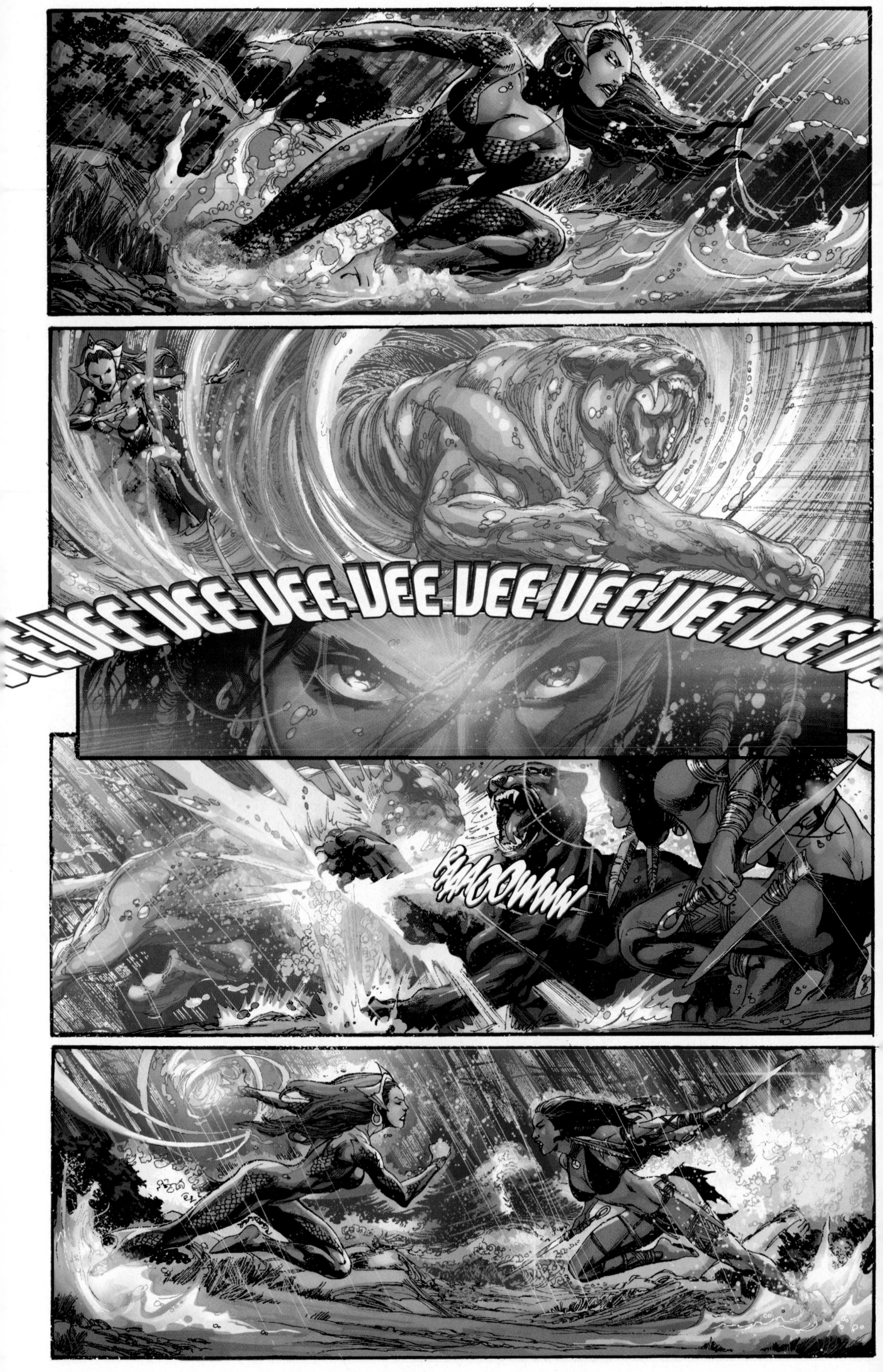
VEE VEE VEE VEE VEE VEE VEE
RAAOWWW

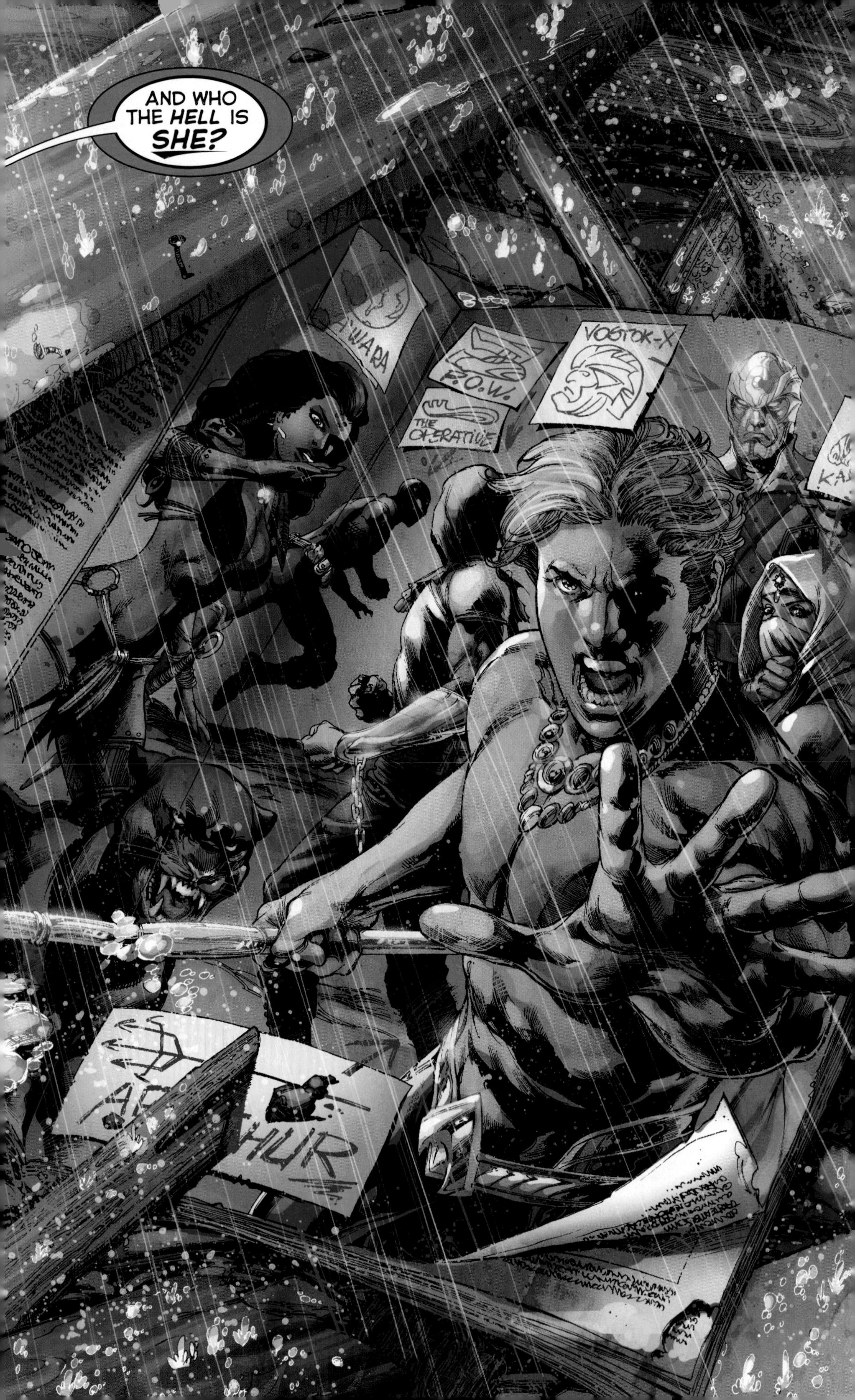
AND WHO THE HELL IS SHE?
A'WARA
P.O.W.
THE OPERATIVE
VOSTOK-X
KA
ARTHUR

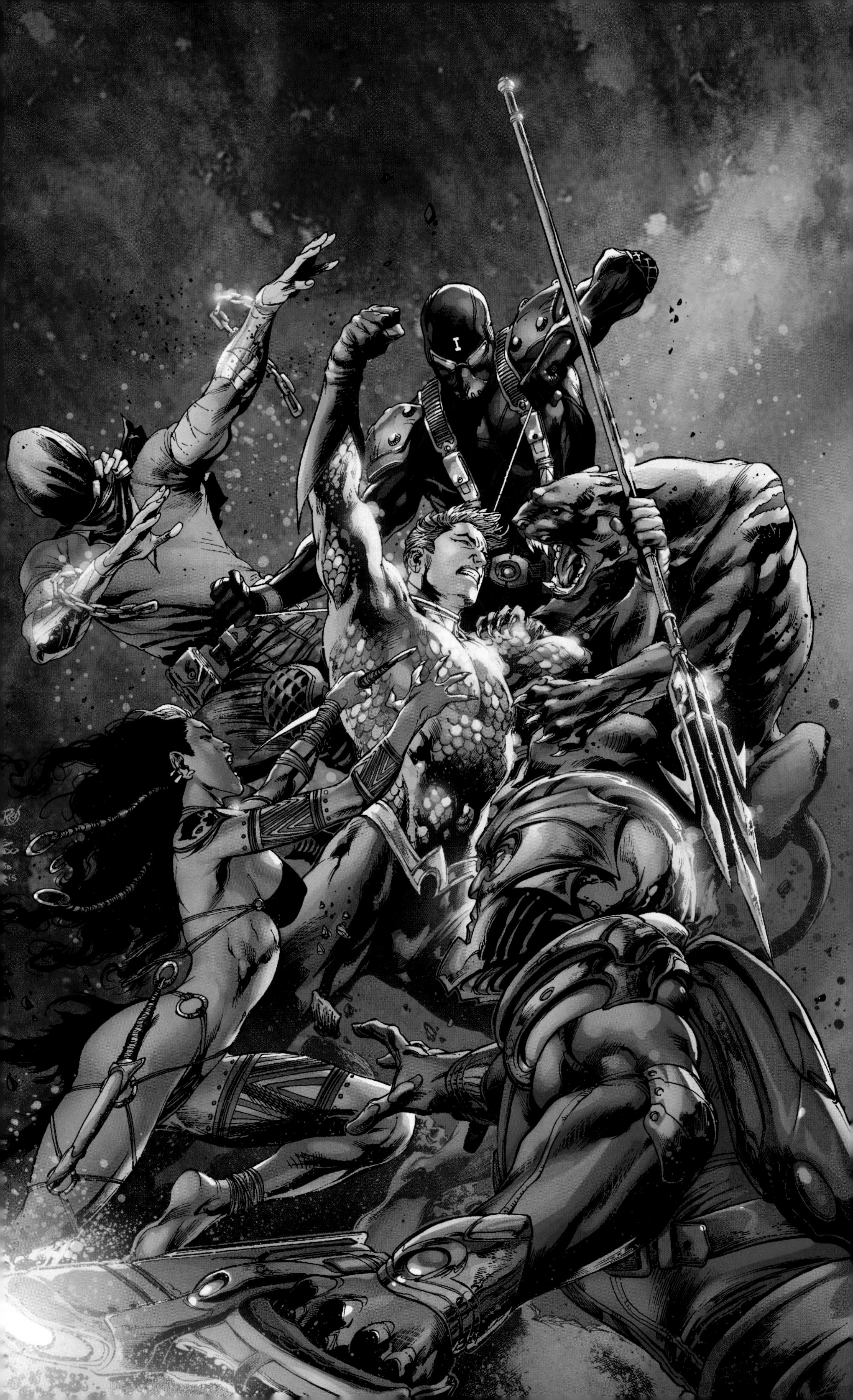

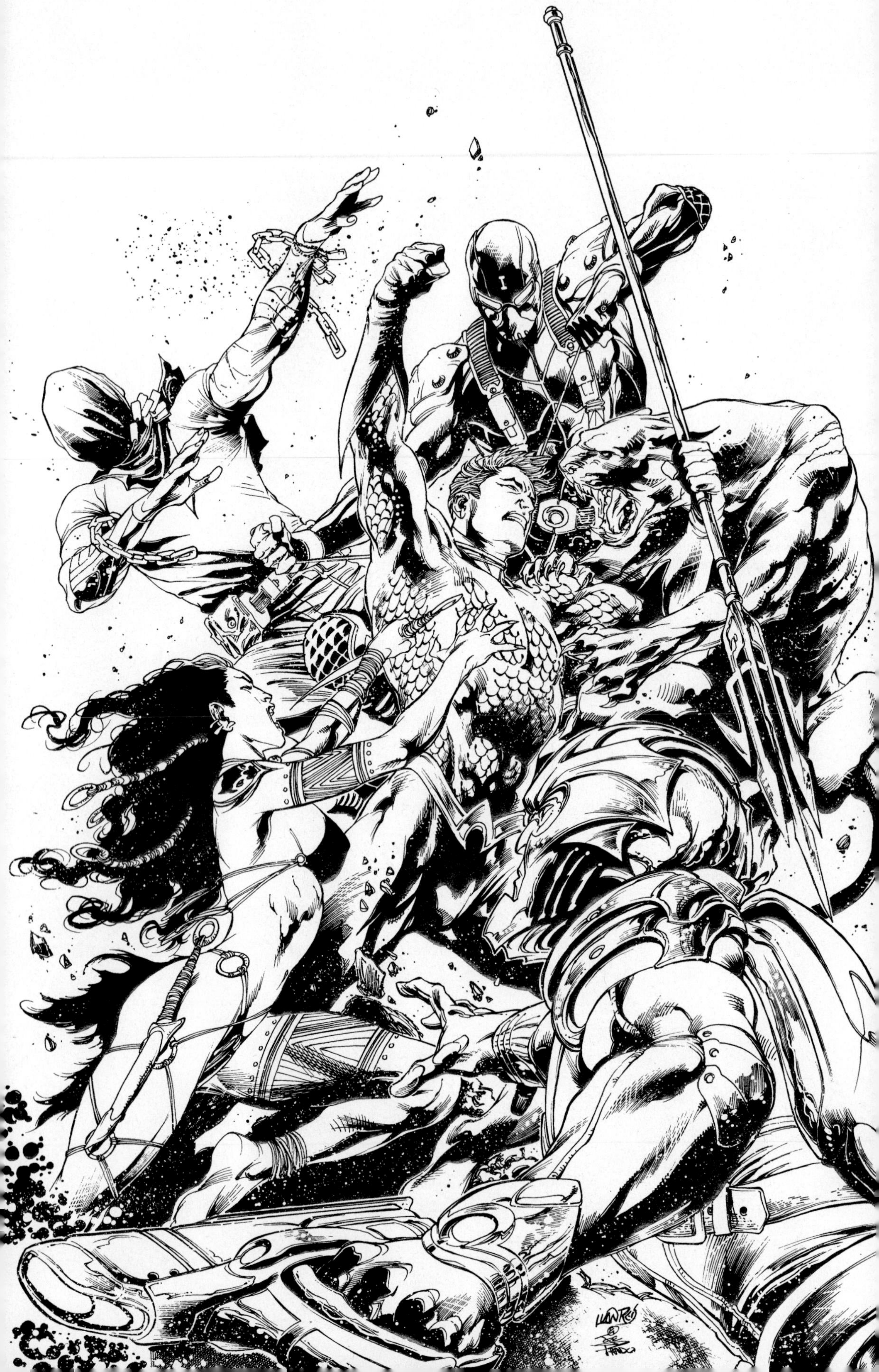

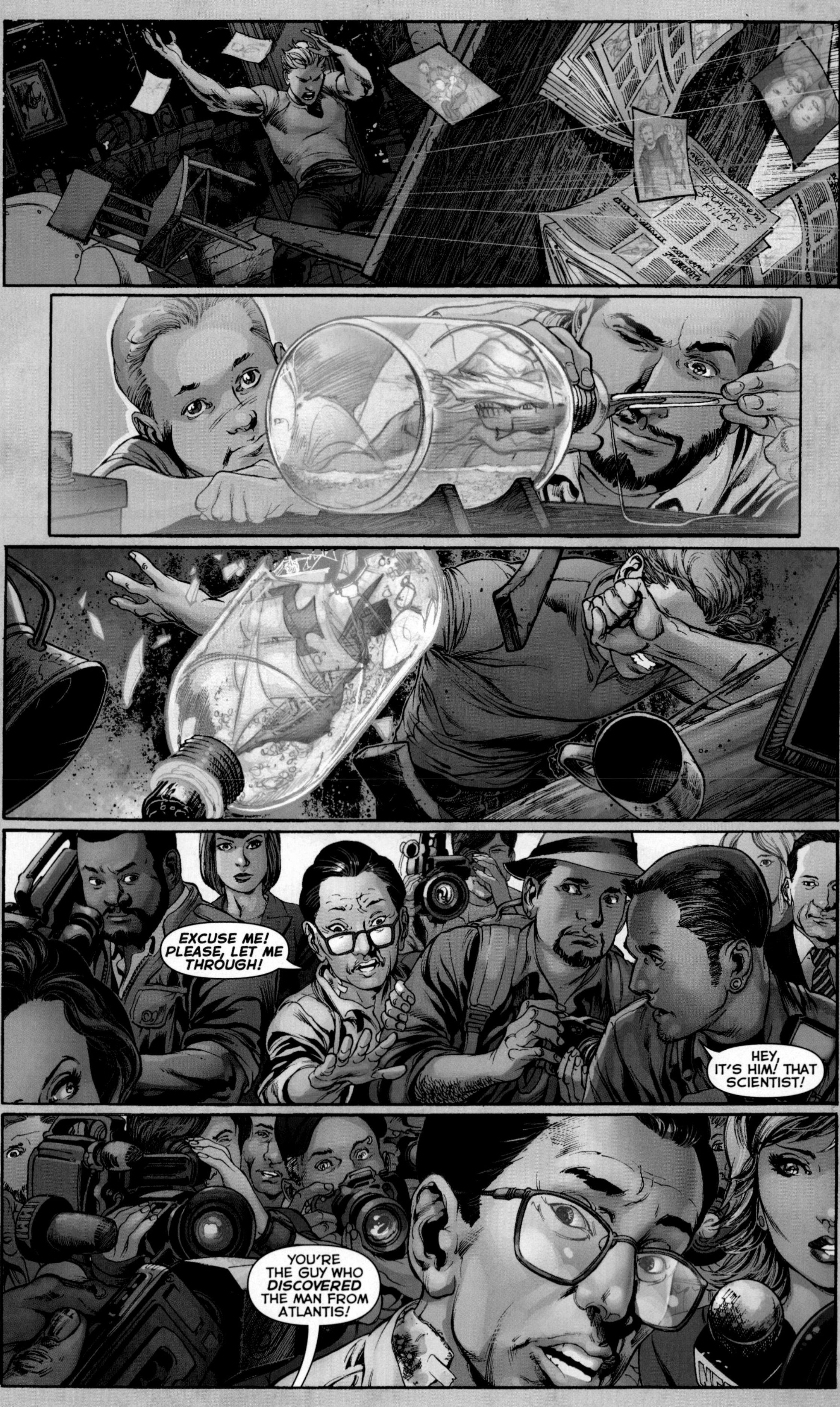
AQUAMAN'S KILLED
EXCUSE ME! PLEASE, LET ME THROUGH!
HEY, IT'S HIM! THAT SCIENTIST!
YOU'RE THE GUY WHO DISCOVERED THE MAN FROM ATLANTIS!

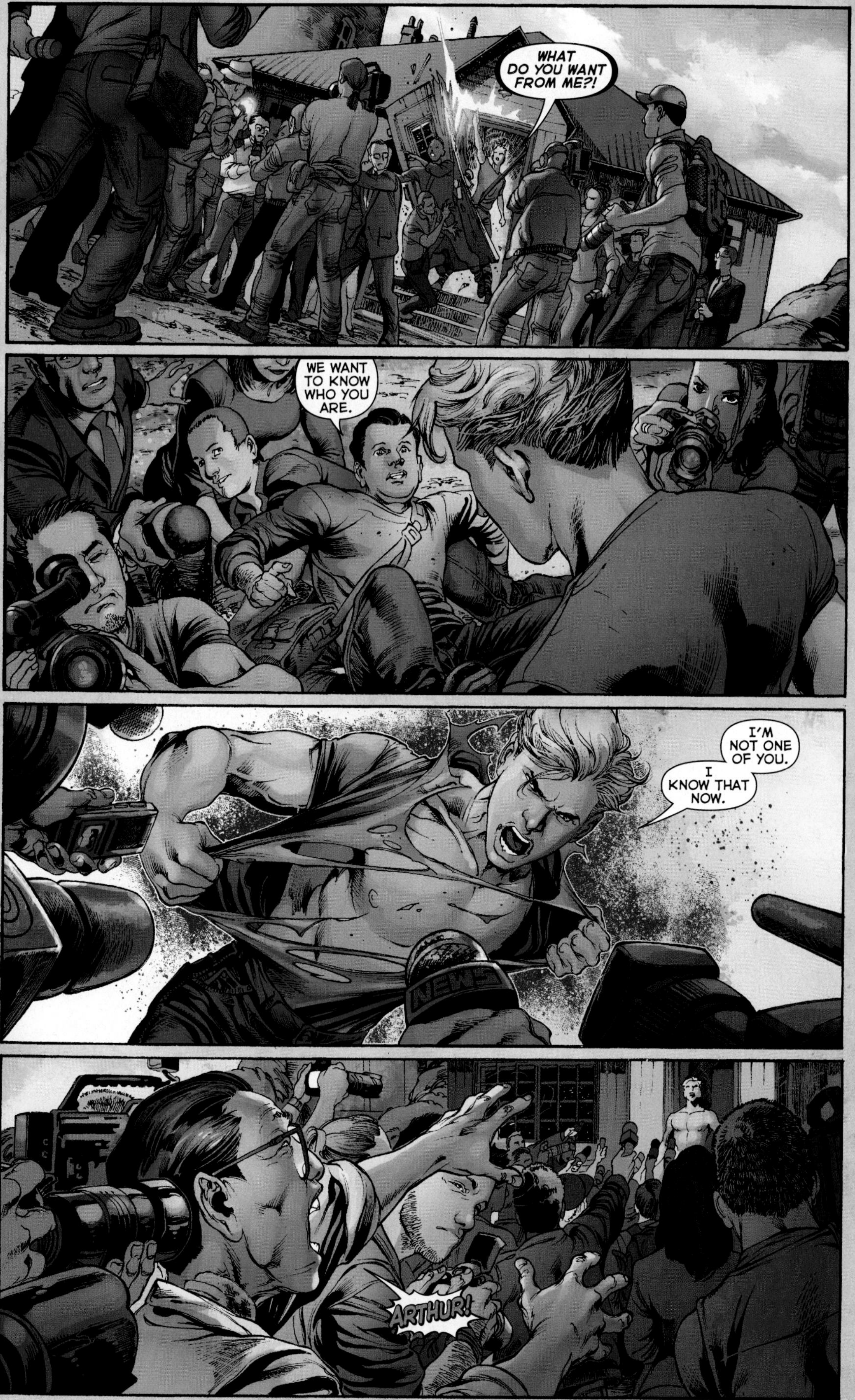

WHAT DO YOU WANT FROM ME?!
WE WANT TO KNOW WHO YOU ARE.
I'M NOT ONE OF YOU.
I KNOW THAT NOW.
NEWS
ARTHUR!

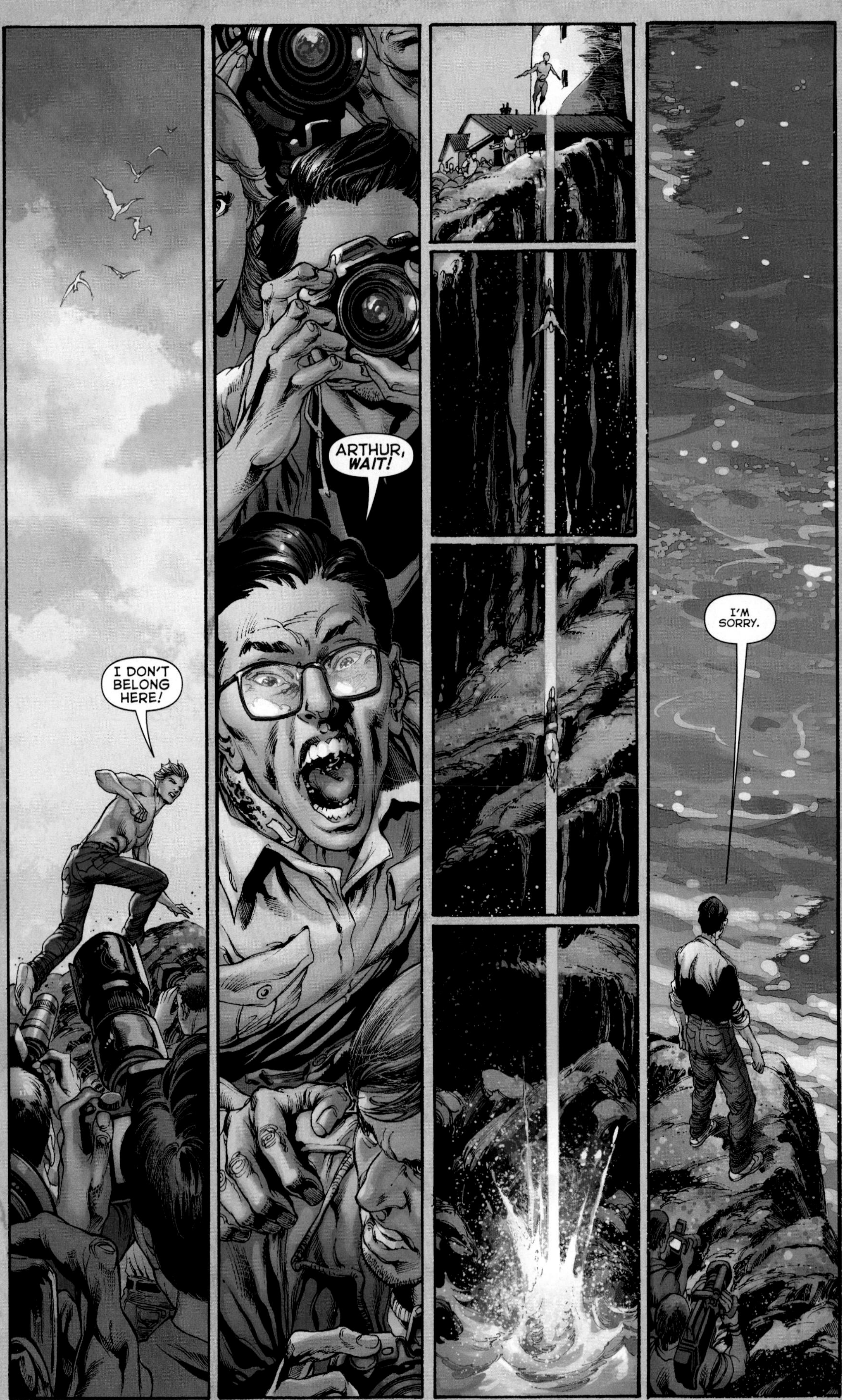
I DON'T BELONG HERE!
ARTHUR, WAIT!
I'M SORRY.

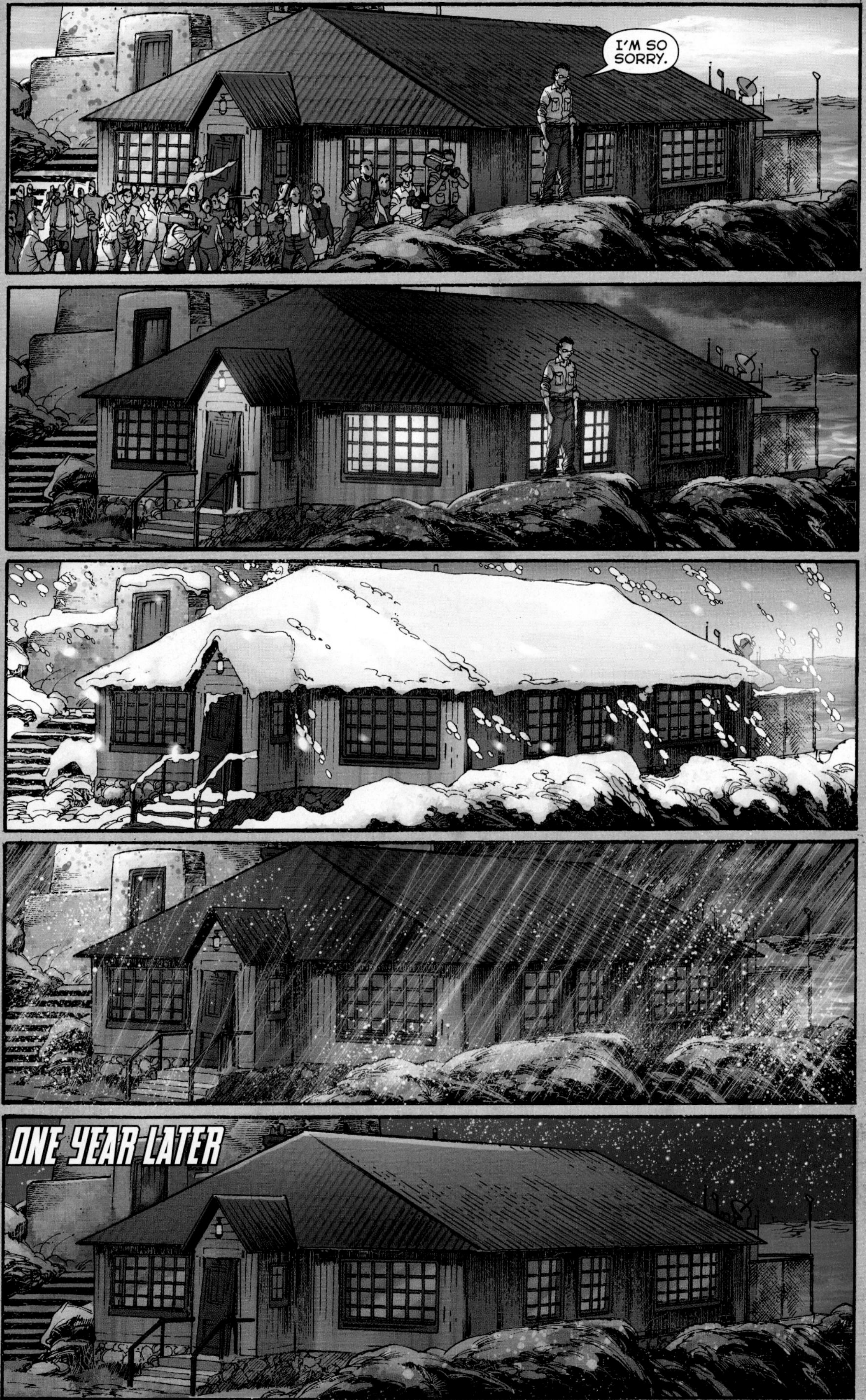
I'M SO SORRY.
ONE YEAR LATER

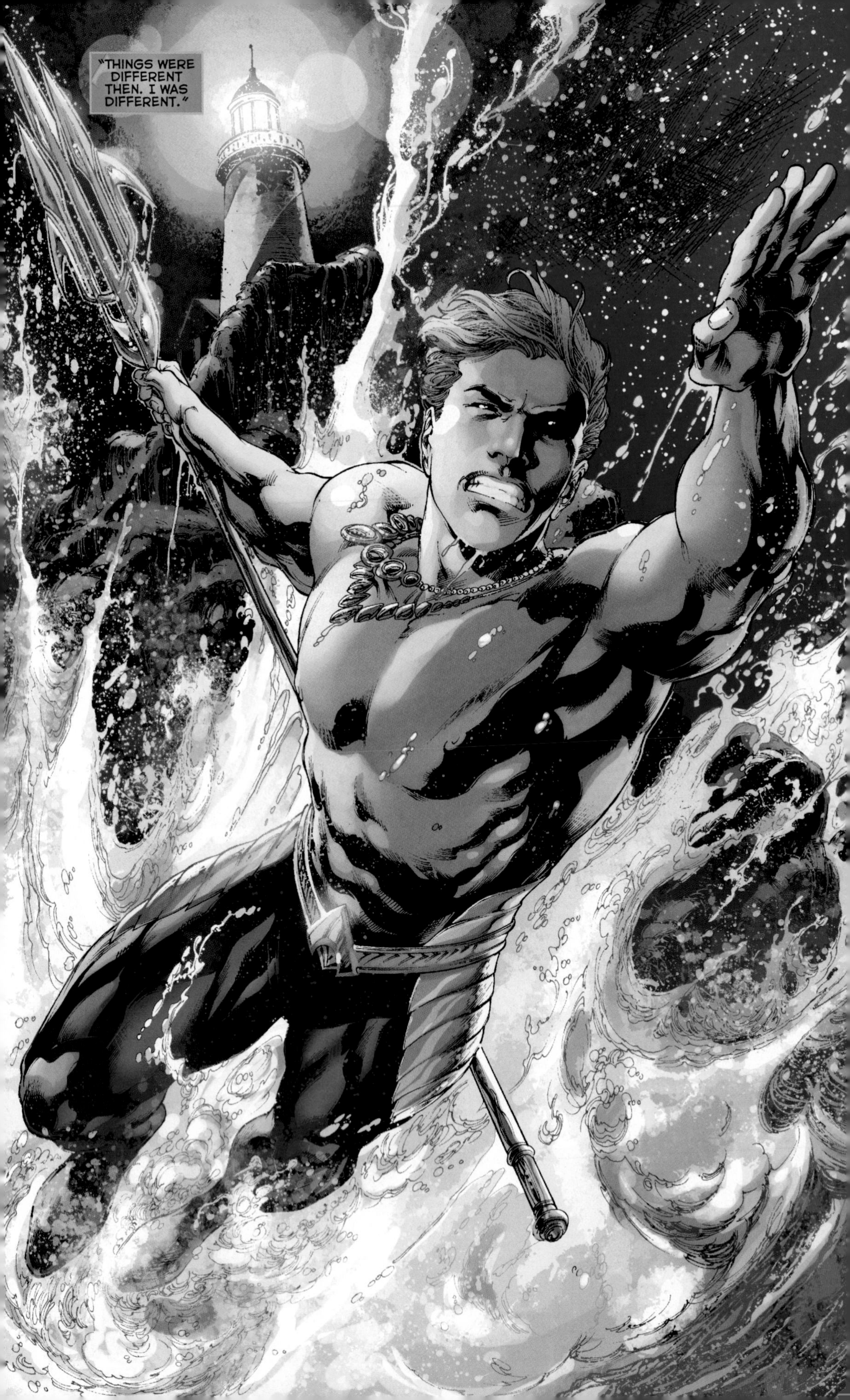
"THINGS WERE DIFFERENT THEN. I WAS DIFFERENT."

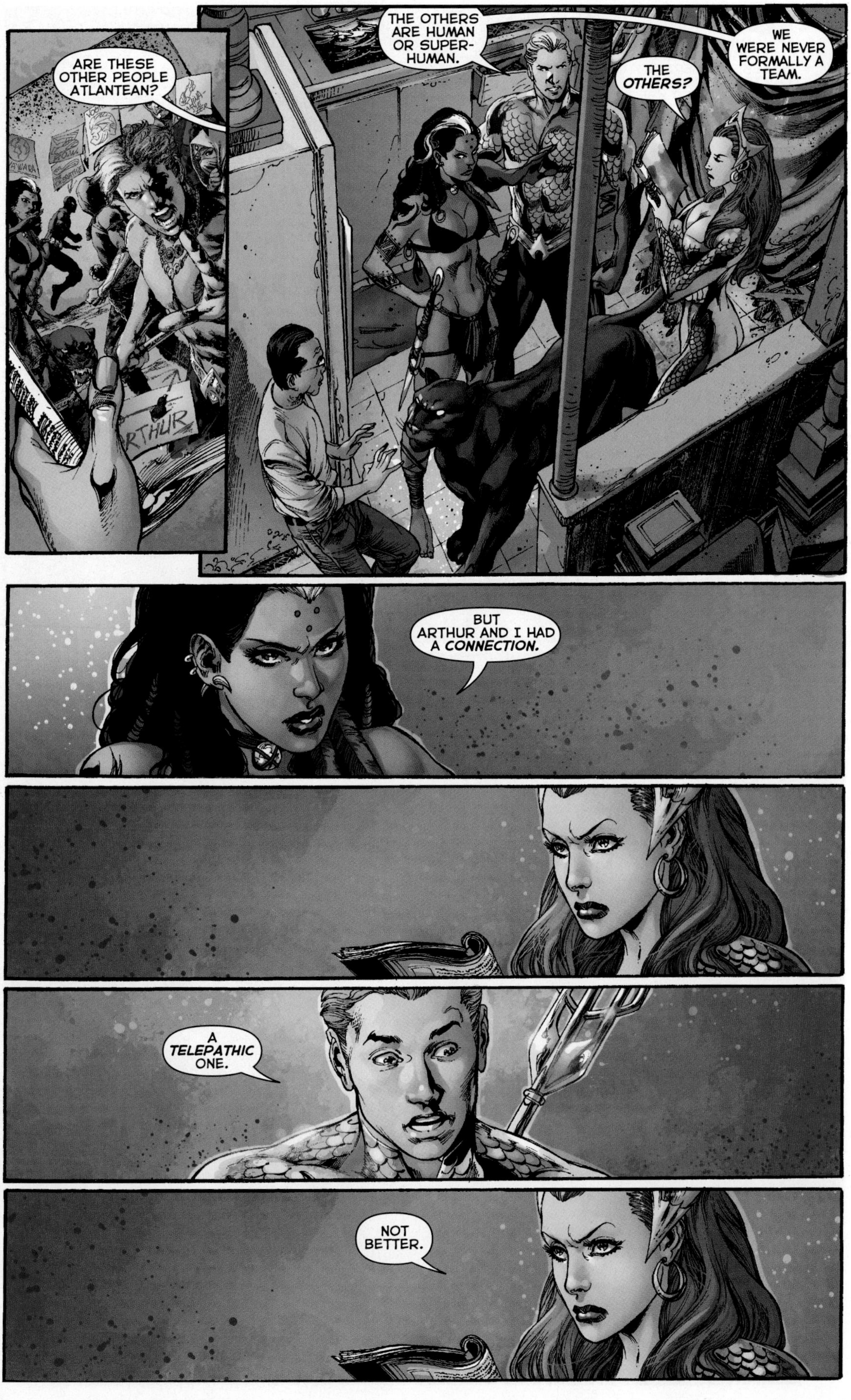
ARE THESE OTHER PEOPLE ATLANTEAN?
THE OTHERS ARE HUMAN OR SUPER-HUMAN.
THE *OTHERS?*
WE WERE NEVER FORMALLY A TEAM.
BUT ARTHUR AND I HAD A *CONNECTION.*
A *TELEPATHIC* ONE.
NOT BETTER.

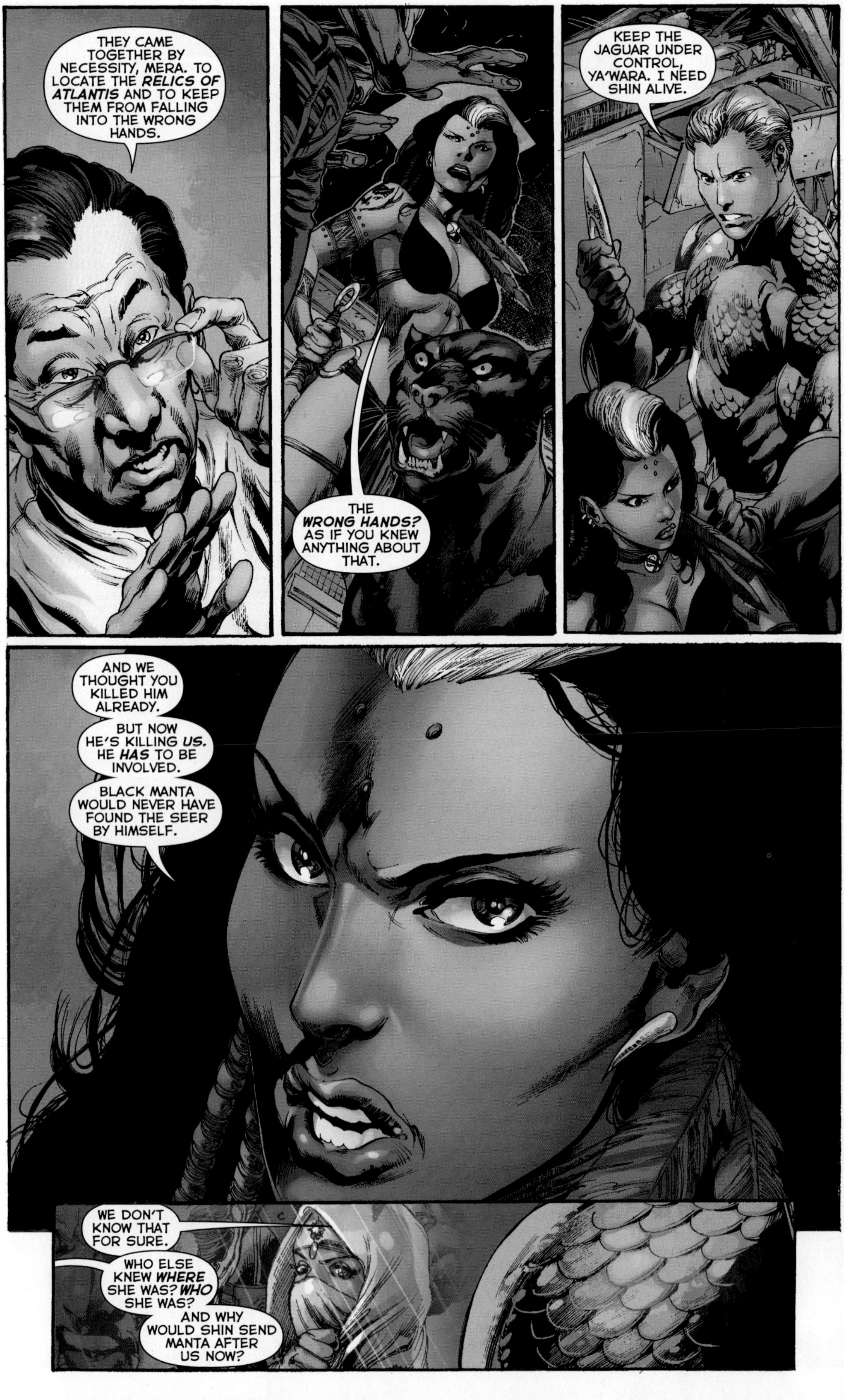
THEY CAME TOGETHER BY NECESSITY, MERA. TO LOCATE THE *RELICS OF ATLANTIS* AND TO KEEP THEM FROM FALLING INTO THE WRONG HANDS.
THE *WRONG HANDS?* AS IF YOU KNEW ANYTHING ABOUT THAT.
KEEP THE JAGUAR UNDER CONTROL, YA'WARA. I NEED SHIN ALIVE.
AND WE THOUGHT YOU KILLED HIM ALREADY.
BUT NOW HE'S KILLING *US.* HE *HAS* TO BE INVOLVED.
BLACK MANTA WOULD NEVER HAVE FOUND THE SEER BY HIMSELF.
WE DON'T KNOW THAT FOR SURE.
WHO ELSE KNEW *WHERE* SHE WAS? *WHO* SHE WAS?
AND WHY WOULD SHIN SEND MANTA AFTER US NOW?

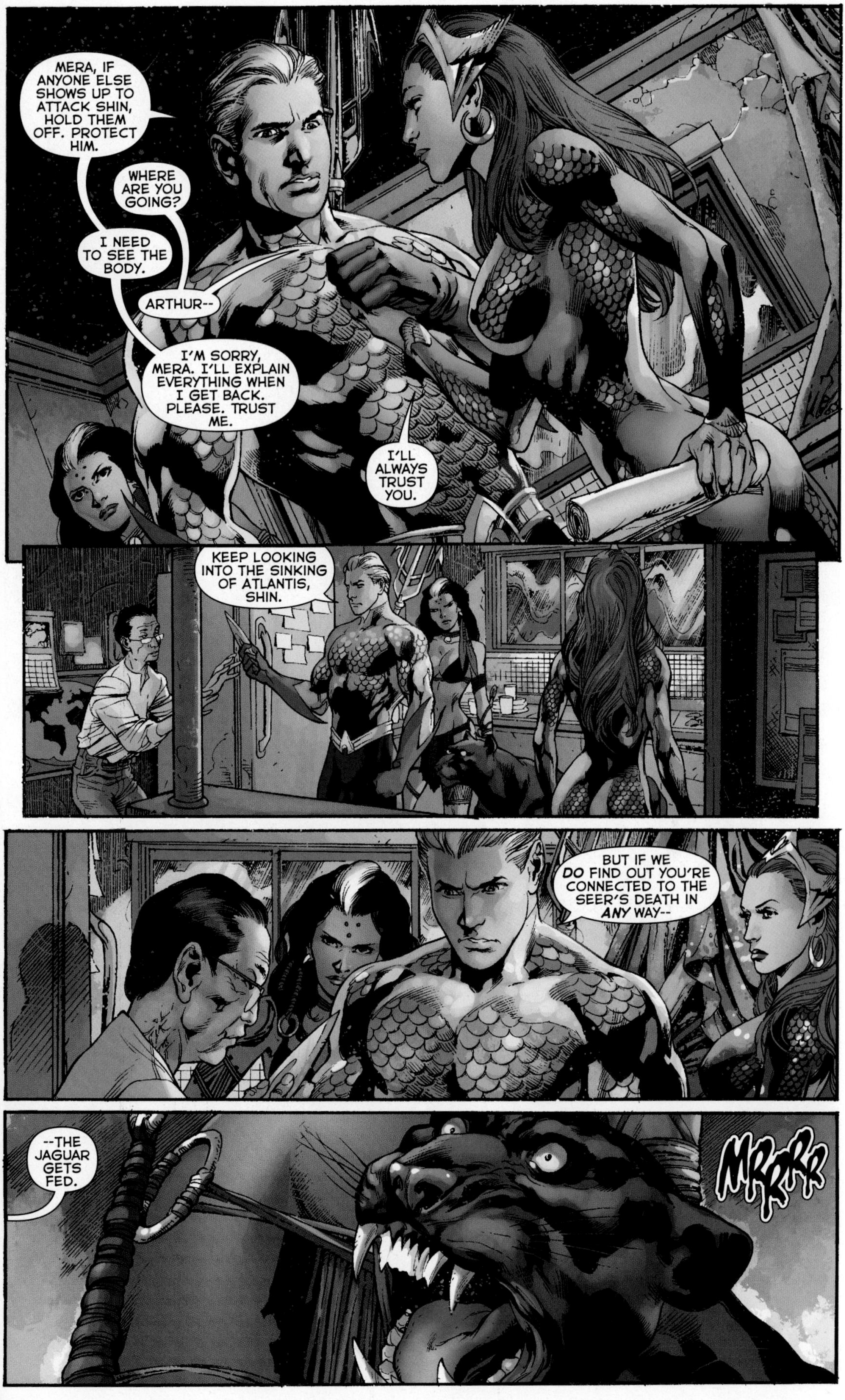
MERA, IF ANYONE ELSE SHOWS UP TO ATTACK SHIN, HOLD THEM OFF. PROTECT HIM.
WHERE ARE YOU GOING?
I NEED TO SEE THE BODY.
ARTHUR--
I'M SORRY, MERA. I'LL EXPLAIN EVERYTHING WHEN I GET BACK. PLEASE. TRUST ME.
I'LL ALWAYS TRUST YOU.
KEEP LOOKING INTO THE SINKING OF ATLANTIS, SHIN.
BUT IF WE *DO* FIND OUT YOU'RE CONNECTED TO THE SEER'S DEATH IN *ANY* WAY--
--THE JAGUAR GETS FED.
MRRRR

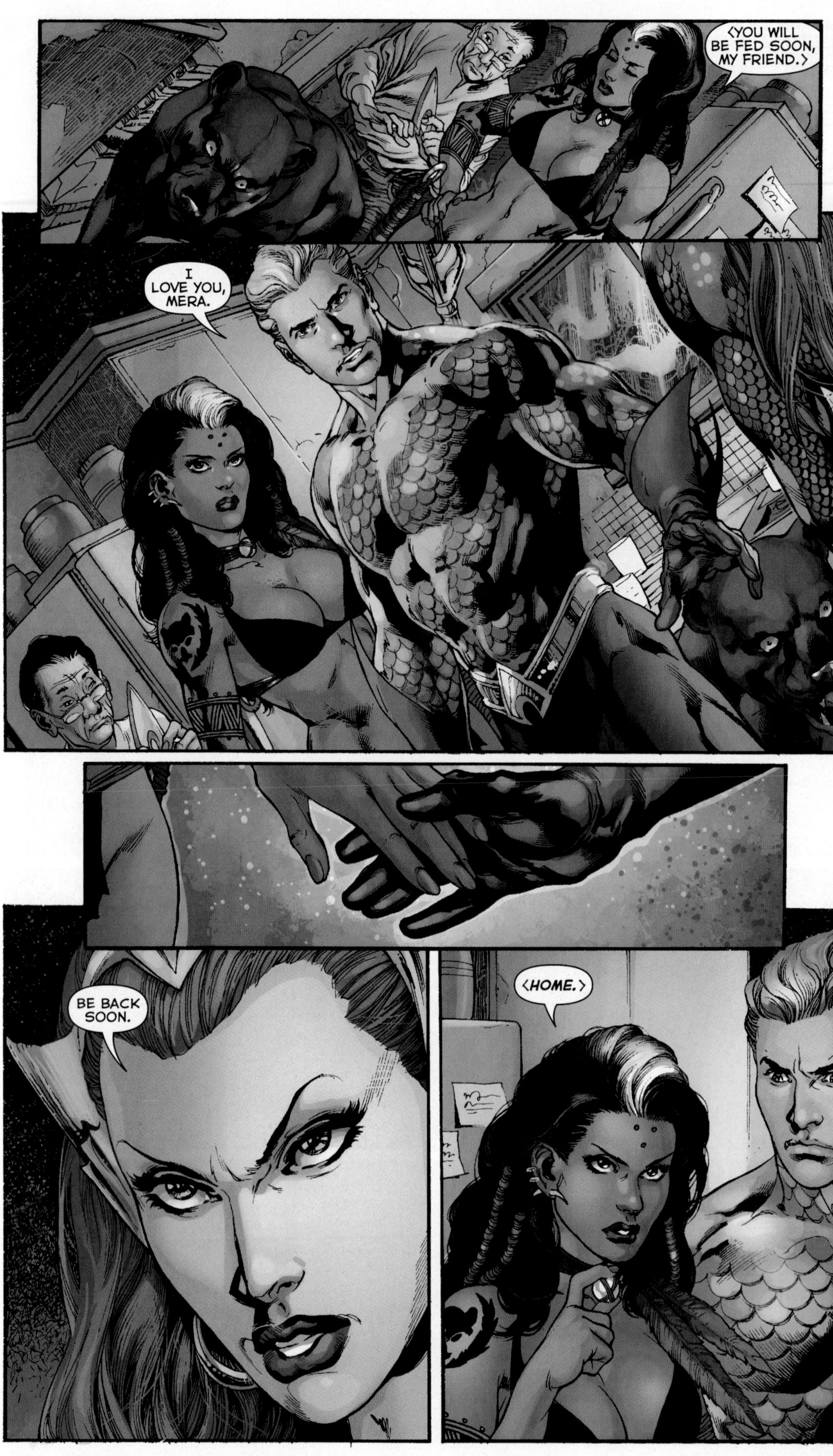
<YOU WILL BE FED SOON, MY FRIEND.>
I LOVE YOU, MERA.
BE BACK SOON.
<HOME.>

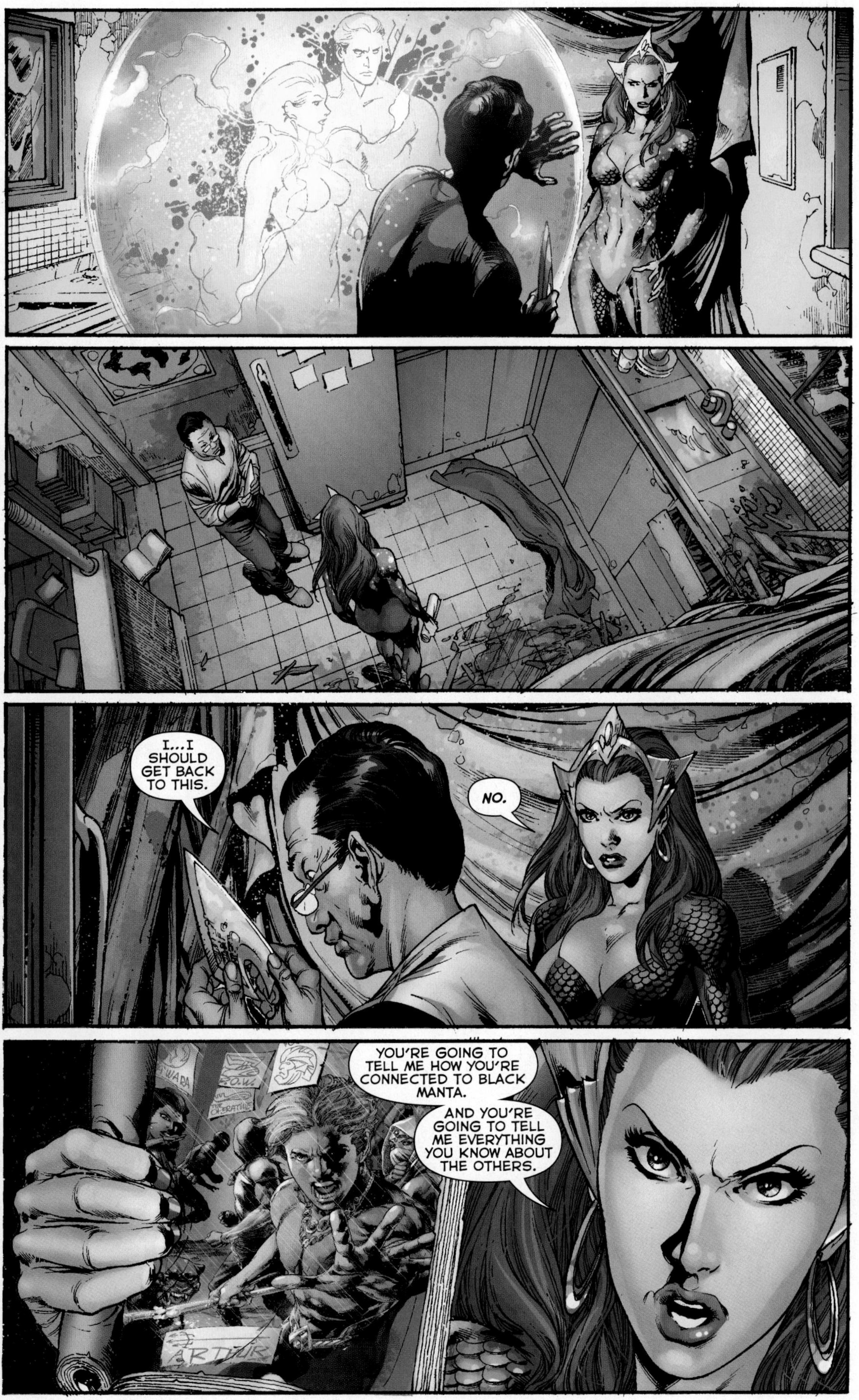
I...I SHOULD GET BACK TO THIS.
NO.
YOU'RE GOING TO TELL ME HOW YOU'RE CONNECTED TO BLACK MANTA.
AND YOU'RE GOING TO TELL ME EVERYTHING YOU KNOW ABOUT THE OTHERS.

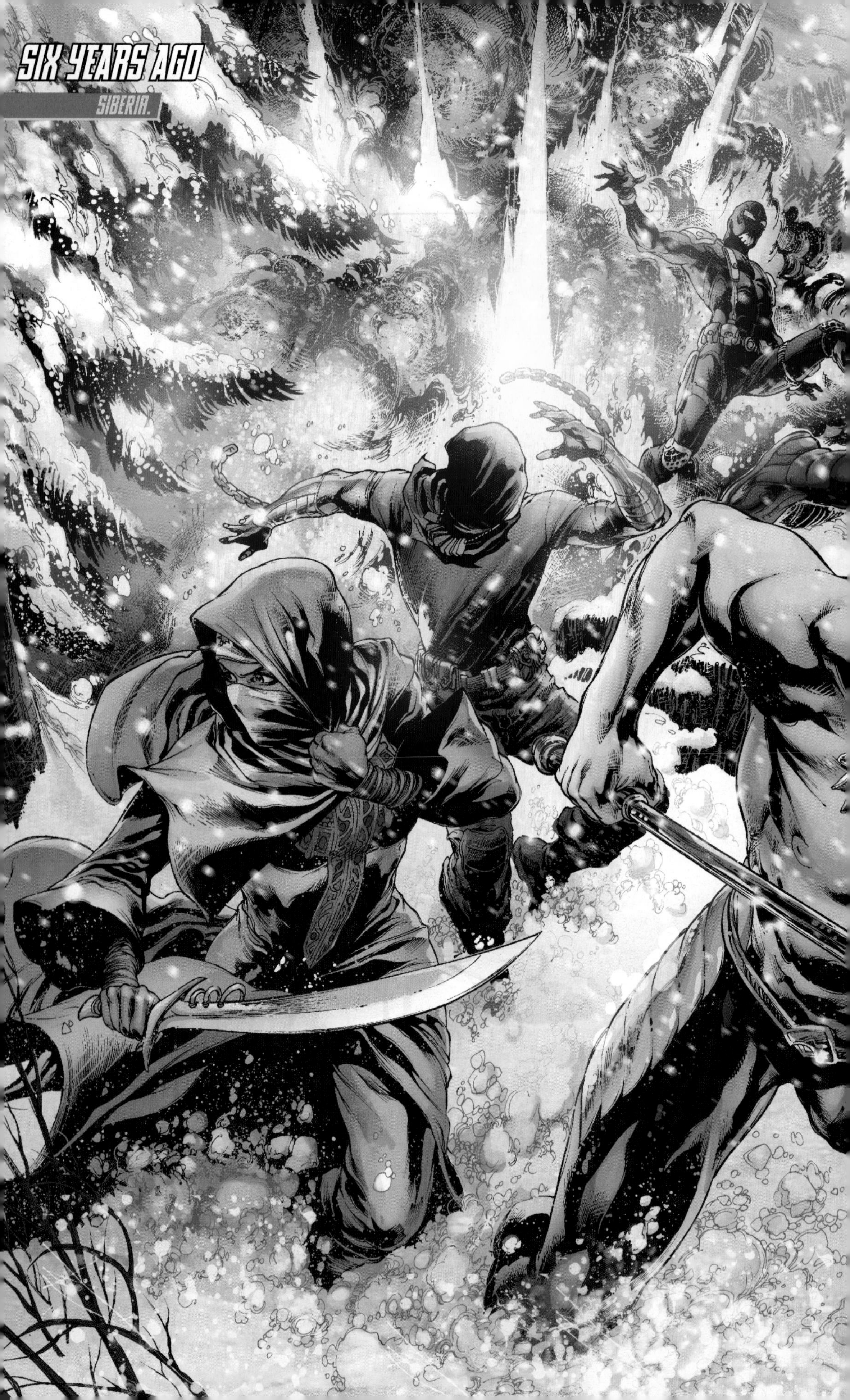
SIX YEARS AGO
SIBERIA.

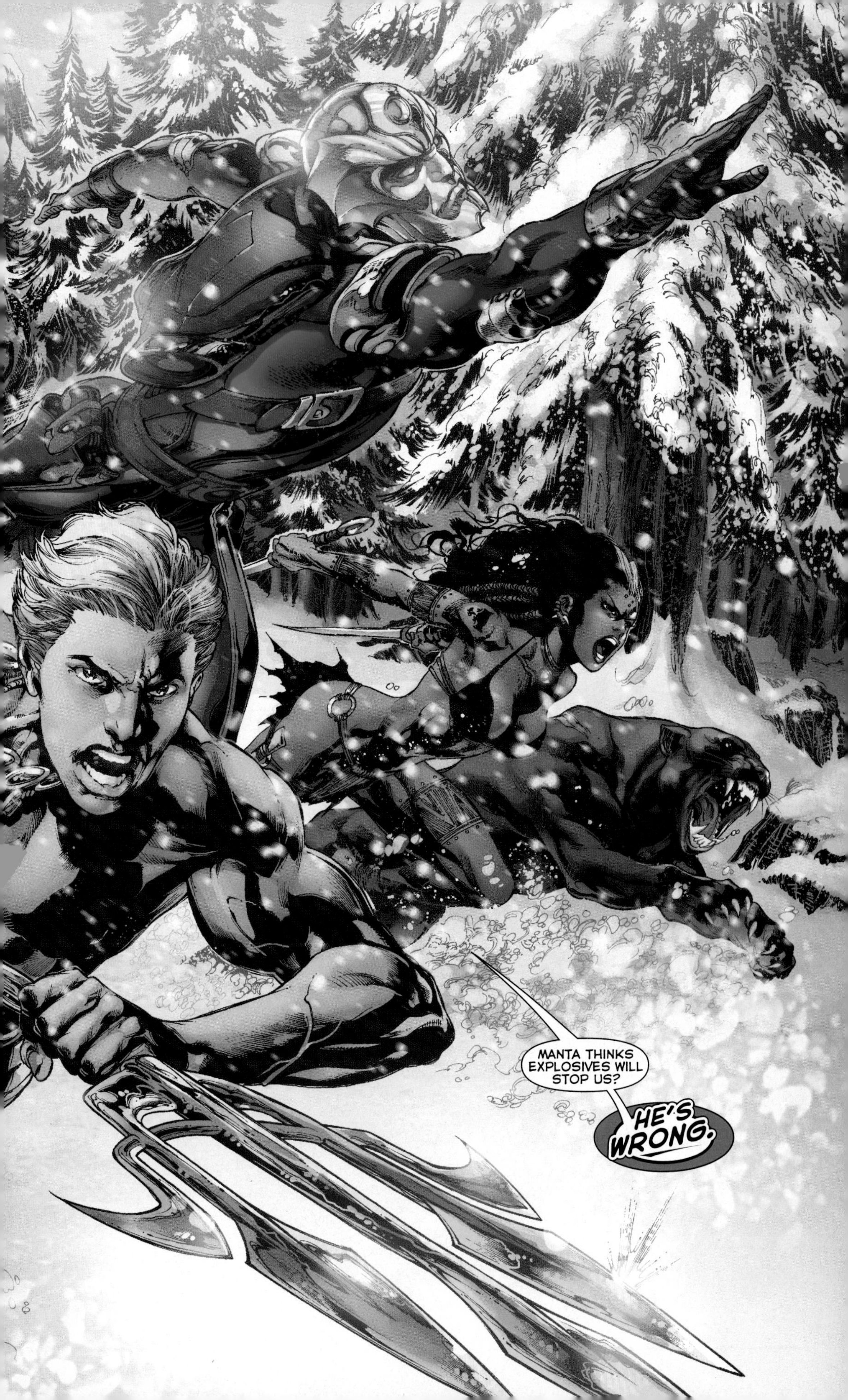
MANTA THINKS EXPLOSIVES WILL STOP US?
HE'S WRONG.

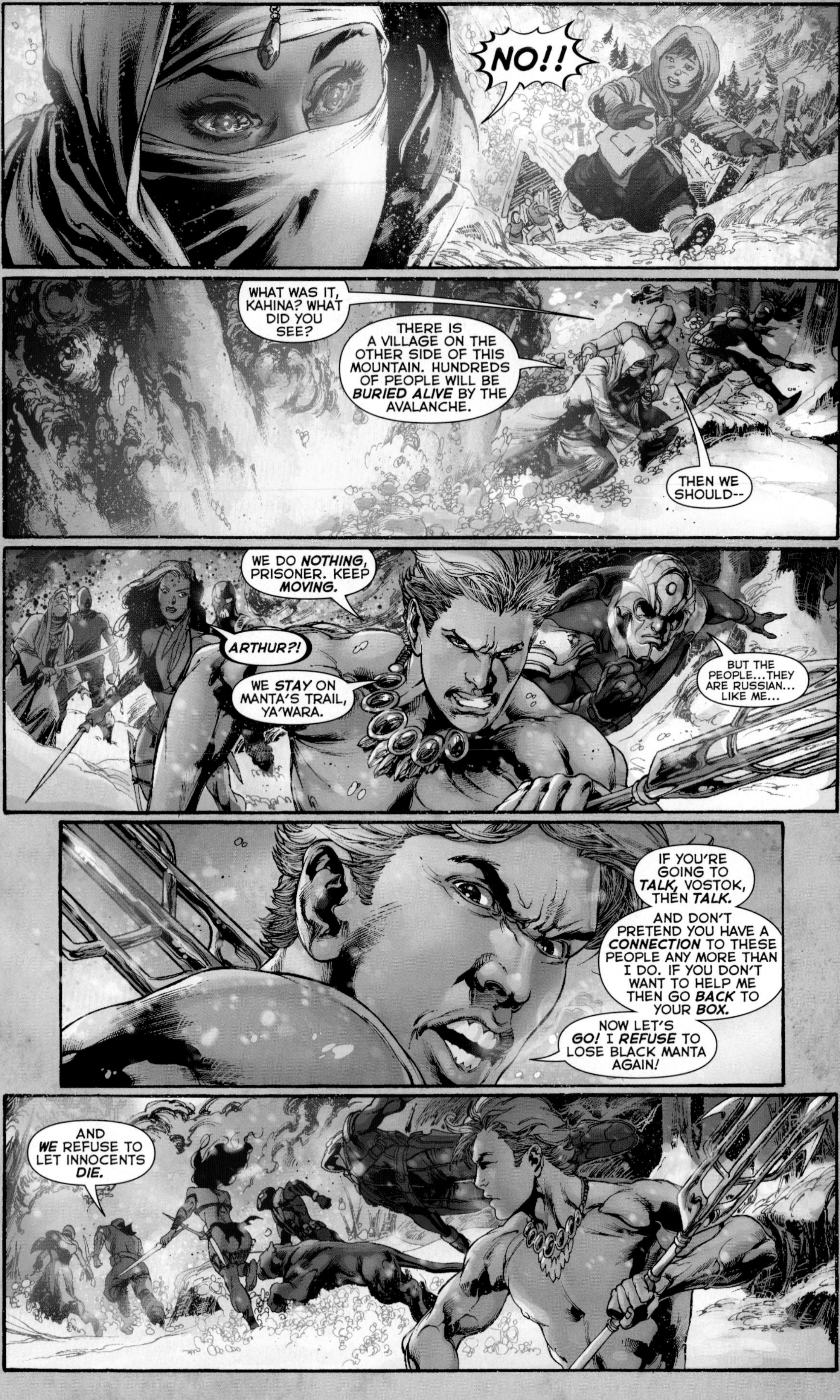
NO!!
WHAT WAS IT, KAHINA? WHAT DID YOU SEE?
THERE IS A VILLAGE ON THE OTHER SIDE OF THIS MOUNTAIN. HUNDREDS OF PEOPLE WILL BE BURIED ALIVE BY THE AVALANCHE.
THEN WE SHOULD--
WE DO NOTHING, PRISONER. KEEP MOVING.
ARTHUR?!
WE STAY ON MANTA'S TRAIL, YA'WARA.
BUT THE PEOPLE...THEY ARE RUSSIAN... LIKE ME...
IF YOU'RE GOING TO TALK, VOSTOK, THEN TALK.
AND DON'T PRETEND YOU HAVE A CONNECTION TO THESE PEOPLE ANY MORE THAN I DO. IF YOU DON'T WANT TO HELP ME THEN GO BACK TO YOUR BOX.
NOW LET'S GO! I REFUSE TO LOSE BLACK MANTA AGAIN!
AND WE REFUSE TO LET INNOCENTS DIE.

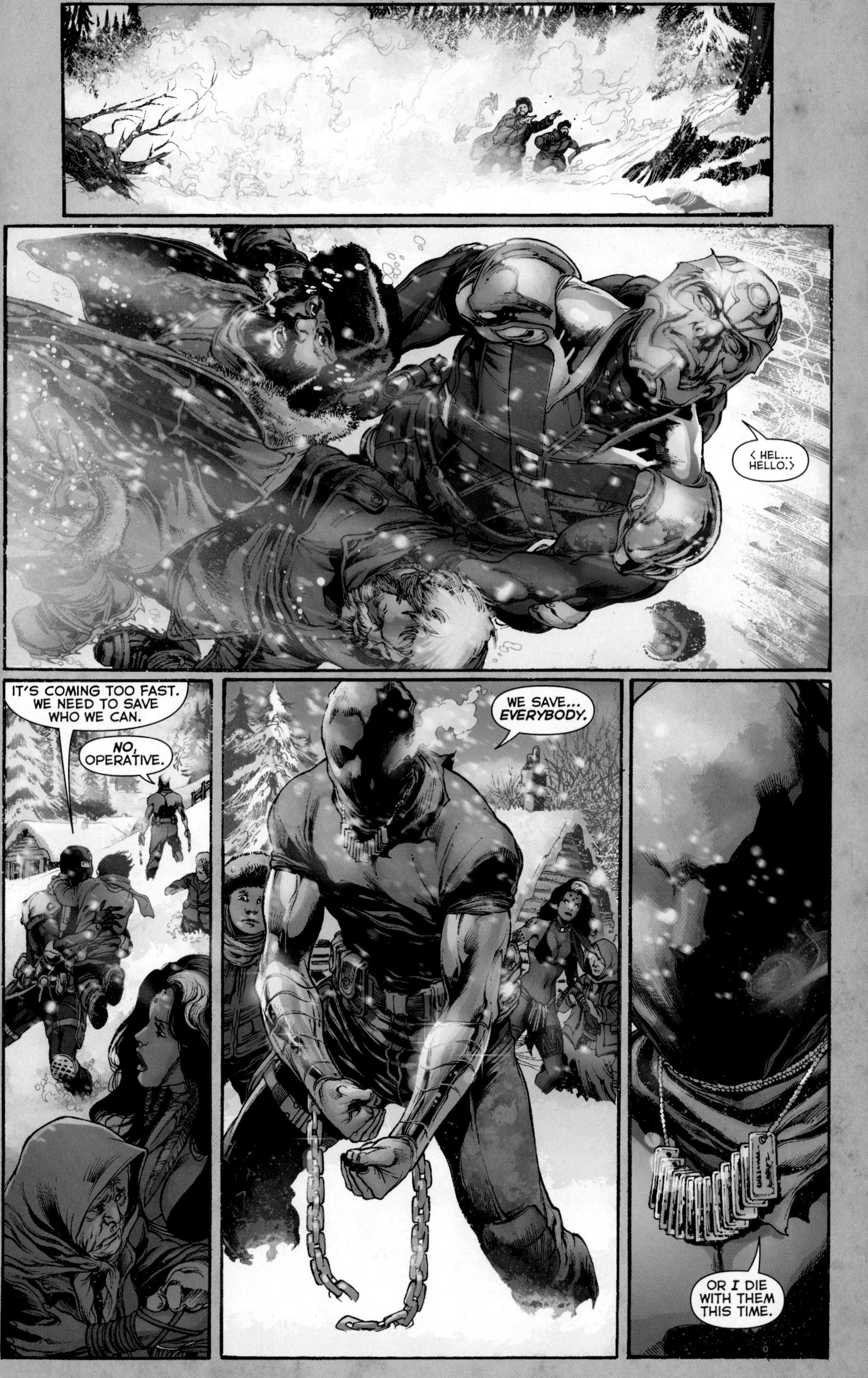

< HEL... HELLO.>
IT'S COMING TOO FAST. WE NEED TO SAVE WHO WE CAN.
NO, OPERATIVE.
WE SAVE... EVERYBODY.
OR I DIE WITH THEM THIS TIME.

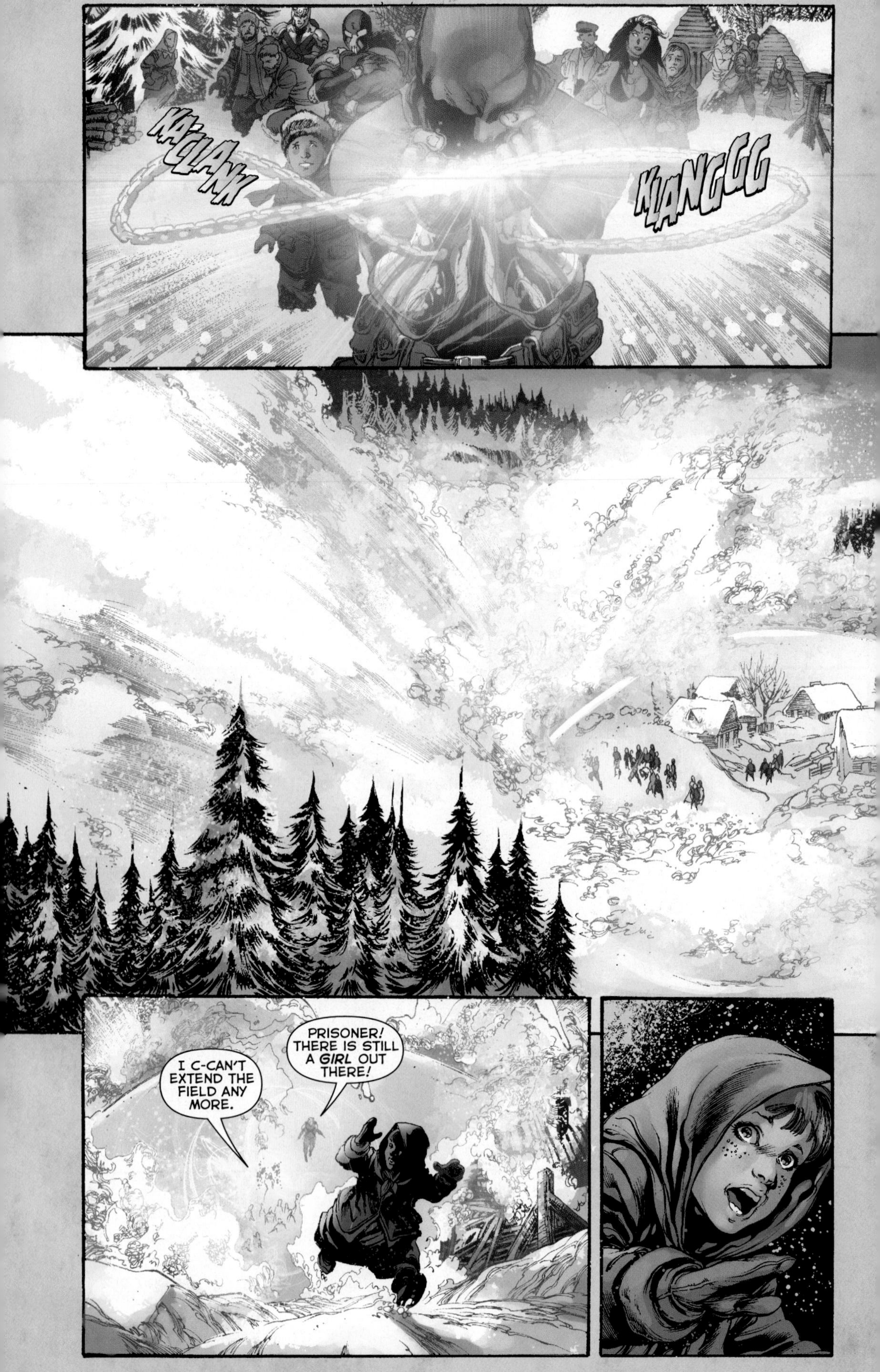
KA-CLANK
KLANGGG
I C-CAN'T EXTEND THE FIELD ANY MORE.
PRISONER! THERE IS STILL A *GIRL* OUT THERE!

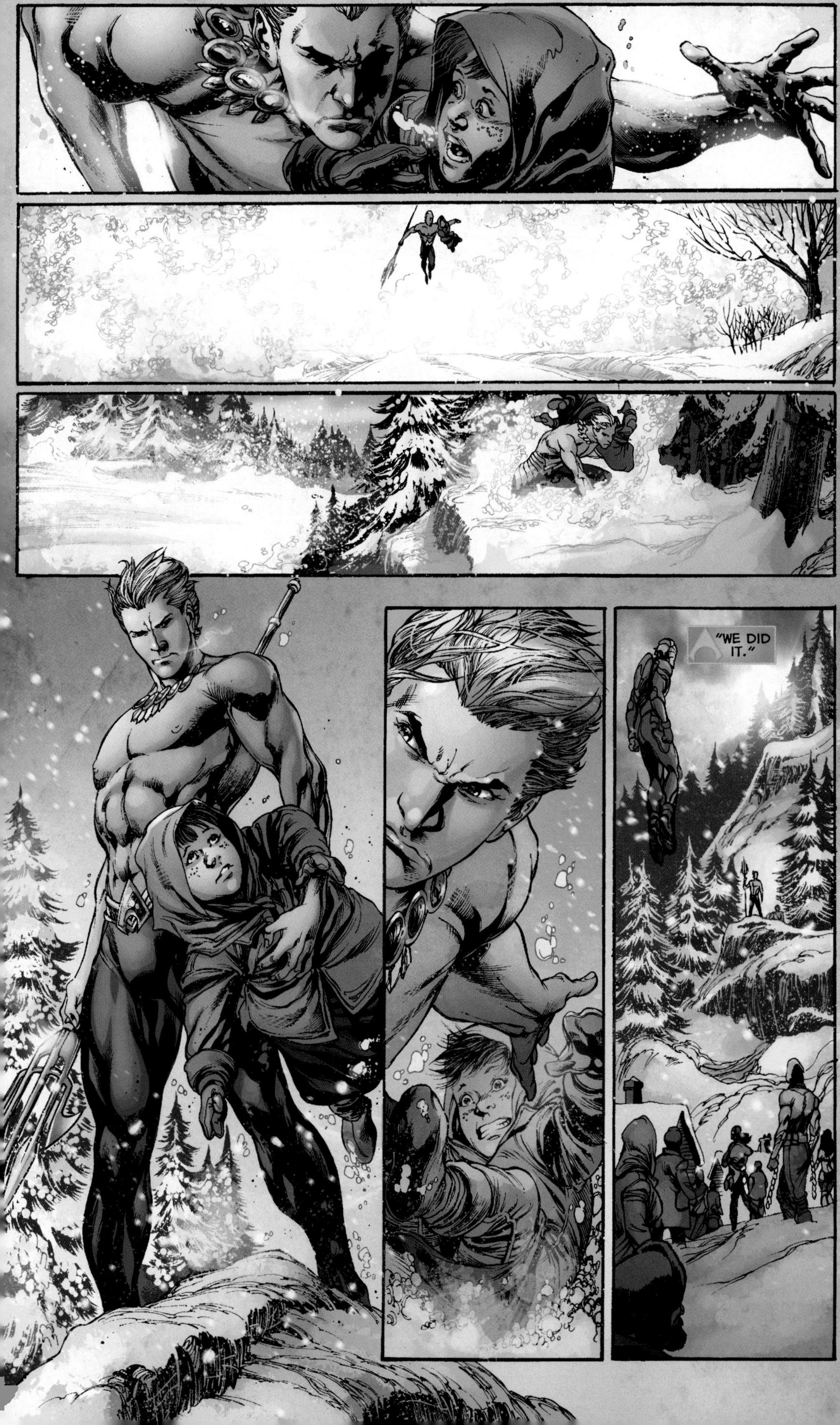
"WE DID IT."

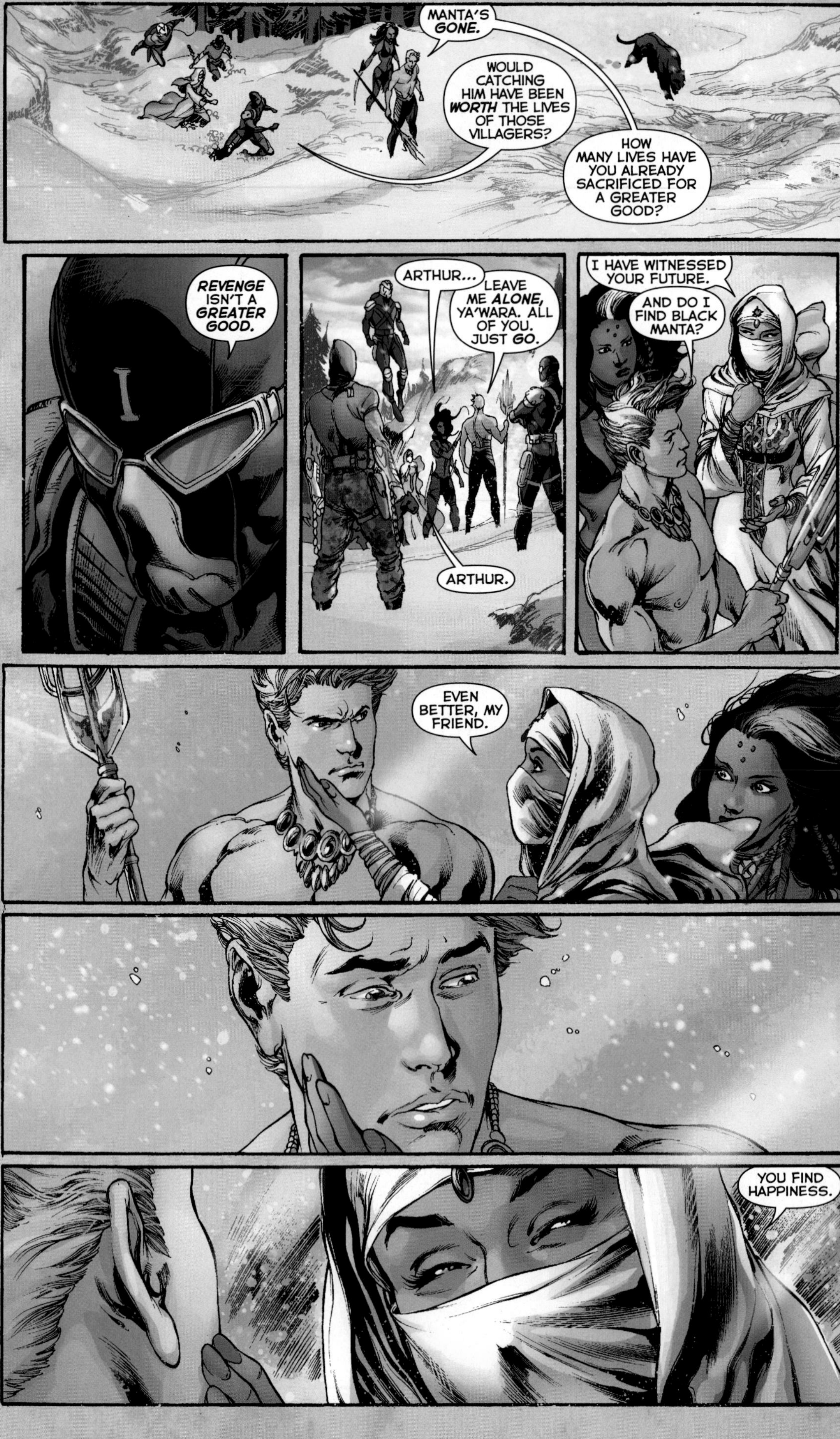
MANTA'S GONE.
WOULD CATCHING HIM HAVE BEEN WORTH THE LIVES OF THOSE VILLAGERS?
HOW MANY LIVES HAVE YOU ALREADY SACRIFICED FOR A GREATER GOOD?
REVENGE ISN'T A GREATER GOOD.
ARTHUR...
LEAVE ME ALONE, YA'WARA. ALL OF YOU. JUST GO.
ARTHUR.
I HAVE WITNESSED YOUR FUTURE.
AND DO I FIND BLACK MANTA?
EVEN BETTER, MY FRIEND.
YOU FIND HAPPINESS.

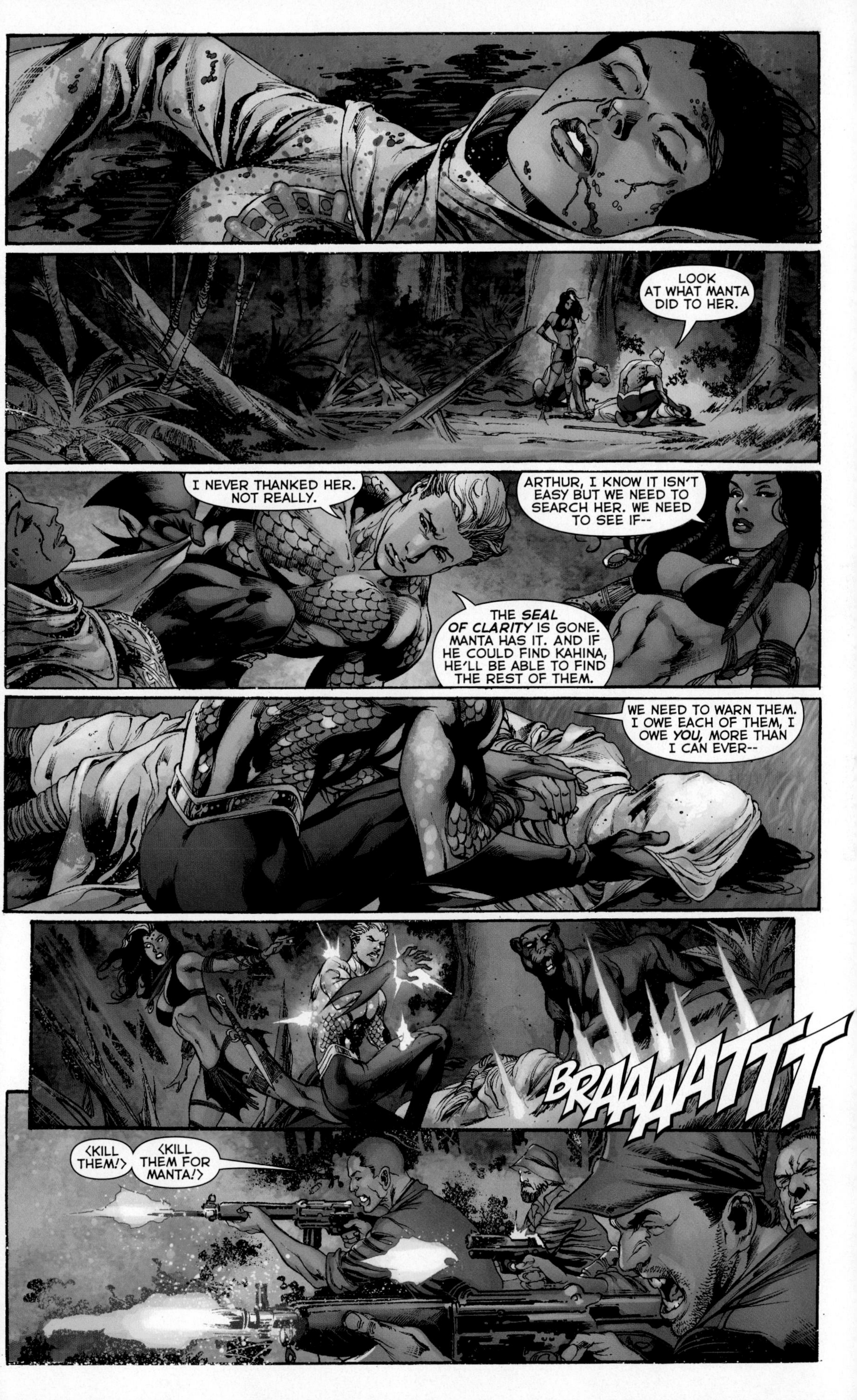
LOOK AT WHAT MANTA DID TO HER.
I NEVER THANKED HER. NOT REALLY.
ARTHUR, I KNOW IT ISN'T EASY BUT WE NEED TO SEARCH HER. WE NEED TO SEE IF--
THE SEAL OF CLARITY IS GONE. MANTA HAS IT. AND IF HE COULD FIND KAHINA, HE'LL BE ABLE TO FIND THE REST OF THEM.
WE NEED TO WARN THEM. I OWE EACH OF THEM, I OWE YOU, MORE THAN I CAN EVER--
BRAAAATTT
<KILL THEM!>
<KILL THEM FOR MANTA!>

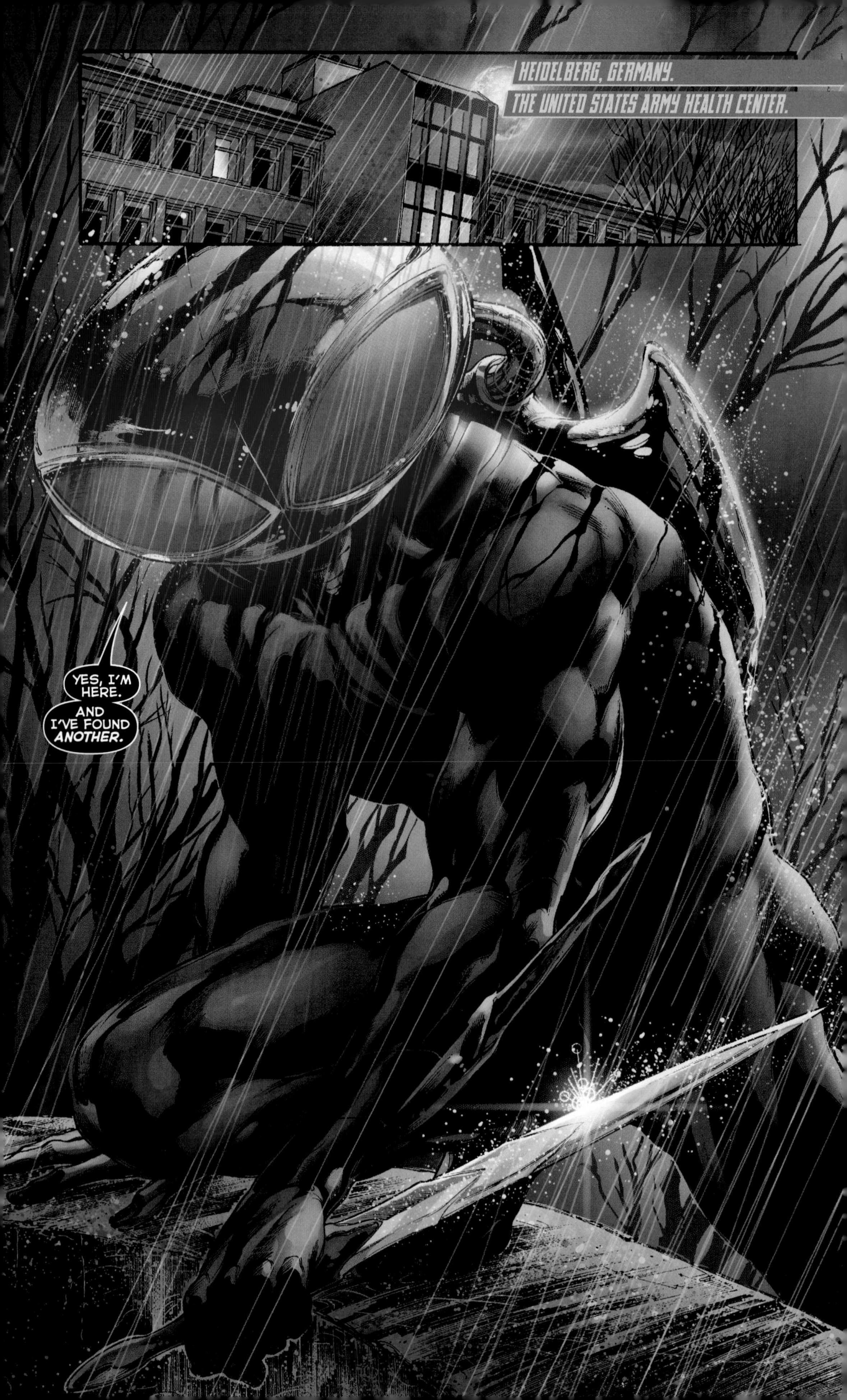
HEIDELBERG, GERMANY.
THE UNITED STATES ARMY HEALTH CENTER.
YES, I'M HERE.
AND I'VE FOUND **ANOTHER.**

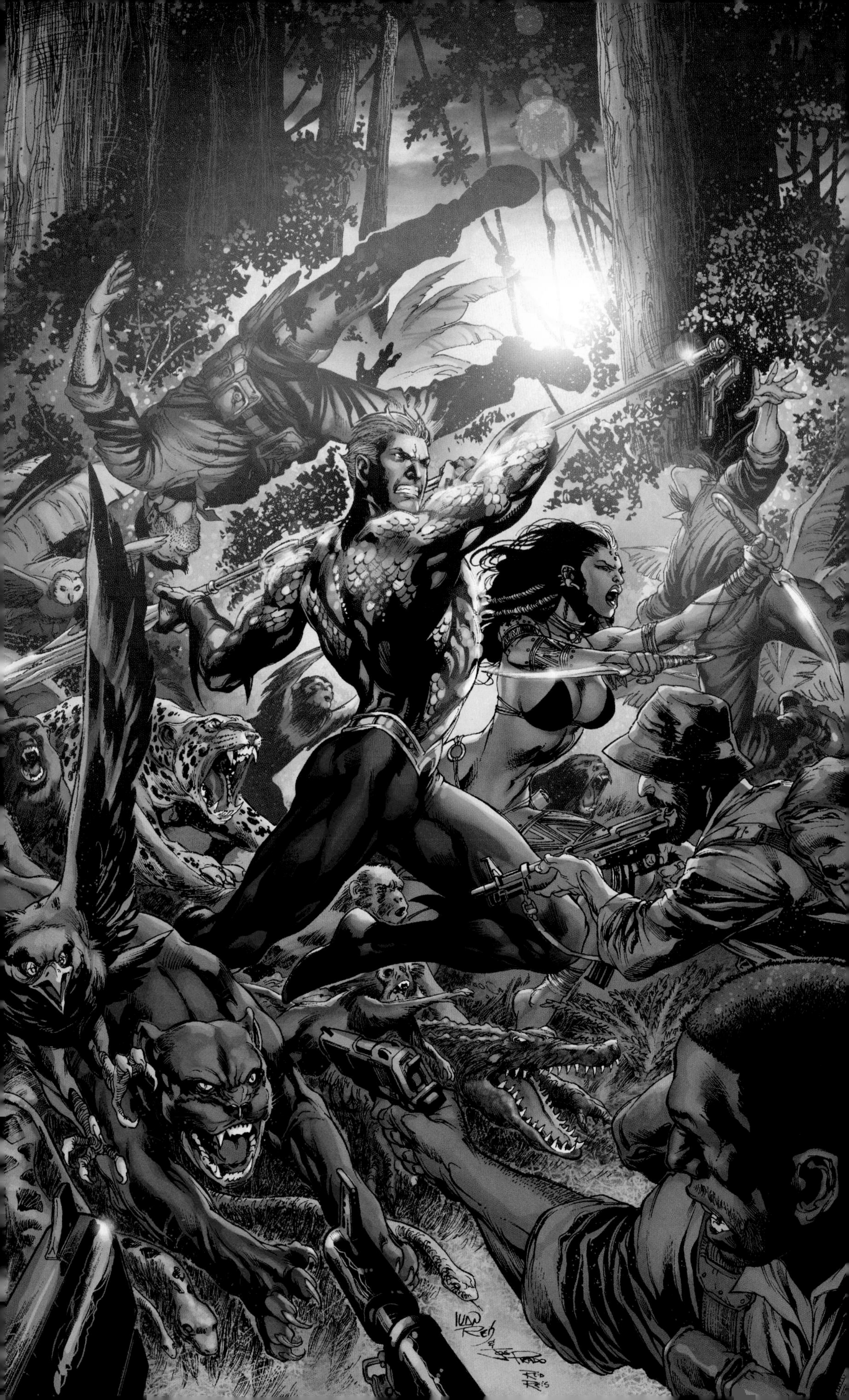

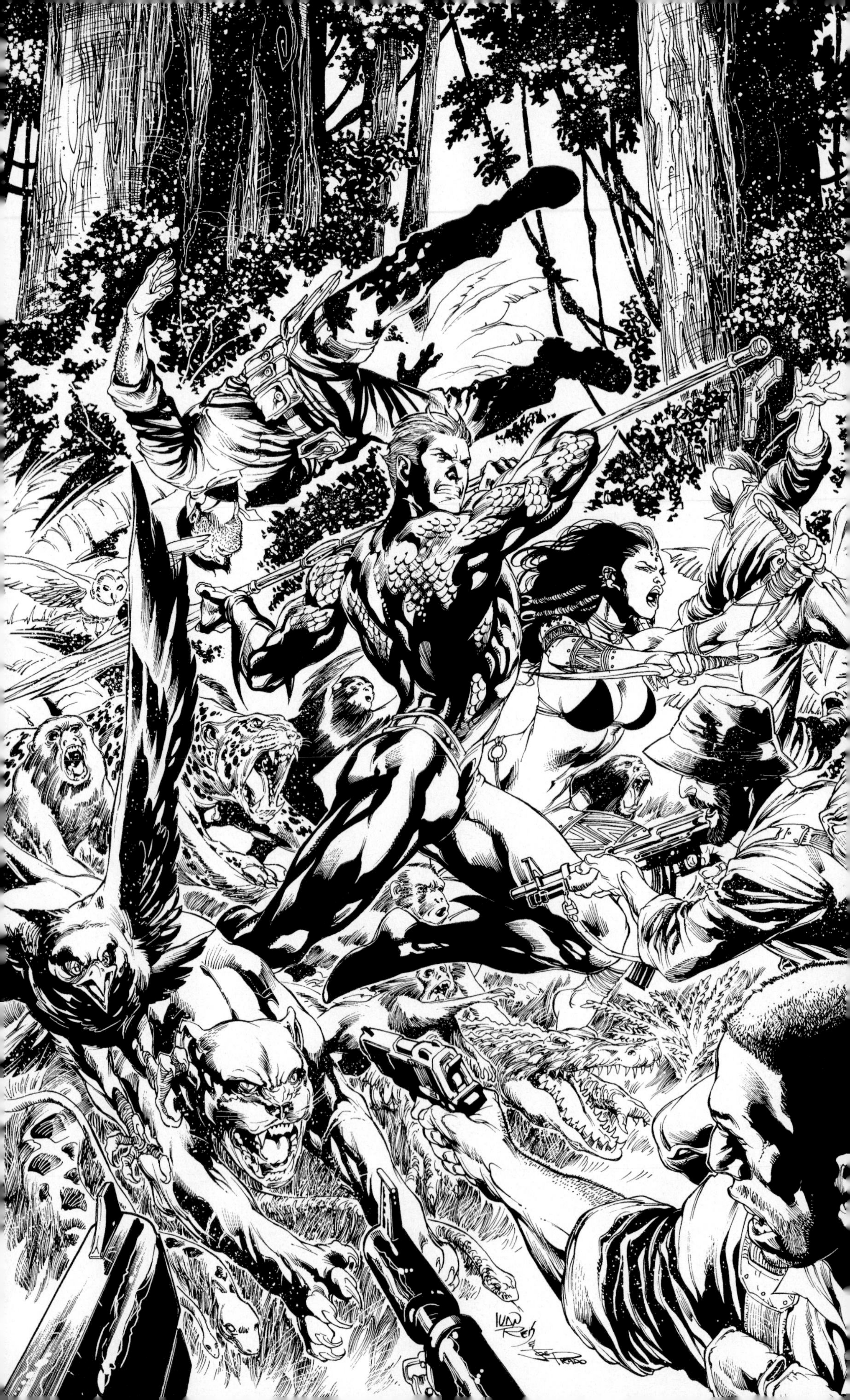

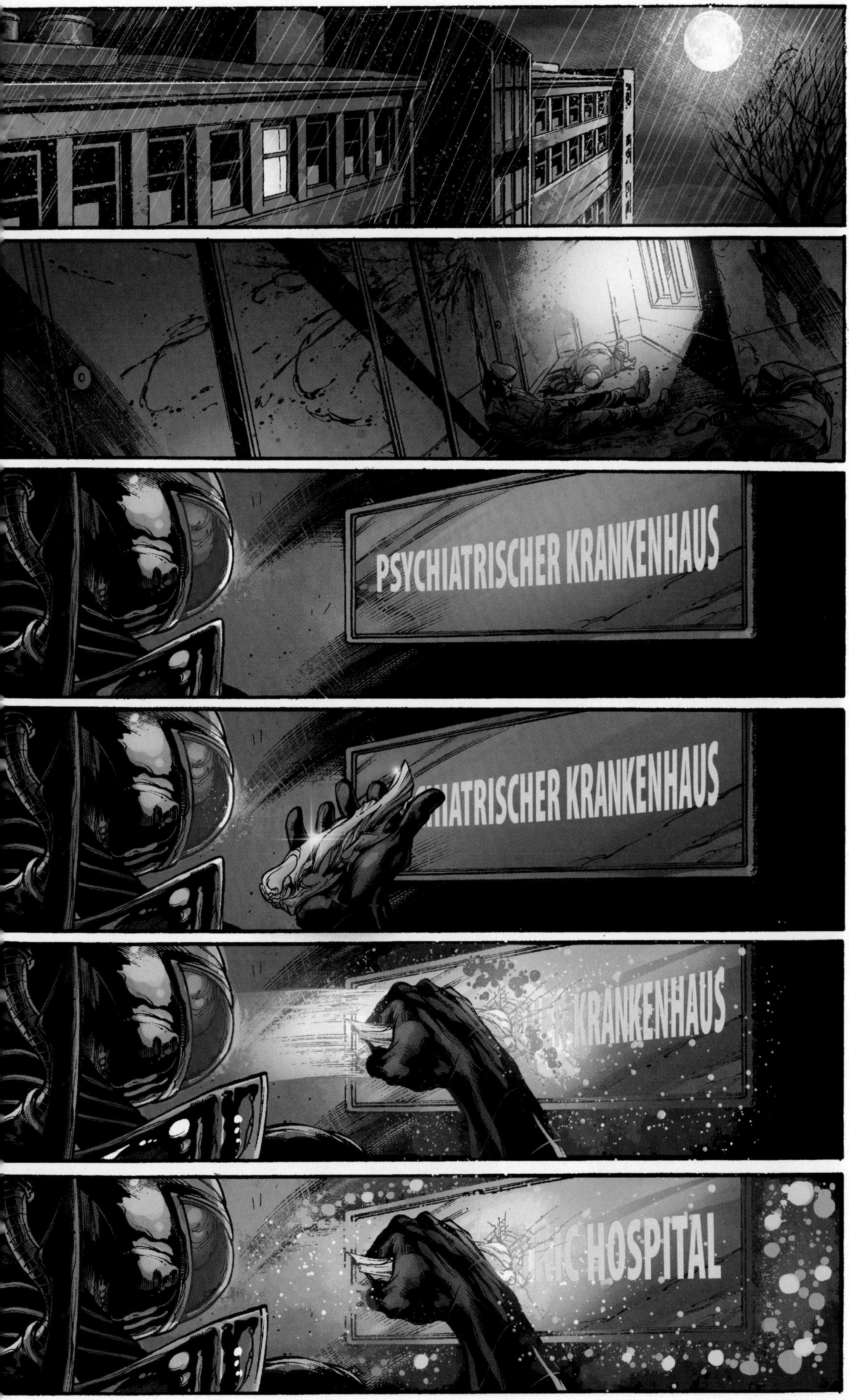
PSYCHIATRISCHER KRANKENHAUS
HIATRISCHER KRANKENHAUS
R KRANKENHAUS
RIC HOSPITAL

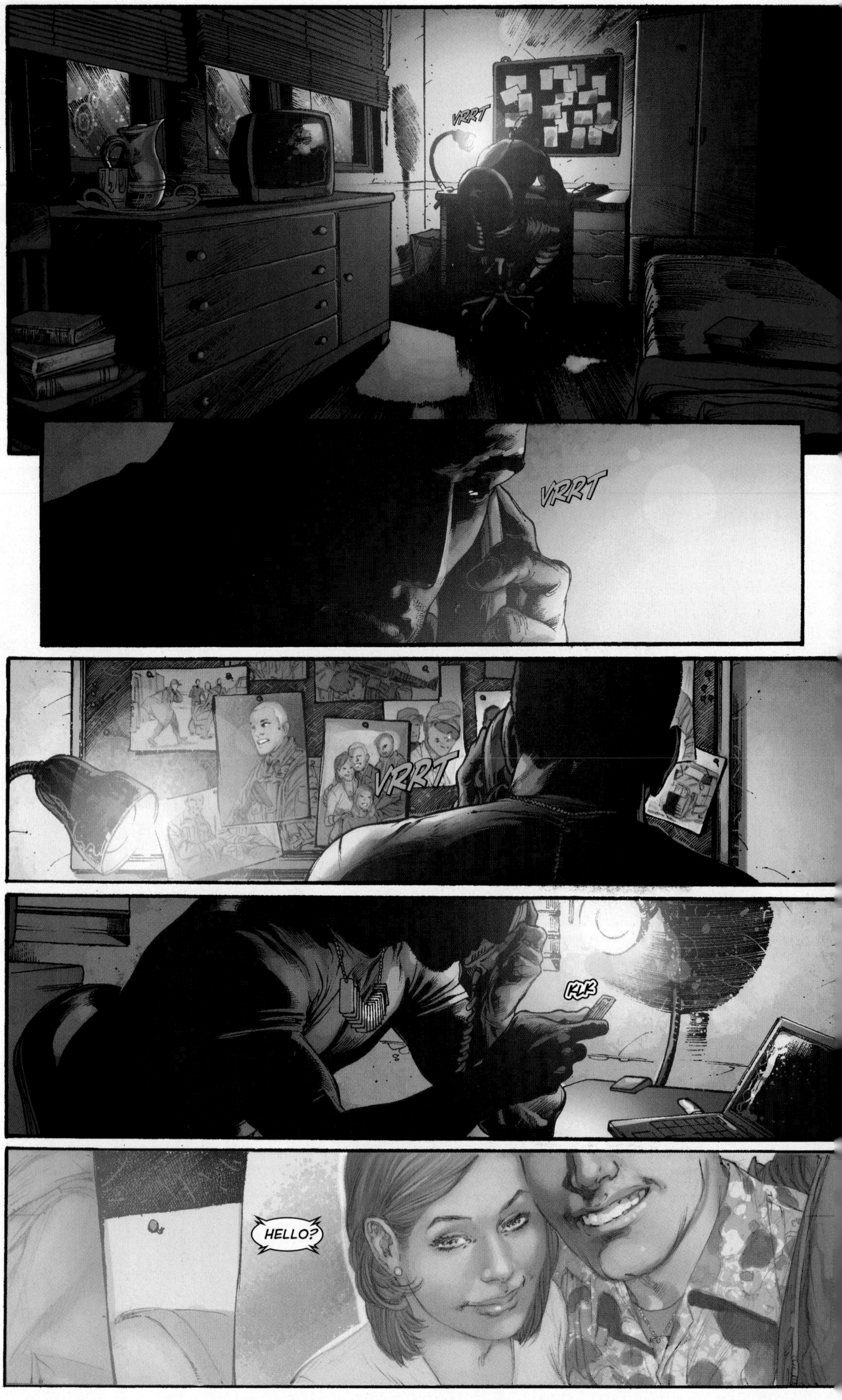
VRRT
VRRT
VRRT
KLIK
HELLO?

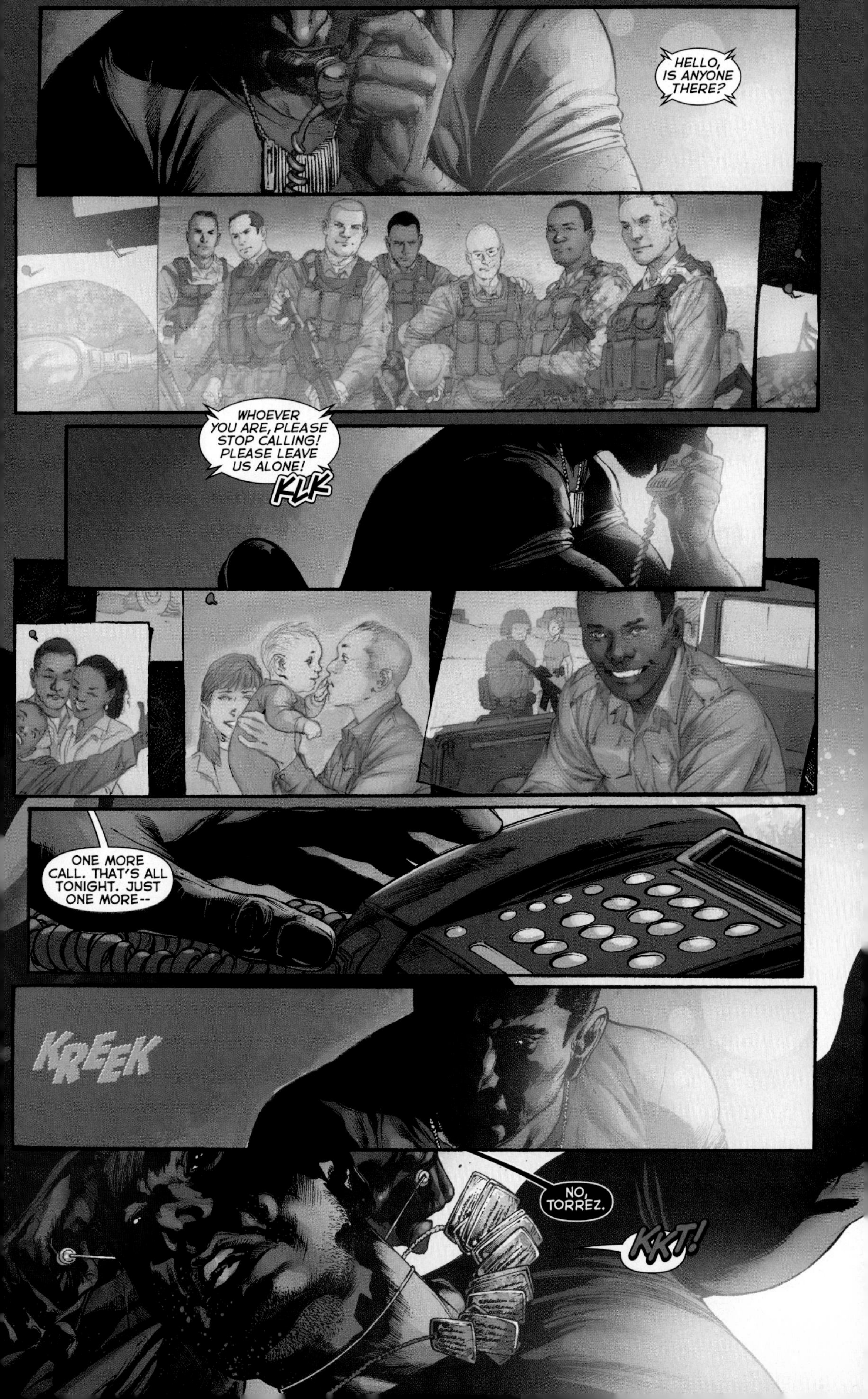
HELLO, IS ANYONE THERE?
WHOEVER YOU ARE, PLEASE STOP CALLING! PLEASE LEAVE US ALONE!
KLIK
ONE MORE CALL. THAT'S ALL TONIGHT. JUST ONE MORE--
KREEK
NO, TORREZ.
KKT!

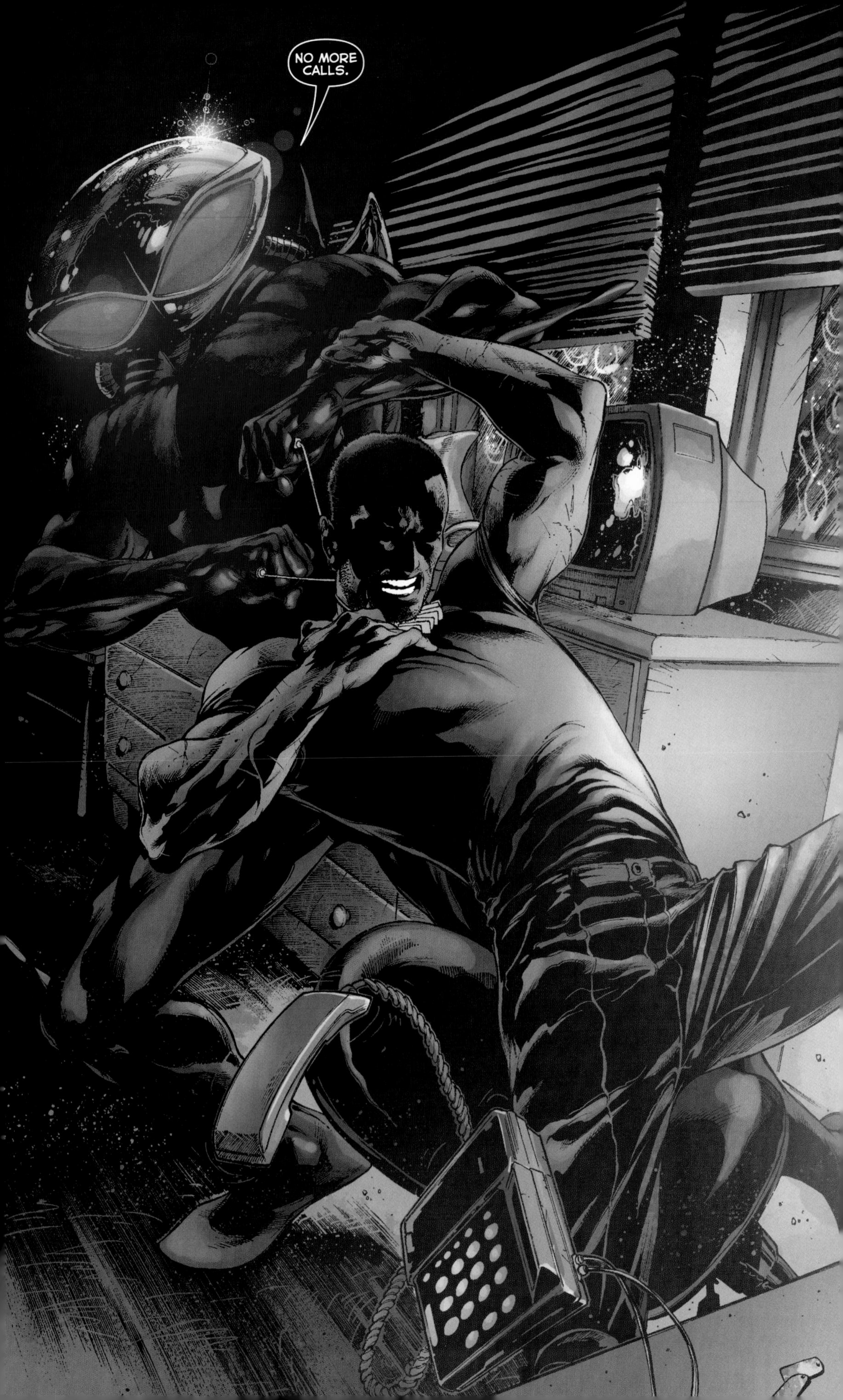
NO MORE CALLS.

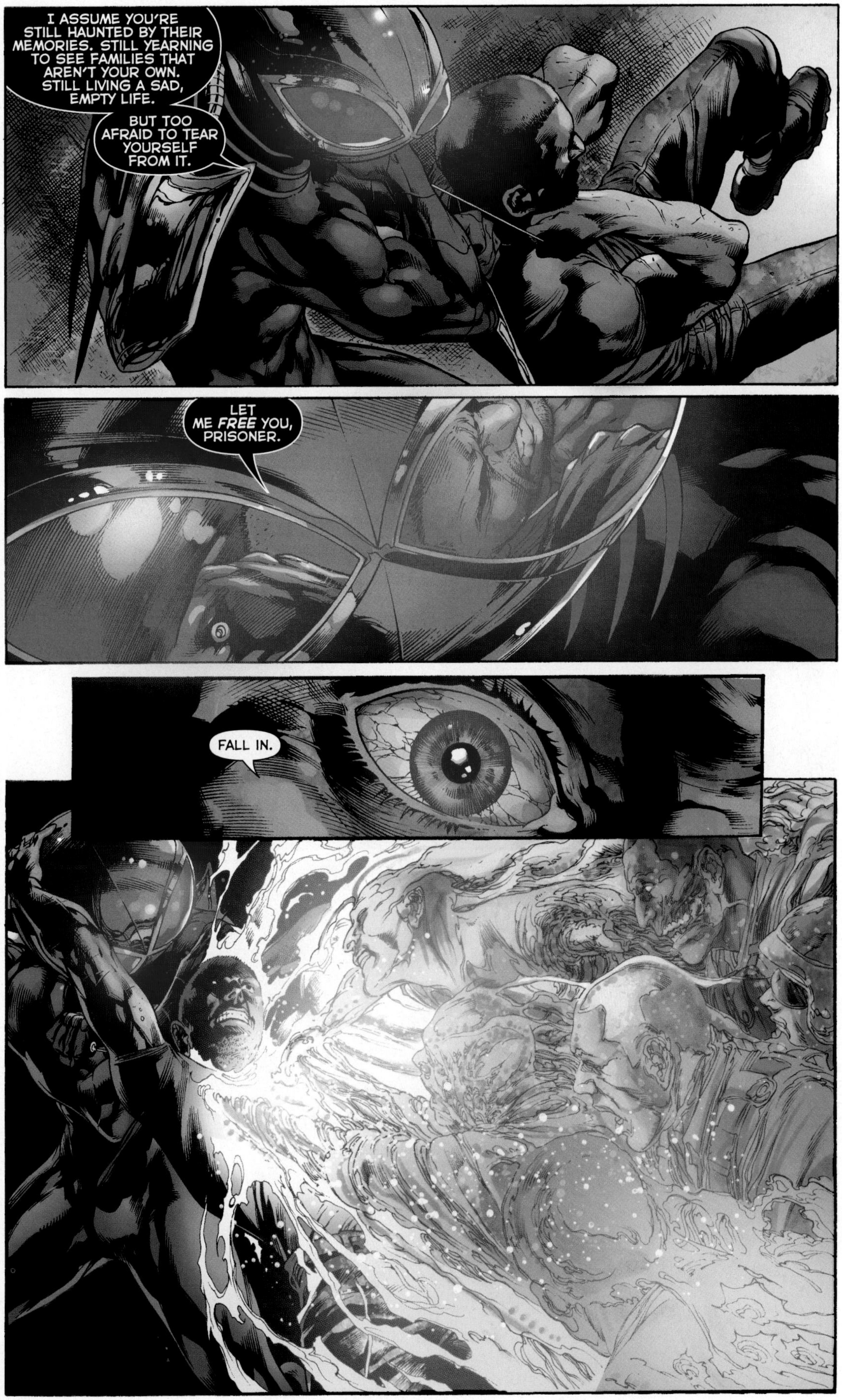
I ASSUME YOU'RE STILL HAUNTED BY THEIR MEMORIES. STILL YEARNING TO SEE FAMILIES THAT AREN'T YOUR OWN. STILL LIVING A SAD, EMPTY LIFE.
BUT TOO AFRAID TO TEAR YOURSELF FROM IT.
LET ME *FREE* YOU, PRISONER.
FALL IN.

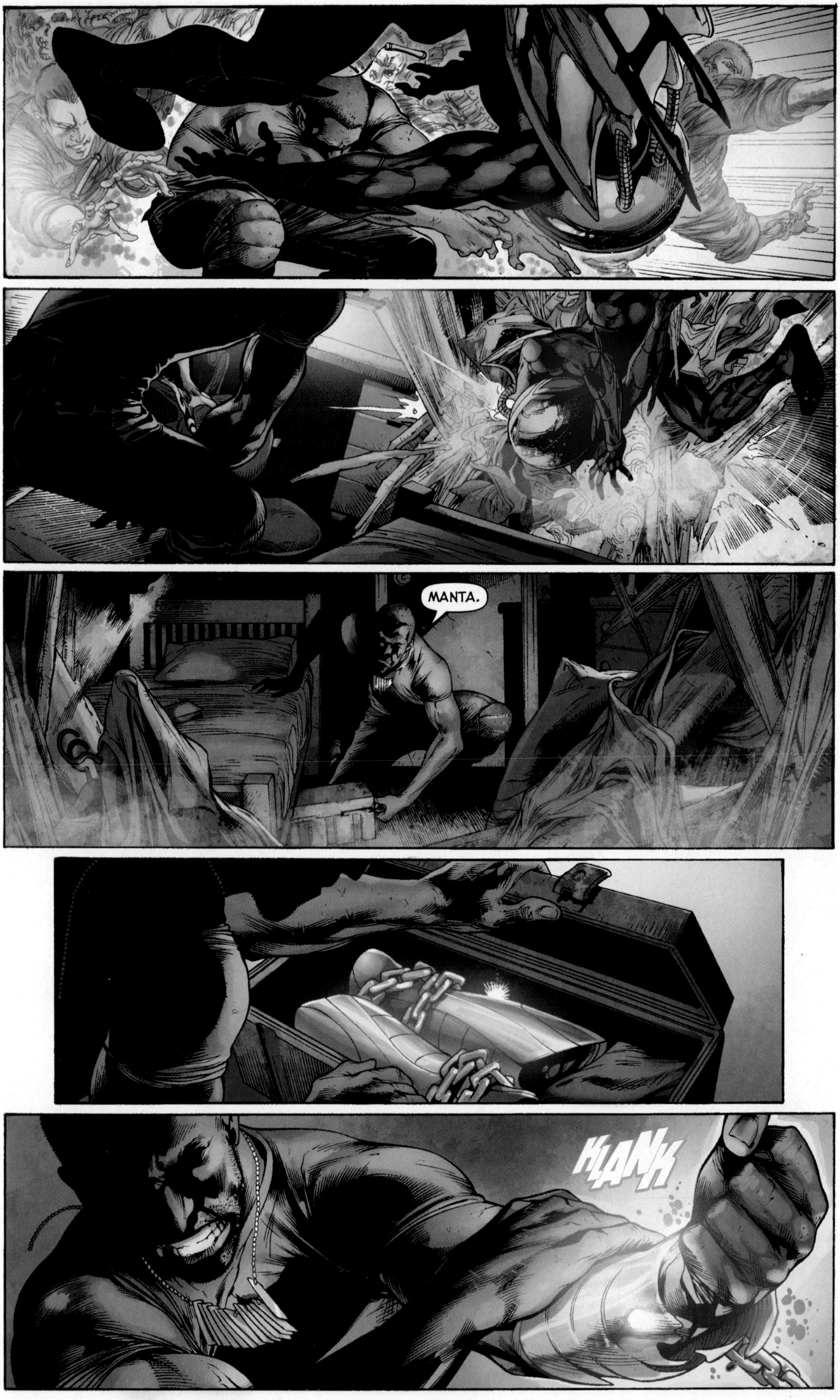
MANTA.
KLANK

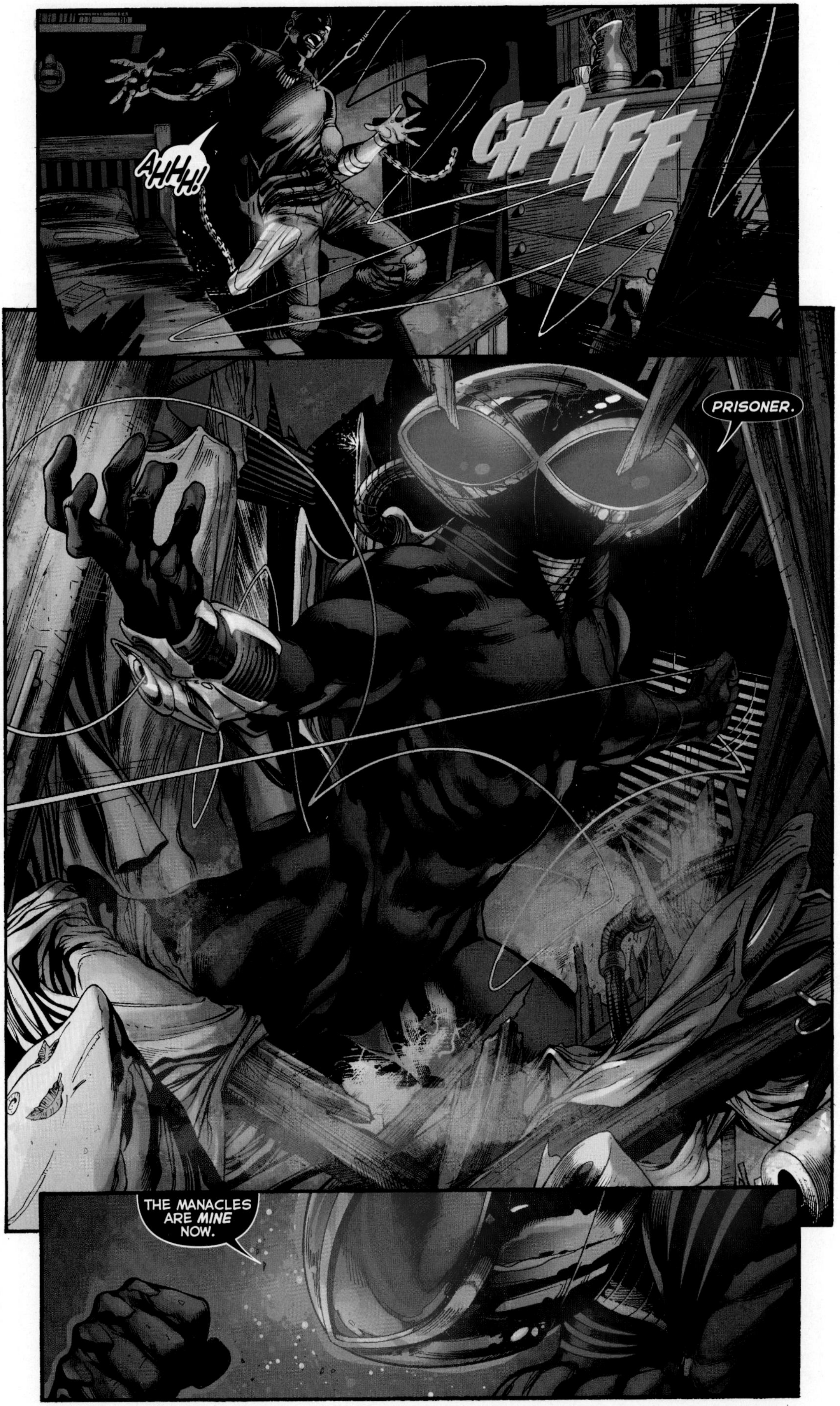

AHHH!
CHANKFF
PRISONER.
THE MANACLES ARE *MINE* NOW.

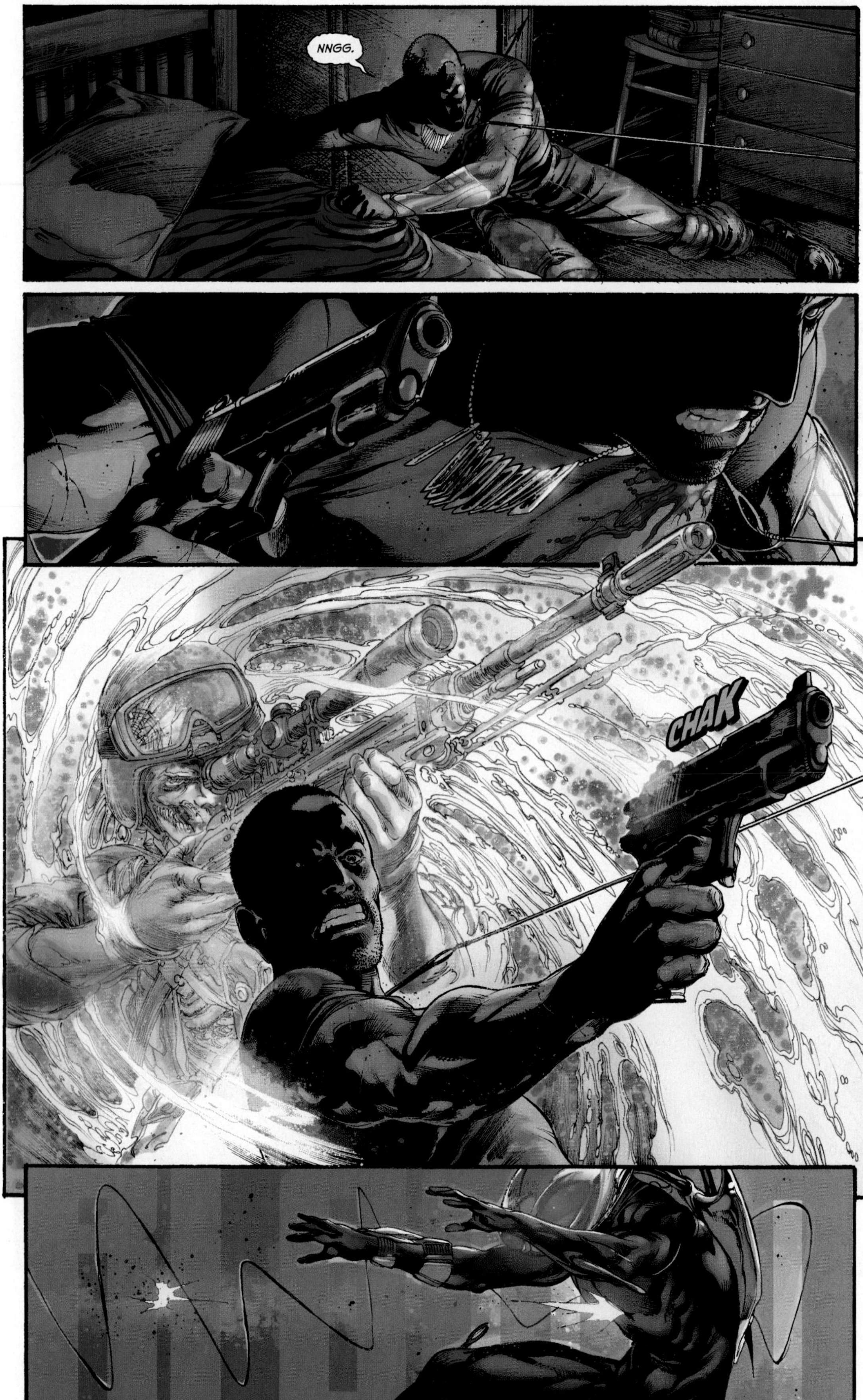
NNGG.
CHAK

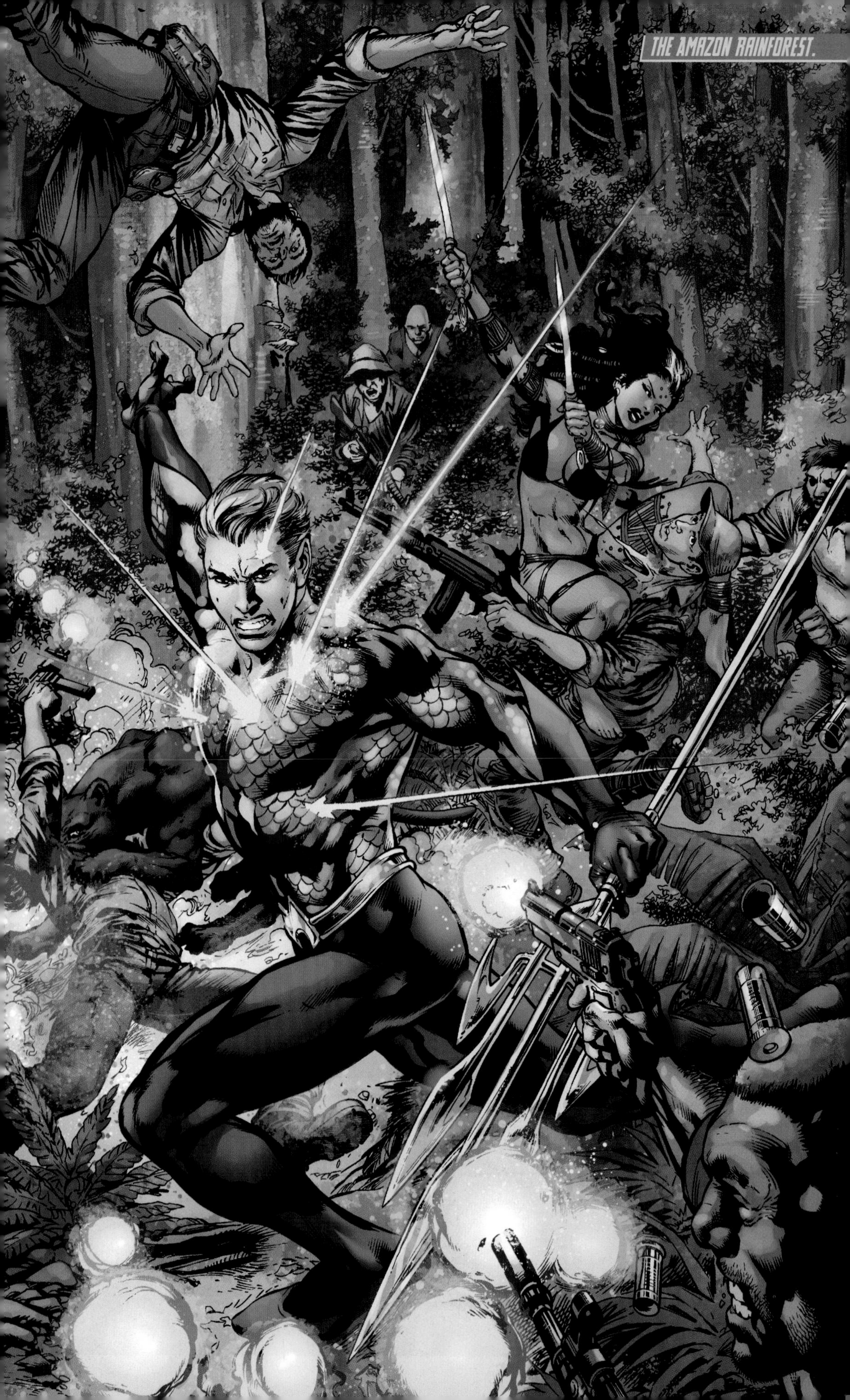
THE AMAZON RAINFOREST.

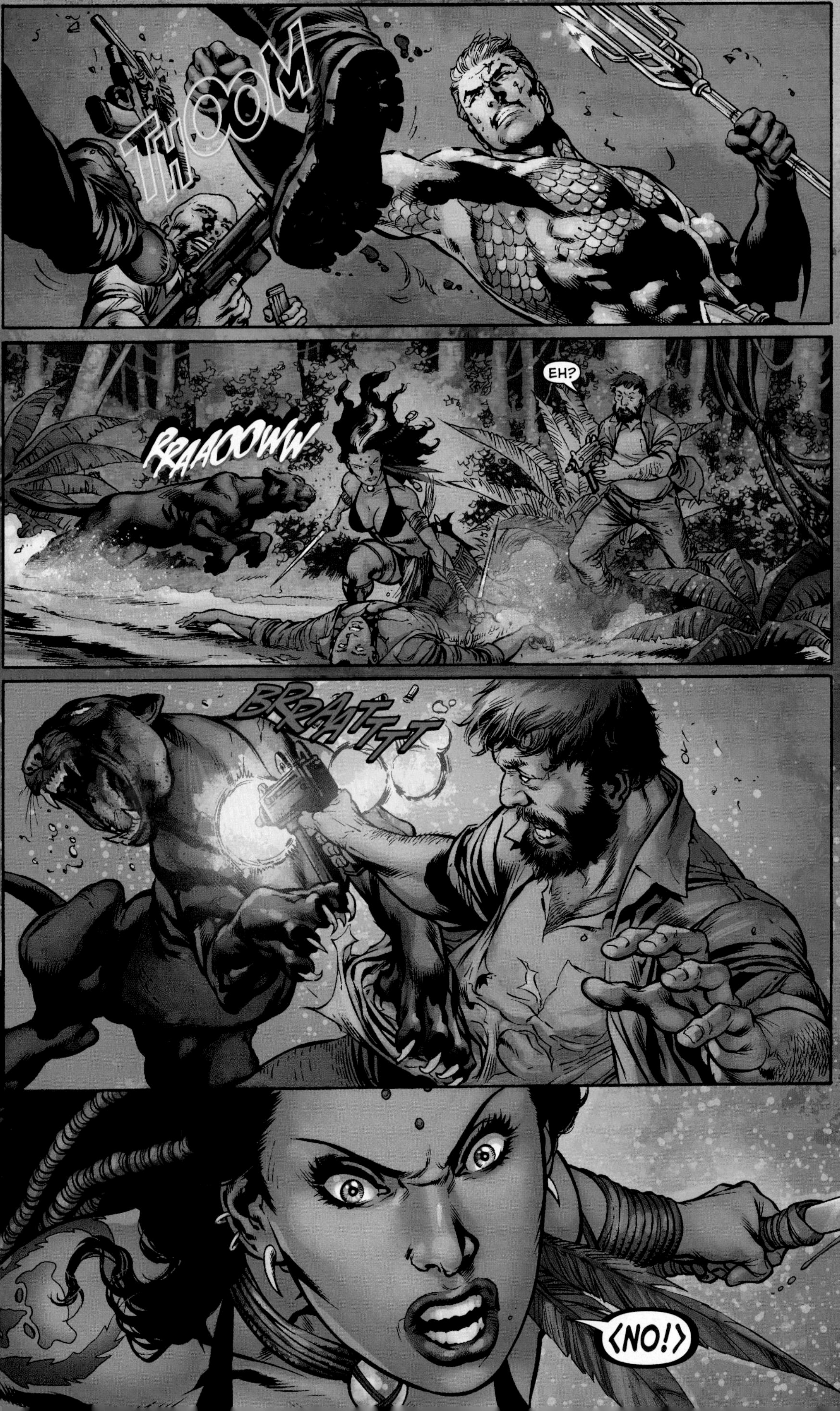
THOOM
EH?
RRAAOOWW
BRRAATTTT
⟨NO!⟩

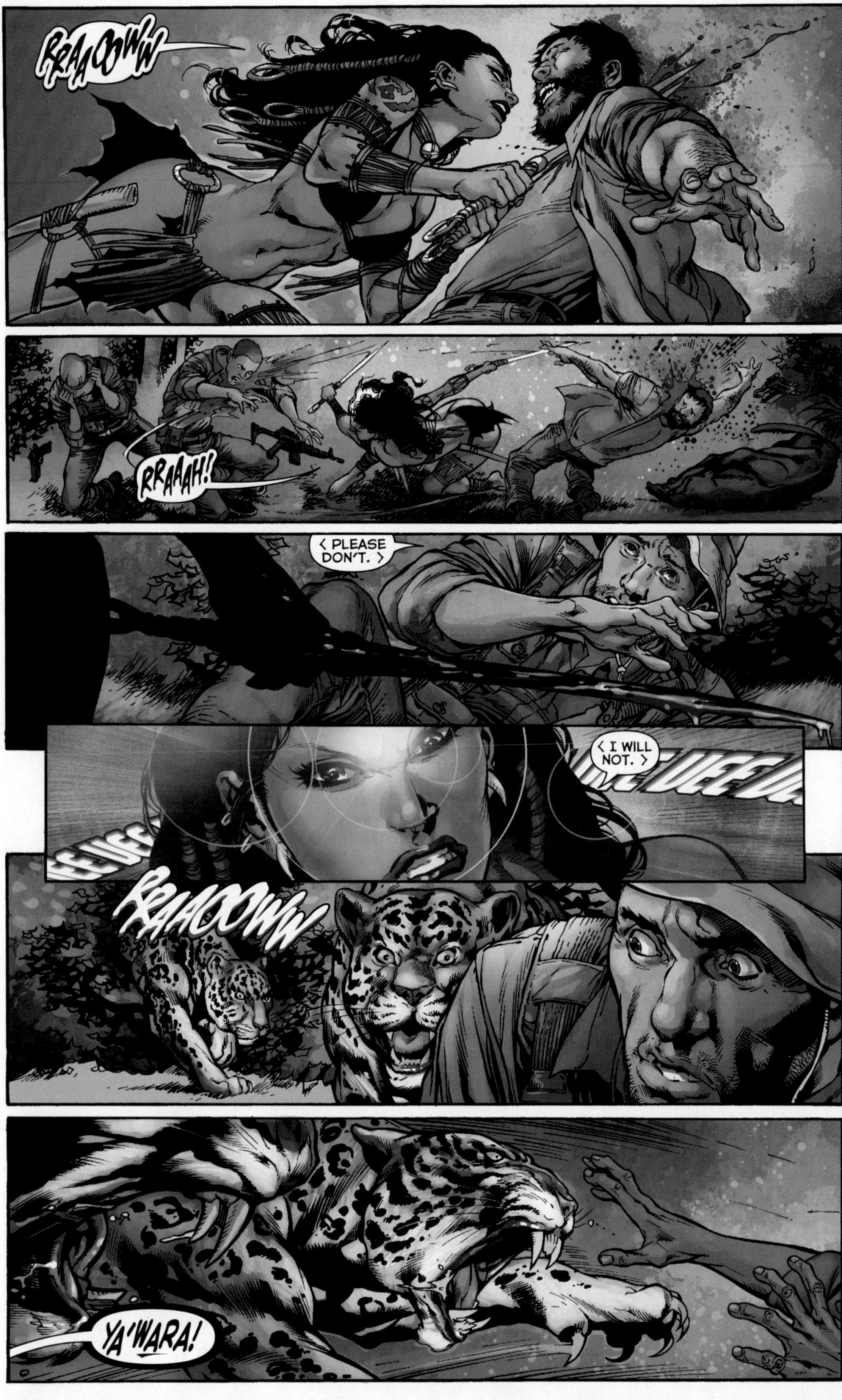
RRAAOOWW
RRAAAH!
< PLEASE DON'T. >
< I WILL NOT. >
RRAAOOWW
YA'WARA!

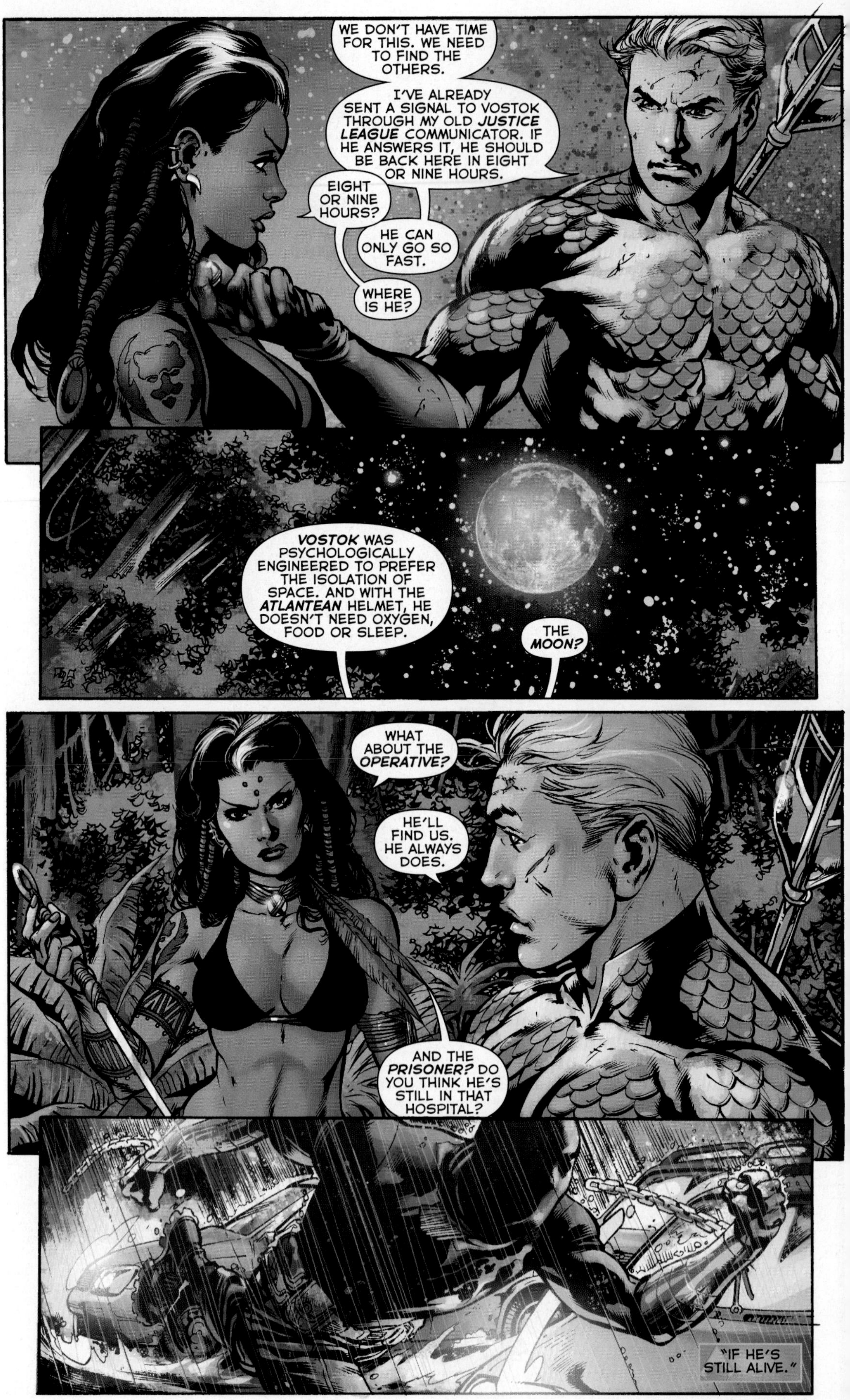
WE DON'T HAVE TIME FOR THIS. WE NEED TO FIND THE OTHERS.
I'VE ALREADY SENT A SIGNAL TO VOSTOK THROUGH MY OLD JUSTICE LEAGUE COMMUNICATOR. IF HE ANSWERS IT, HE SHOULD BE BACK HERE IN EIGHT OR NINE HOURS.
EIGHT OR NINE HOURS?
HE CAN ONLY GO SO FAST.
WHERE IS HE?
VOSTOK WAS PSYCHOLOGICALLY ENGINEERED TO PREFER THE ISOLATION OF SPACE. AND WITH THE ATLANTEAN HELMET, HE DOESN'T NEED OXYGEN, FOOD OR SLEEP.
THE MOON?
WHAT ABOUT THE OPERATIVE?
HE'LL FIND US. HE ALWAYS DOES.
AND THE PRISONER? DO YOU THINK HE'S STILL IN THAT HOSPITAL?
"IF HE'S STILL ALIVE."

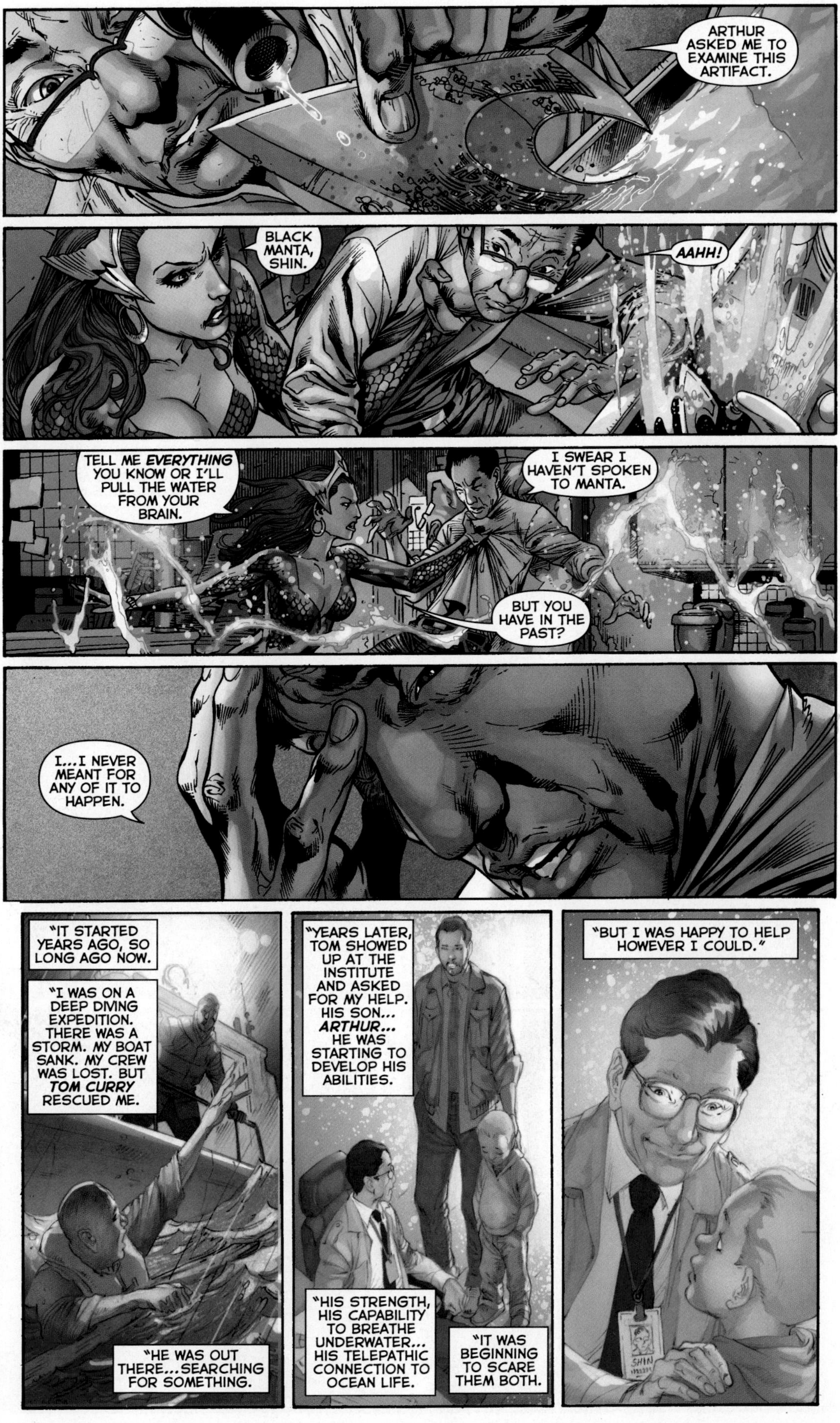
ARTHUR ASKED ME TO EXAMINE THIS ARTIFACT.
BLACK MANTA, SHIN.
AAHH!
TELL ME EVERYTHING YOU KNOW OR I'LL PULL THE WATER FROM YOUR BRAIN.
I SWEAR I HAVEN'T SPOKEN TO MANTA.
BUT YOU HAVE IN THE PAST?
I...I NEVER MEANT FOR ANY OF IT TO HAPPEN.
"IT STARTED YEARS AGO, SO LONG AGO NOW.
"I WAS ON A DEEP DIVING EXPEDITION. THERE WAS A STORM. MY BOAT SANK. MY CREW WAS LOST. BUT TOM CURRY RESCUED ME.
"HE WAS OUT THERE...SEARCHING FOR SOMETHING.
"YEARS LATER, TOM SHOWED UP AT THE INSTITUTE AND ASKED FOR MY HELP. HIS SON... ARTHUR... HE WAS STARTING TO DEVELOP HIS ABILITIES.
"HIS STRENGTH, HIS CAPABILITY TO BREATHE UNDERWATER... HIS TELEPATHIC CONNECTION TO OCEAN LIFE.
"IT WAS BEGINNING TO SCARE THEM BOTH.
"BUT I WAS HAPPY TO HELP HOWEVER I COULD."
SHIN

AND YOU TAUGHT ARTHUR HOW TO CONTROL HIS ABILITIES?

"I TAUGHT HIM HOW TO LOVE THEM. HIS POWERS ARE A MIRACULOUS *GIFT*.

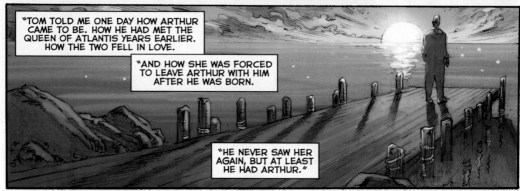

"TOM TOLD ME ONE DAY HOW ARTHUR CAME TO BE. HOW HE HAD MET THE QUEEN OF ATLANTIS YEARS EARLIER. HOW THE TWO FELL IN LOVE.

"AND HOW SHE WAS FORCED TO LEAVE ARTHUR WITH HIM AFTER HE WAS BORN.

"HE NEVER SAW HER AGAIN, BUT AT LEAST HE HAD ARTHUR."

AND THAT BOY WOULD BE THE MOST SIGNIFICANT SCIENTIFIC DISCOVERY OF OUR ERA.

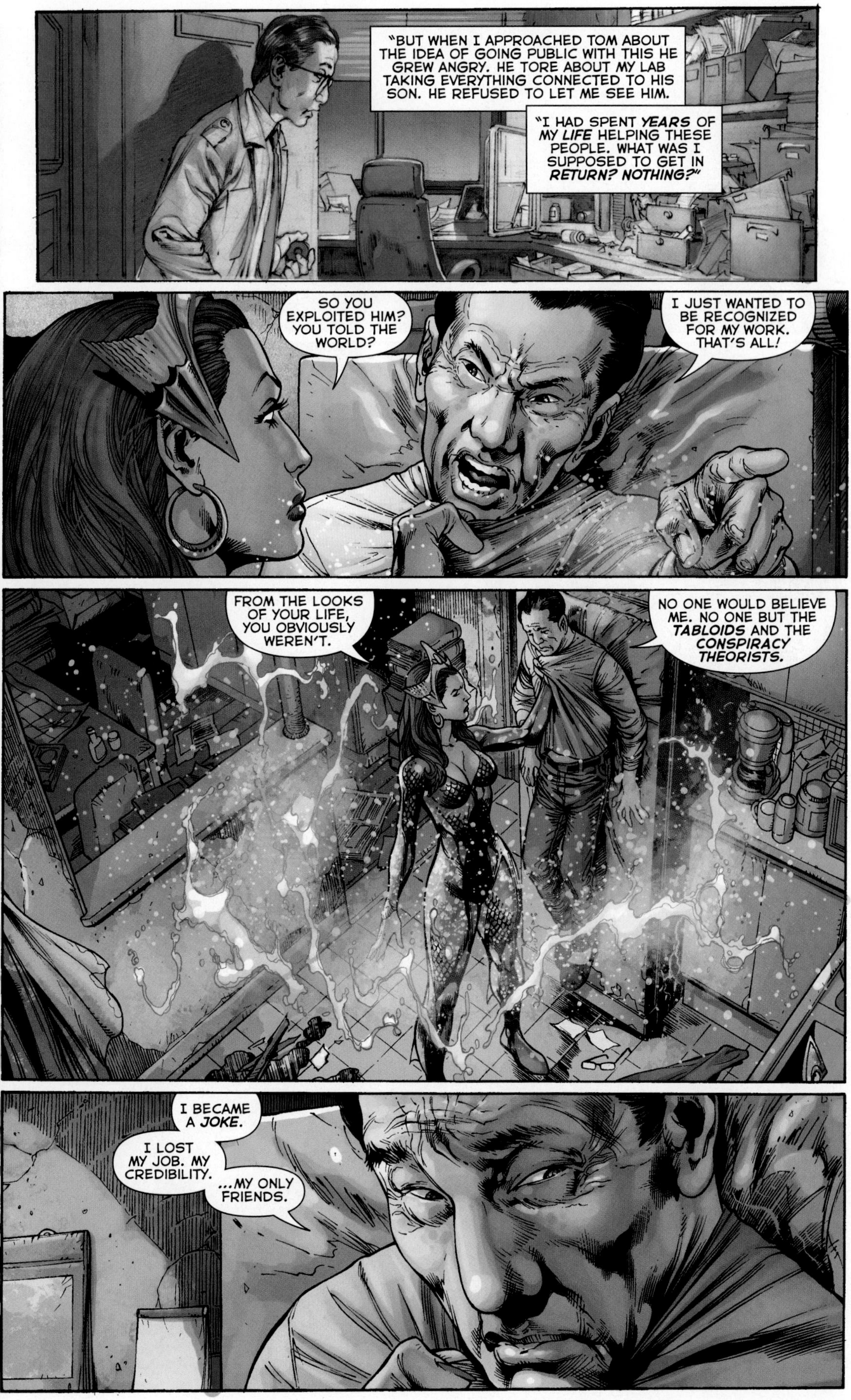
"BUT WHEN I APPROACHED TOM ABOUT THE IDEA OF GOING PUBLIC WITH THIS HE GREW ANGRY. HE TORE ABOUT MY LAB TAKING EVERYTHING CONNECTED TO HIS SON. HE REFUSED TO LET ME SEE HIM.
"I HAD SPENT *YEARS* OF MY *LIFE* HELPING THESE PEOPLE. WHAT WAS I SUPPOSED TO GET IN *RETURN? NOTHING?*"
SO YOU EXPLOITED HIM? YOU TOLD THE WORLD?
I JUST WANTED TO BE RECOGNIZED FOR MY WORK. THAT'S ALL!
FROM THE LOOKS OF YOUR LIFE, YOU OBVIOUSLY WEREN'T.
NO ONE WOULD BELIEVE ME. NO ONE BUT THE *TABLOIDS* AND THE *CONSPIRACY THEORISTS.*
I BECAME A *JOKE*.
I LOST MY JOB. MY CREDIBILITY.
...MY ONLY FRIENDS.

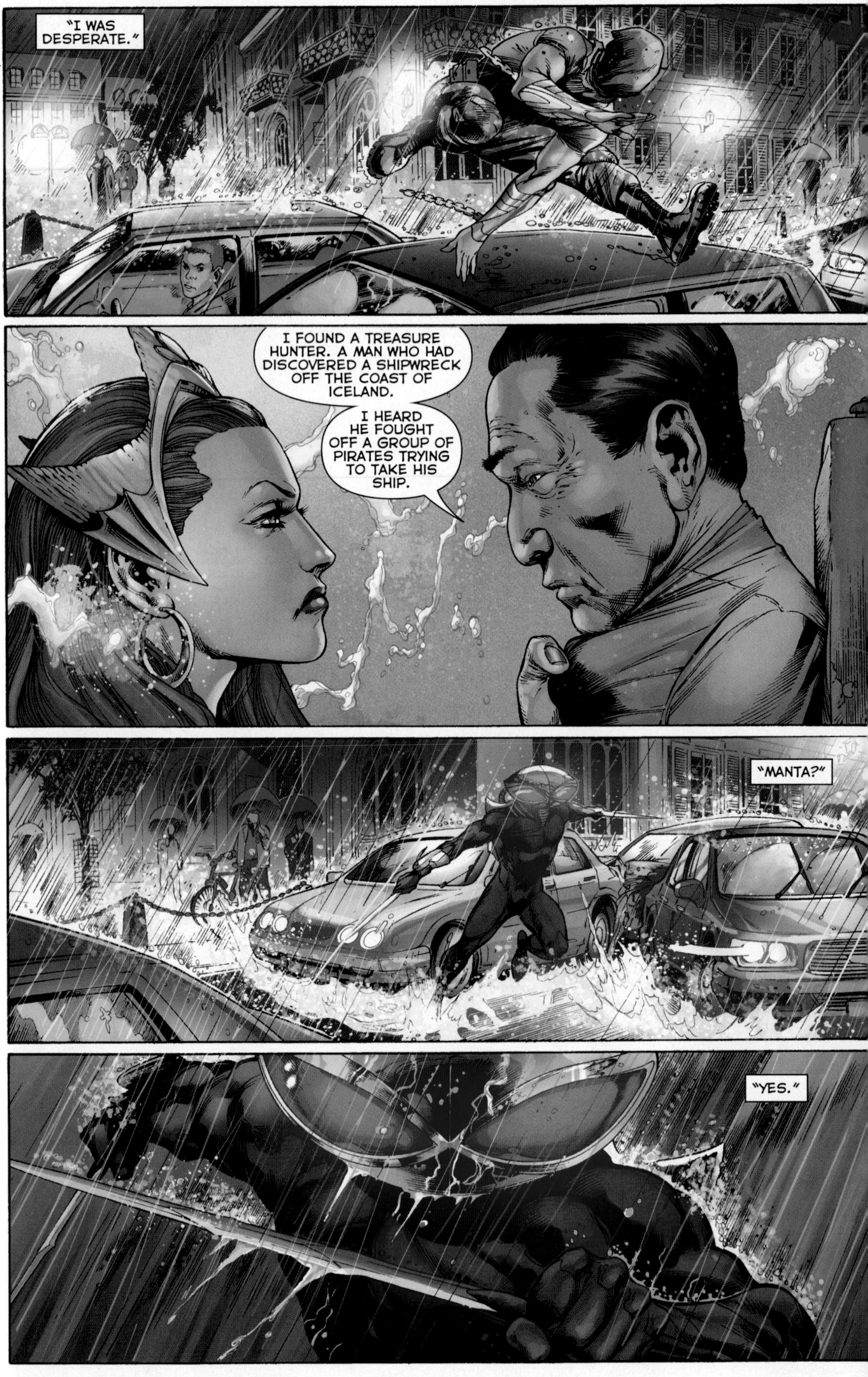
"I WAS DESPERATE."
I FOUND A TREASURE HUNTER. A MAN WHO HAD DISCOVERED A SHIPWRECK OFF THE COAST OF ICELAND.
I HEARD HE FOUGHT OFF A GROUP OF PIRATES TRYING TO TAKE HIS SHIP.
"MANTA?"
"YES."

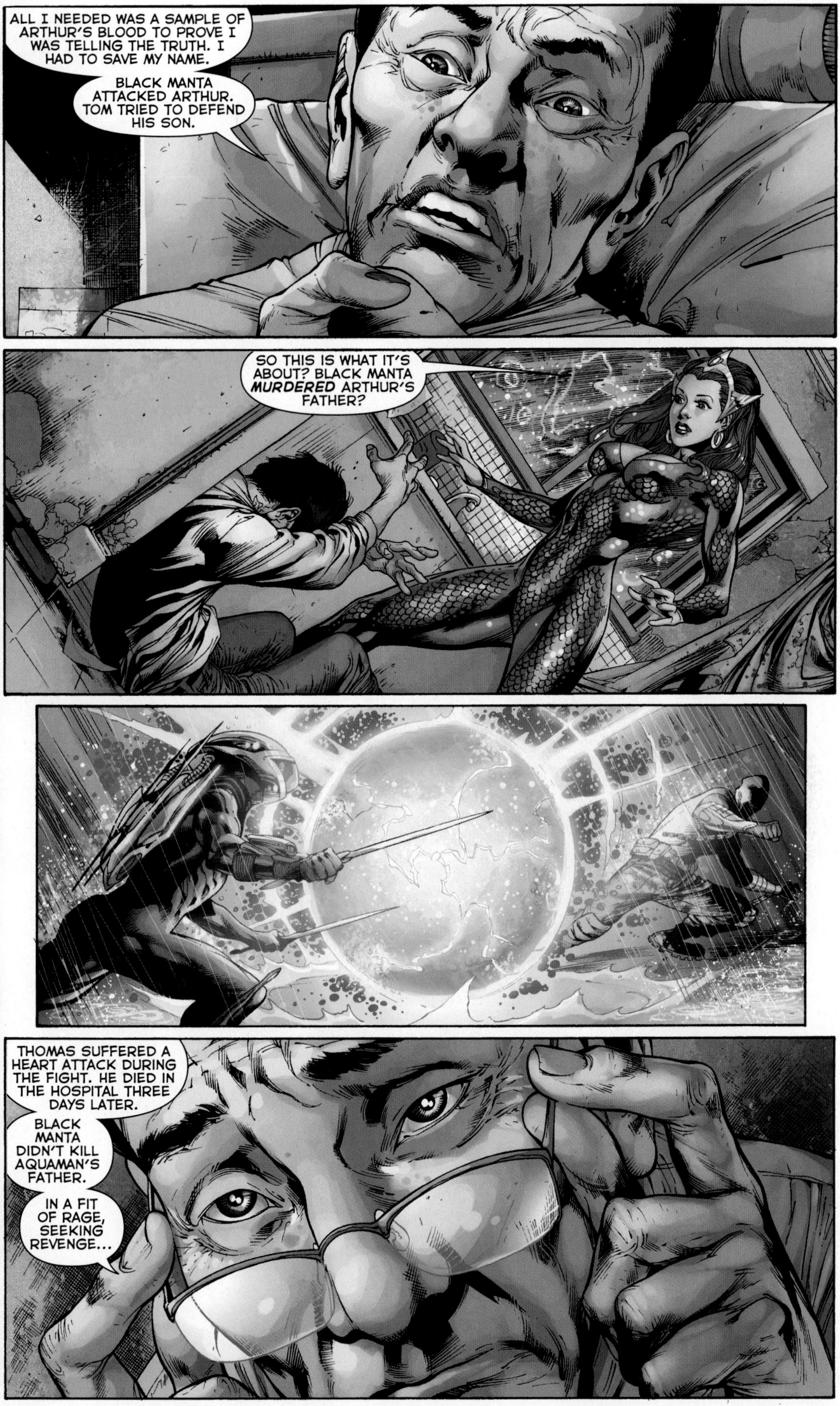
ALL I NEEDED WAS A SAMPLE OF ARTHUR'S BLOOD TO PROVE I WAS TELLING THE TRUTH. I HAD TO SAVE MY NAME.
BLACK MANTA ATTACKED ARTHUR. TOM TRIED TO DEFEND HIS SON.
SO THIS IS WHAT IT'S ABOUT? BLACK MANTA *MURDERED* ARTHUR'S FATHER?
THOMAS SUFFERED A HEART ATTACK DURING THE FIGHT. HE DIED IN THE HOSPITAL THREE DAYS LATER.
BLACK MANTA DIDN'T KILL AQUAMAN'S FATHER.
IN A FIT OF RAGE, SEEKING REVENGE...

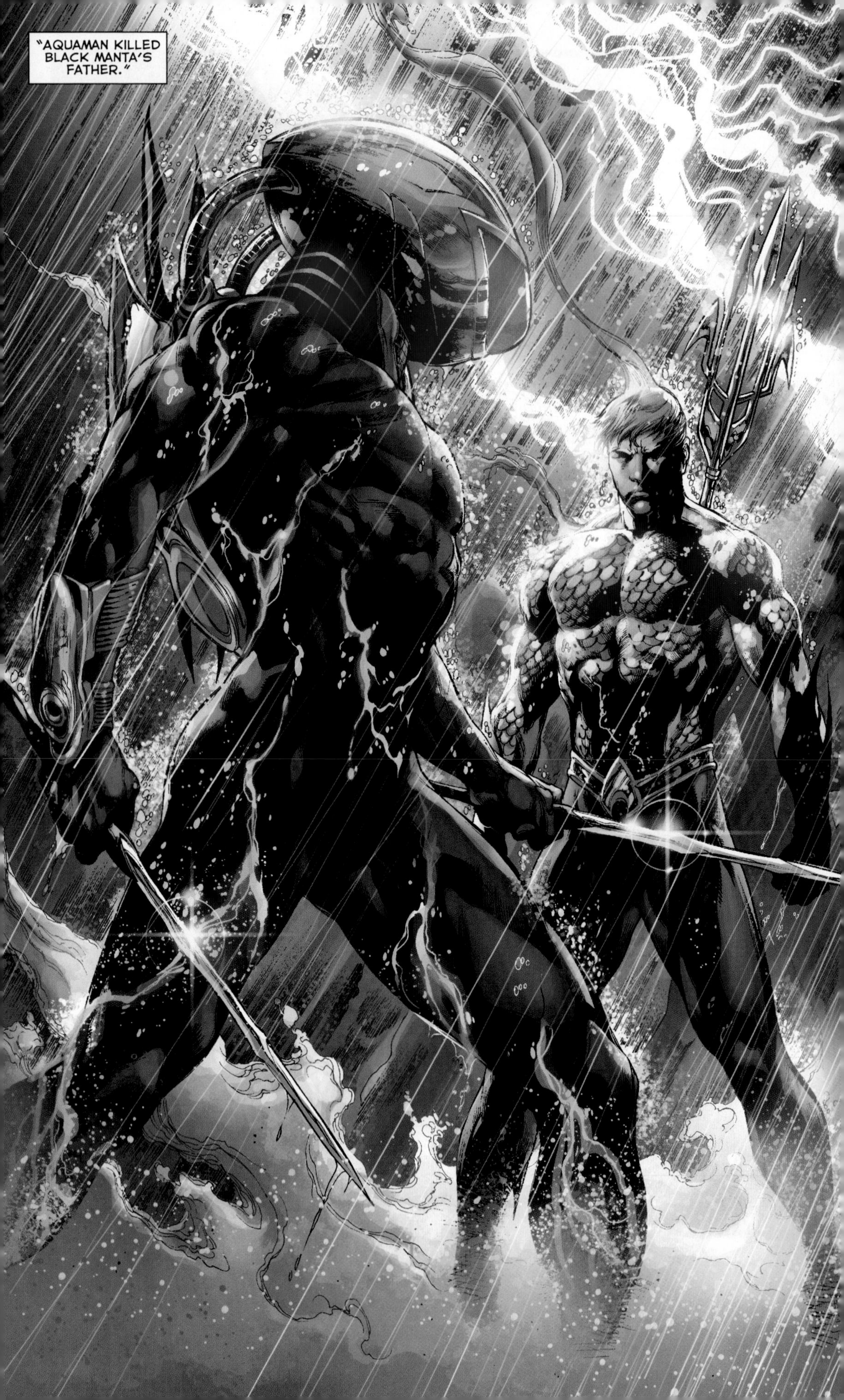
"AQUAMAN KILLED BLACK MANTA'S FATHER."

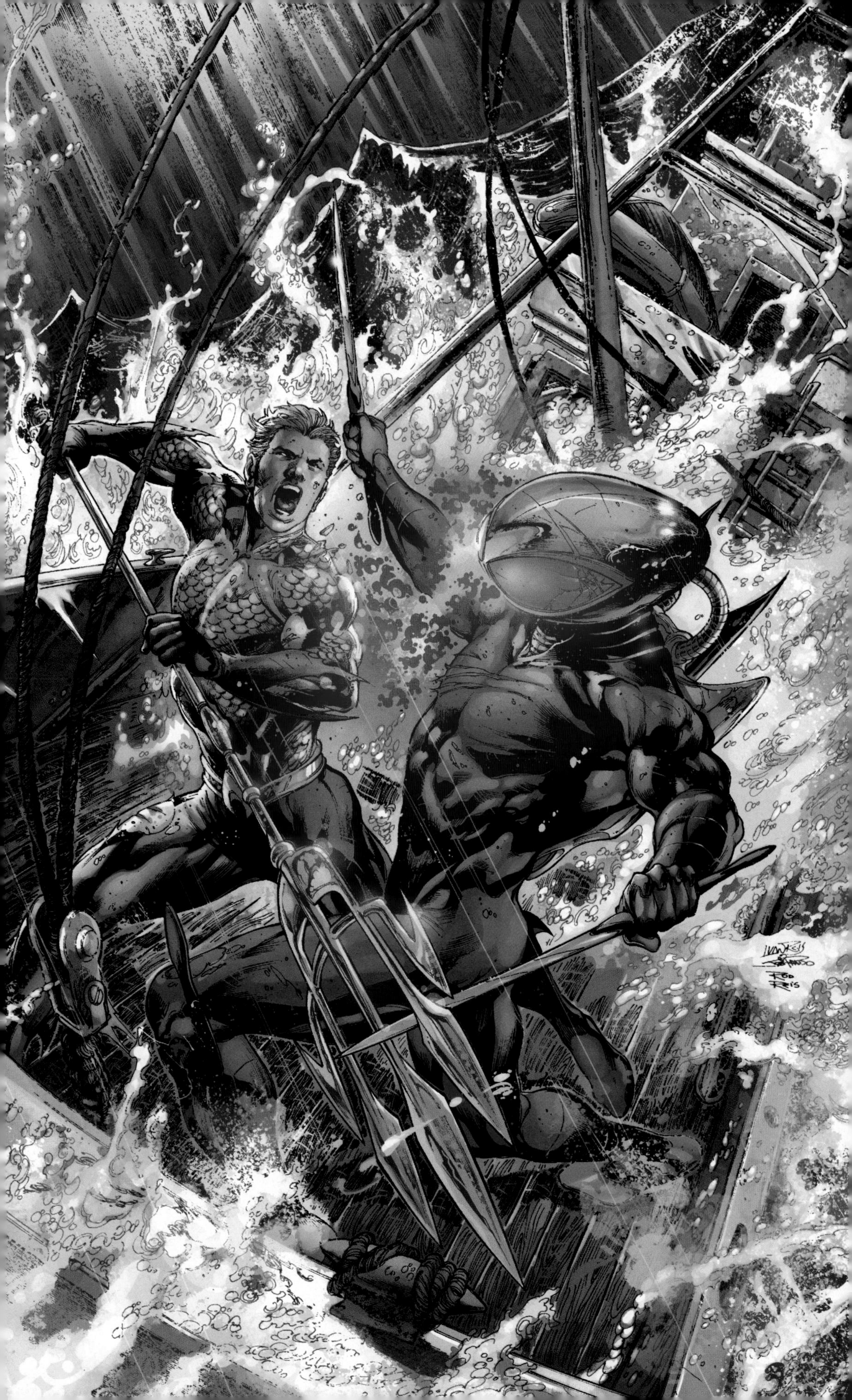

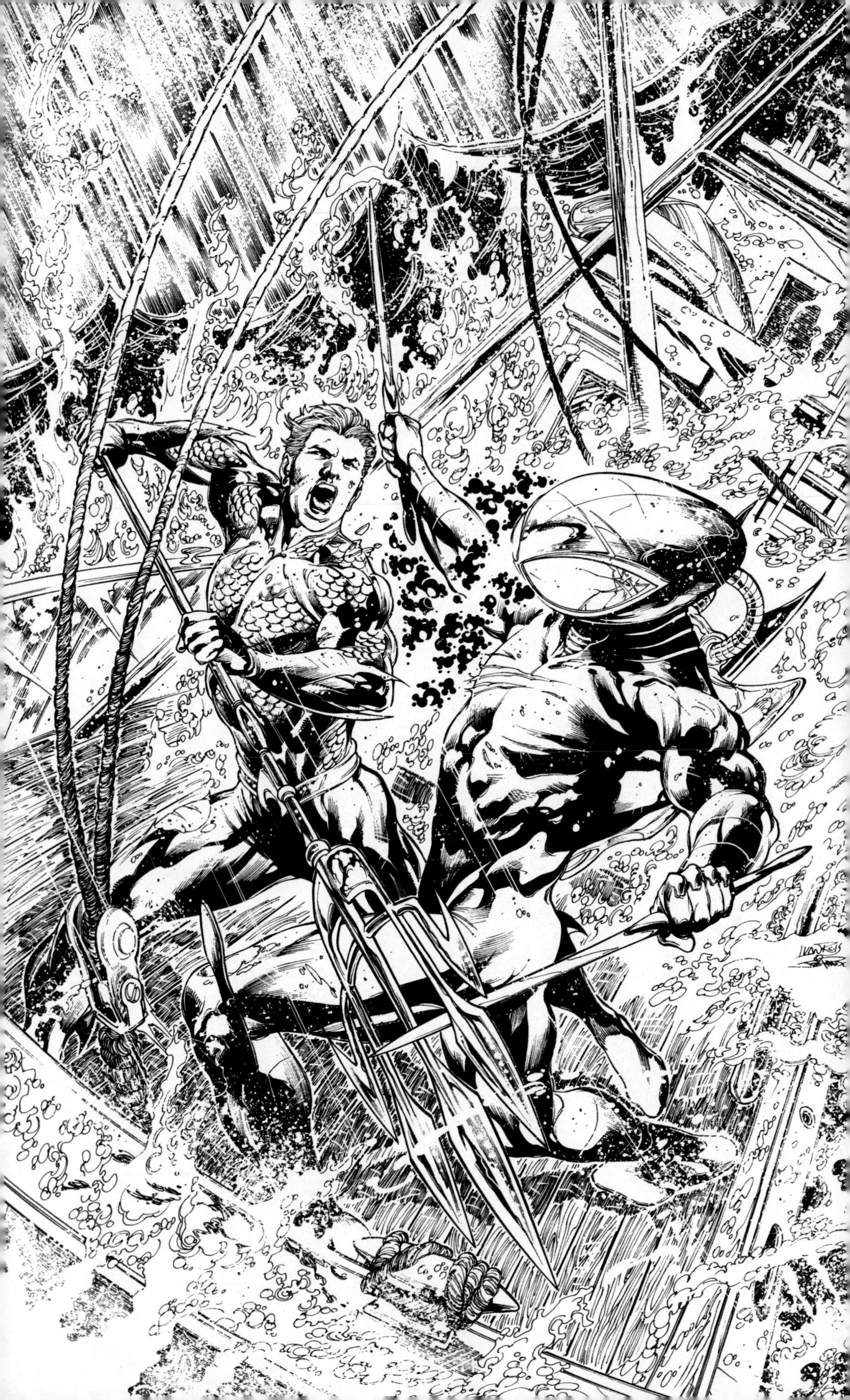

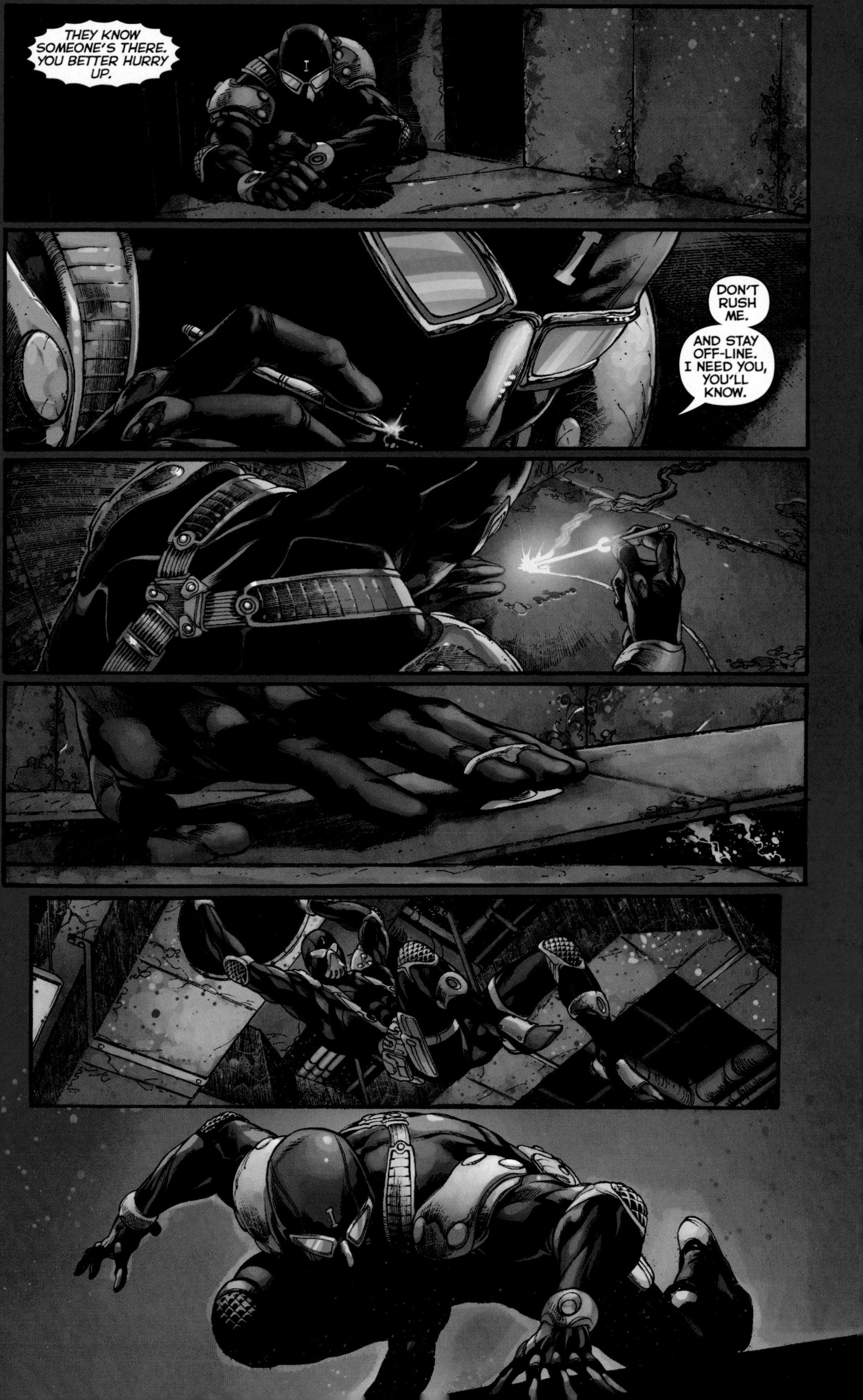
THEY KNOW SOMEONE'S THERE. YOU BETTER HURRY UP.
DON'T RUSH ME.
AND STAY OFF-LINE. I NEED YOU, YOU'LL KNOW.

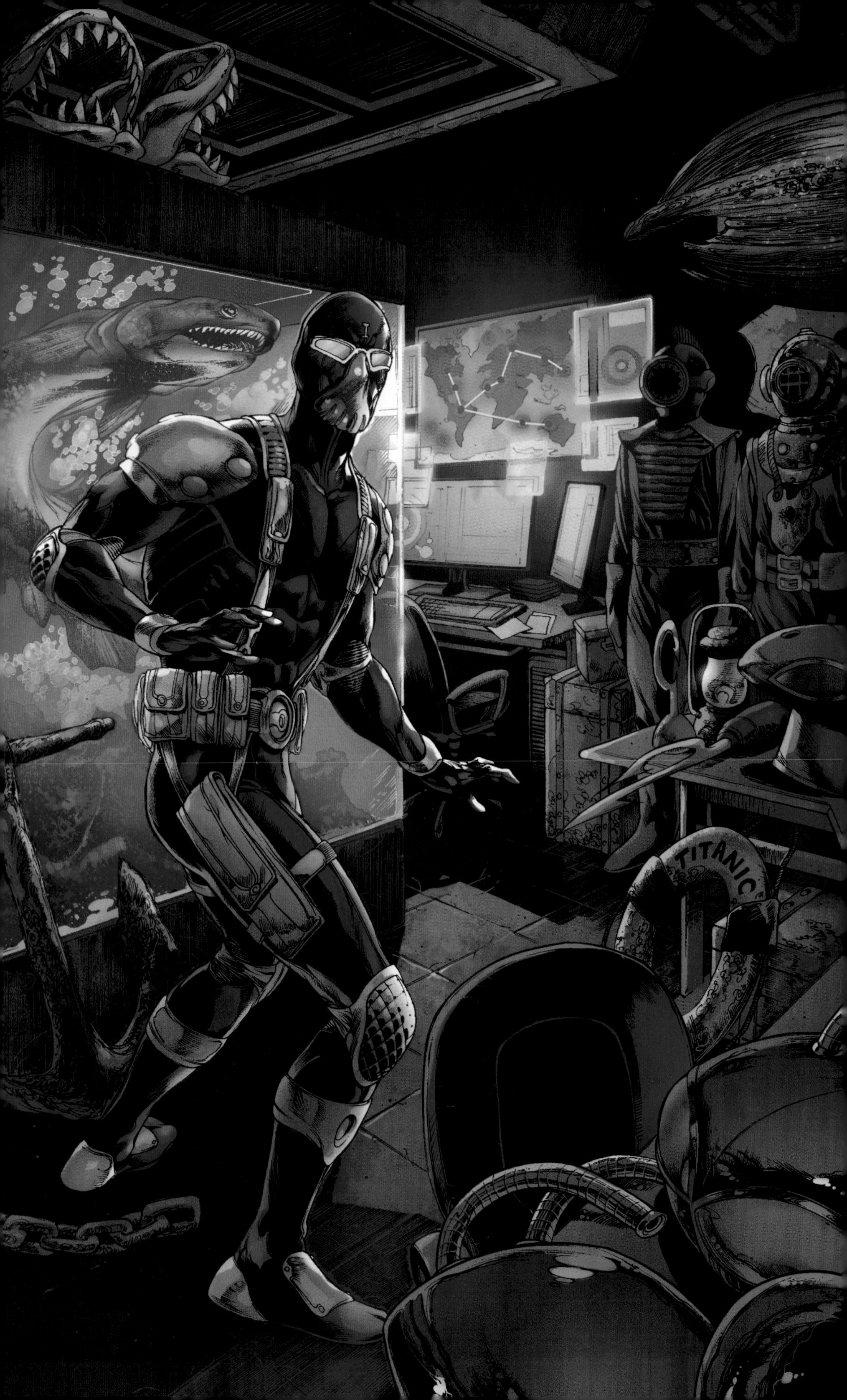
TITANIC

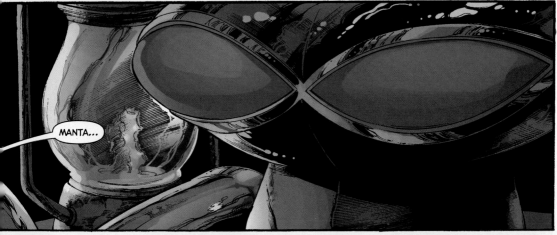

MANTA...

HOW DID YOU FIND US?

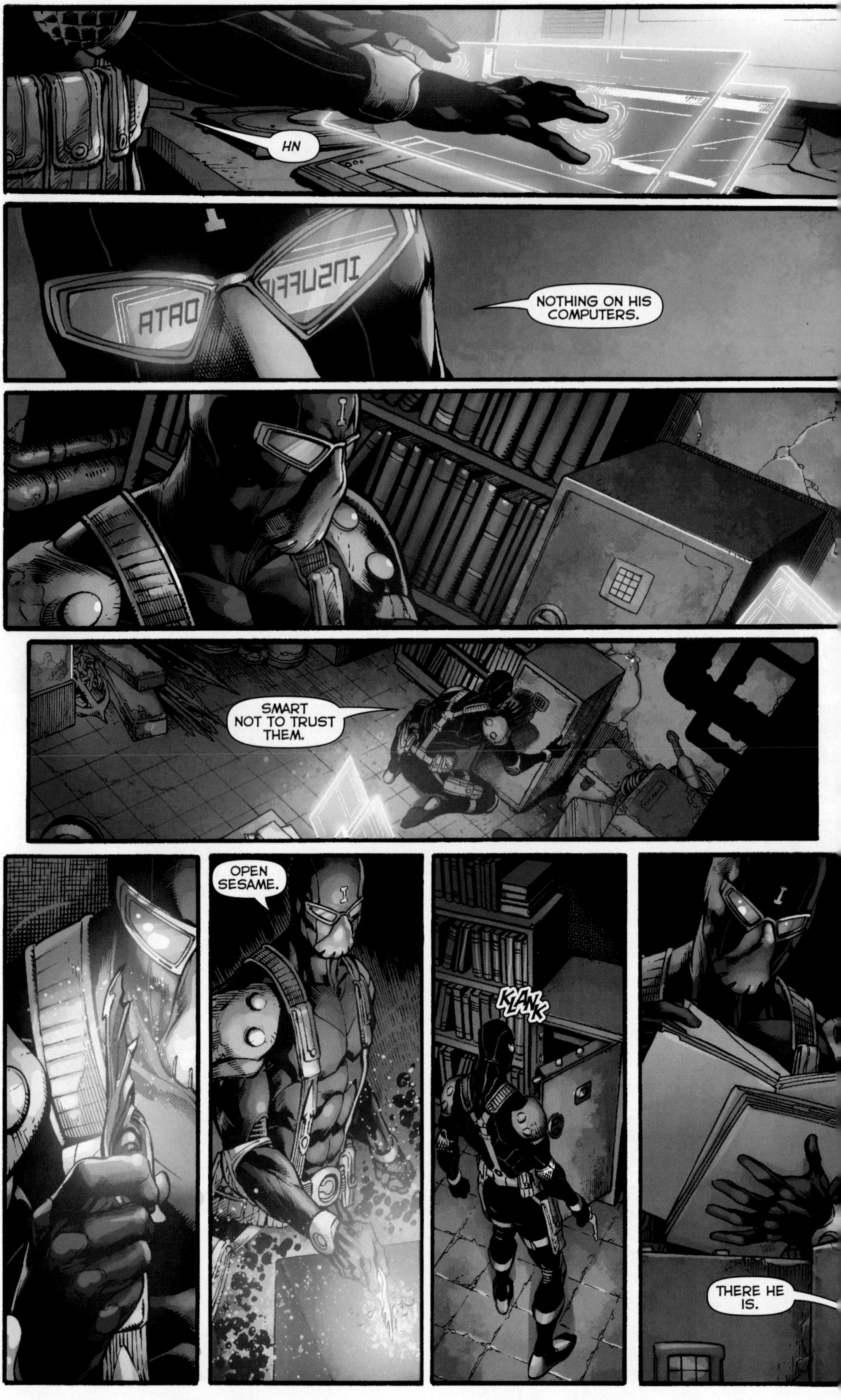
HN
NOTHING ON HIS COMPUTERS.
SMART NOT TO TRUST THEM.
OPEN SESAME.
KLANK
THERE HE IS.

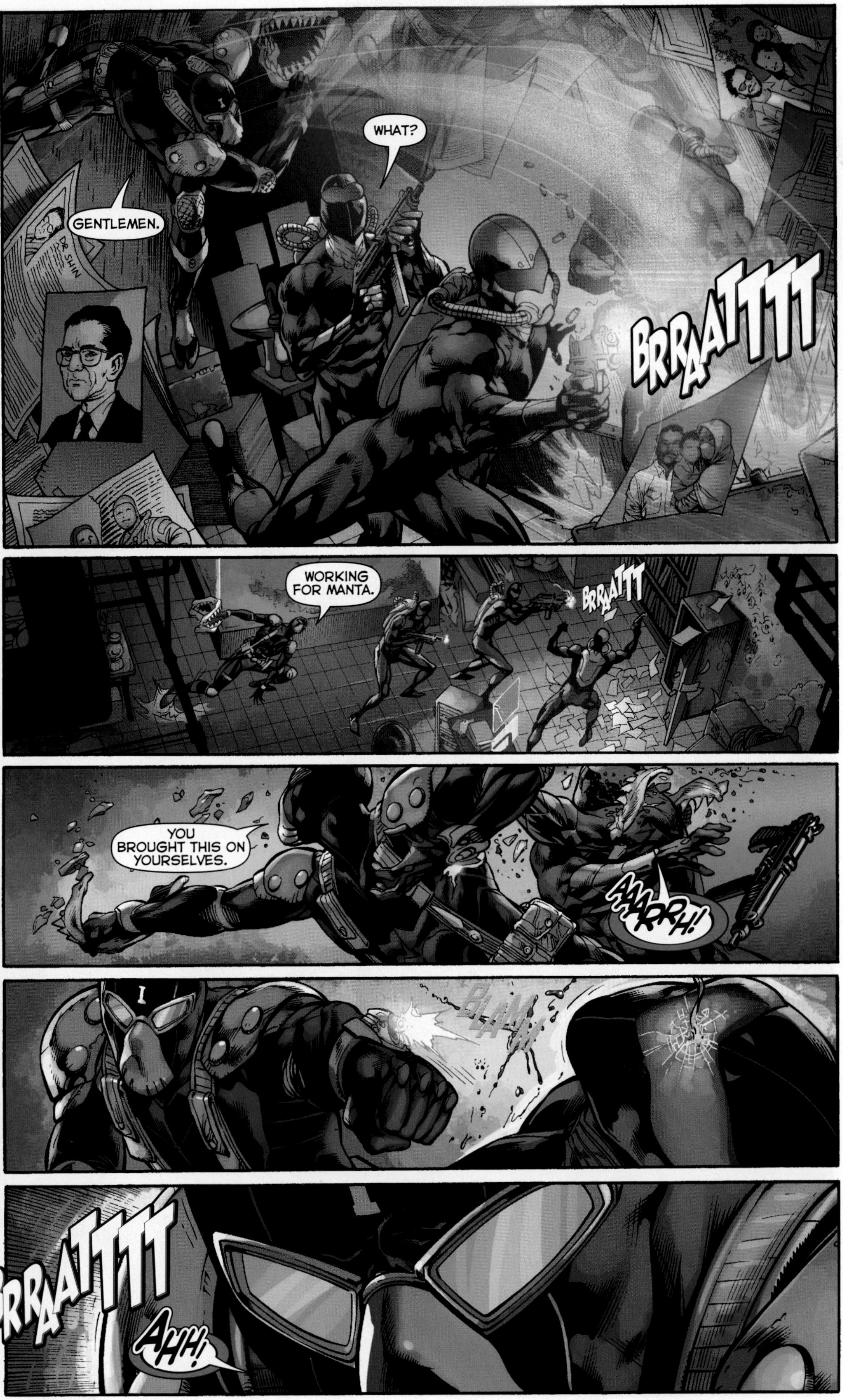

WHAT?
GENTLEMEN.
DR SHIN
BRRAATTTT
WORKING FOR MANTA.
BRRAATTT
YOU BROUGHT THIS ON YOURSELVES.
AAARRH!
BLAM
RRAATTTT
AHH!

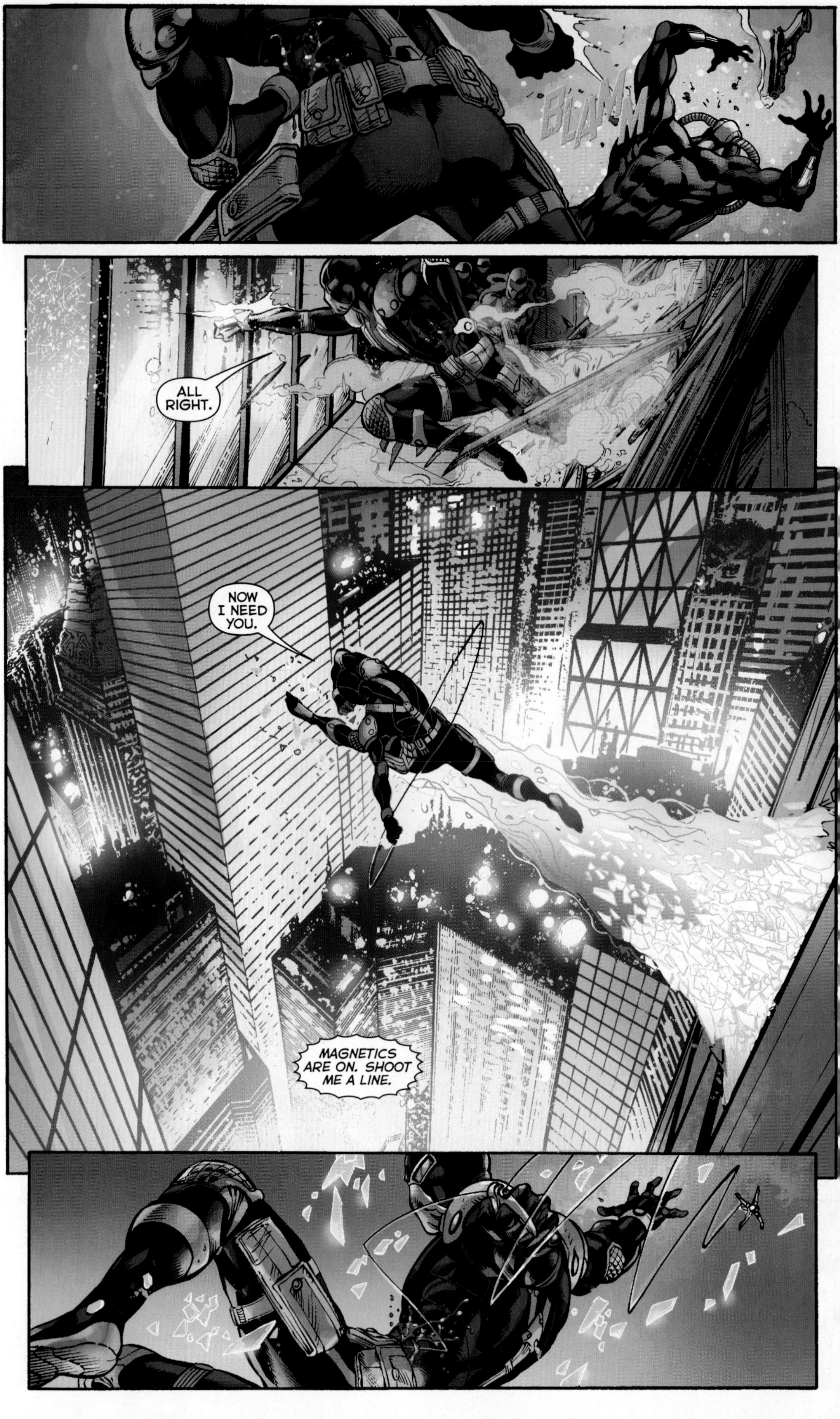
BLAMM
ALL RIGHT.
NOW I NEED YOU.
MAGNETICS ARE ON. SHOOT ME A LINE.

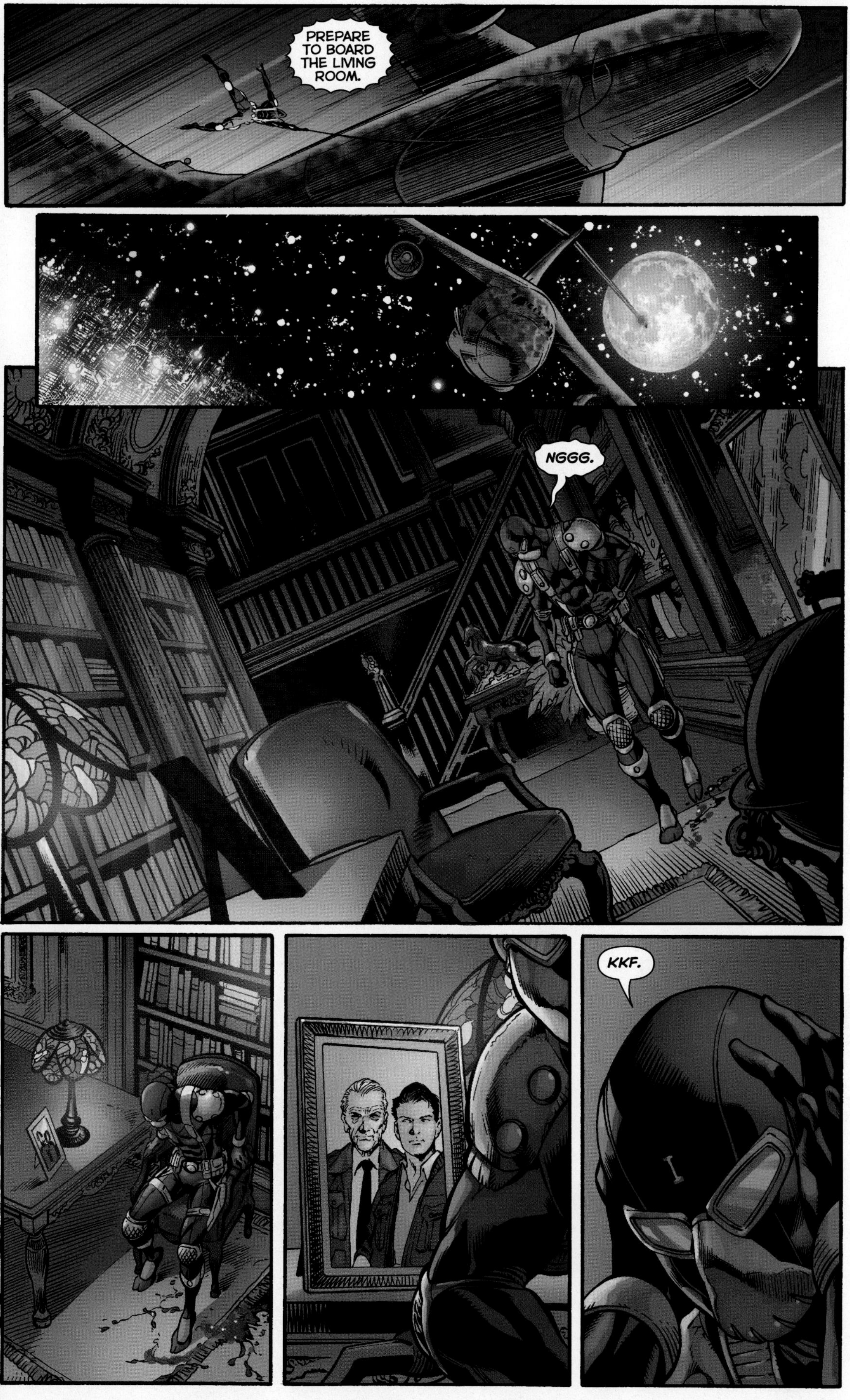
PREPARE TO BOARD THE LIVING ROOM.
NGGG.
KKF.

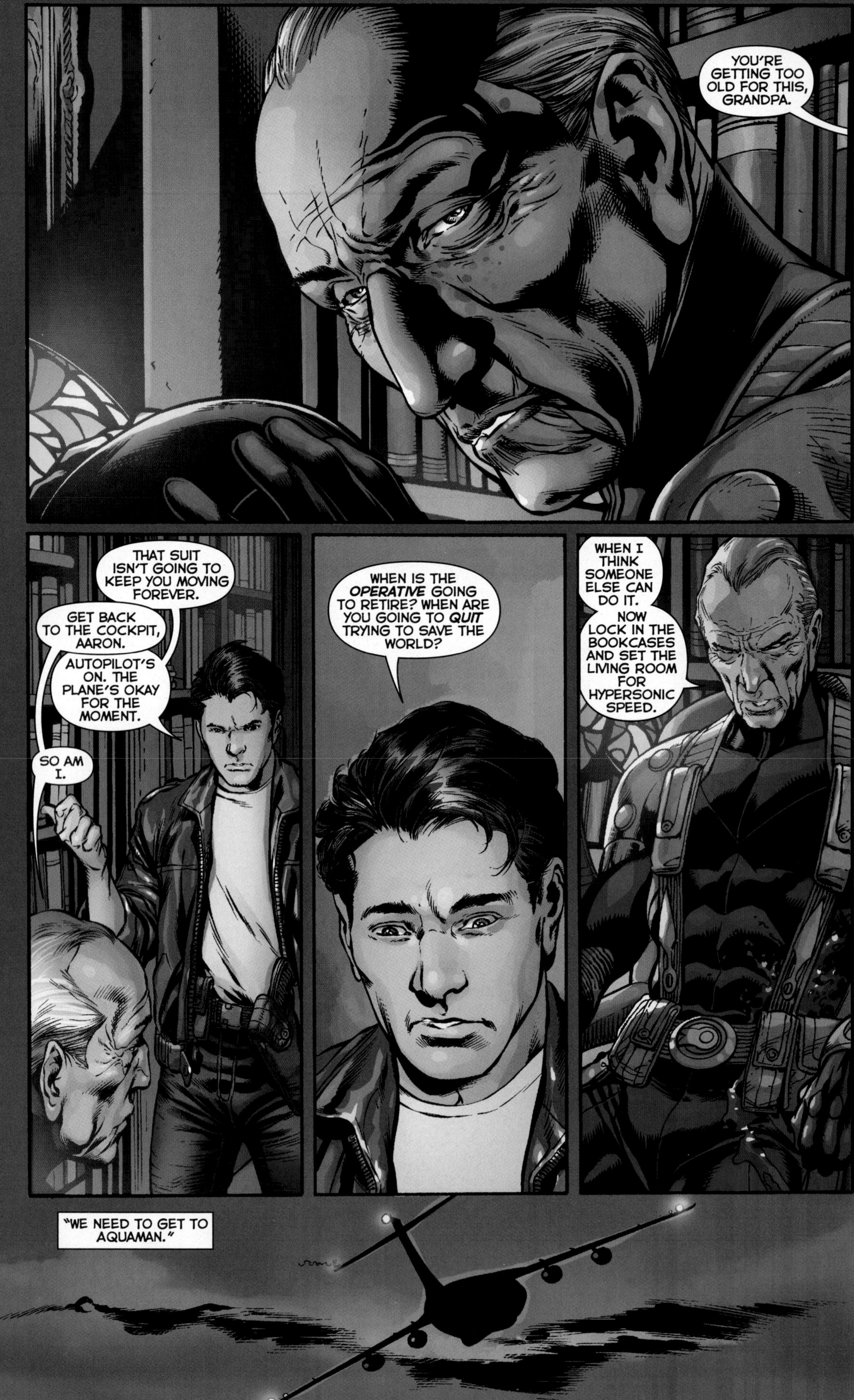
YOU'RE GETTING TOO OLD FOR THIS, GRANDPA.
THAT SUIT ISN'T GOING TO KEEP YOU MOVING FOREVER.
GET BACK TO THE COCKPIT, AARON.
AUTOPILOT'S ON. THE PLANE'S OKAY FOR THE MOMENT.
SO AM I.
WHEN IS THE *OPERATIVE* GOING TO RETIRE? WHEN ARE YOU GOING TO *QUIT* TRYING TO SAVE THE WORLD?
WHEN I THINK SOMEONE ELSE CAN DO IT.
NOW LOCK IN THE BOOKCASES AND SET THE LIVING ROOM FOR HYPERSONIC SPEED.
"WE NEED TO GET TO AQUAMAN."

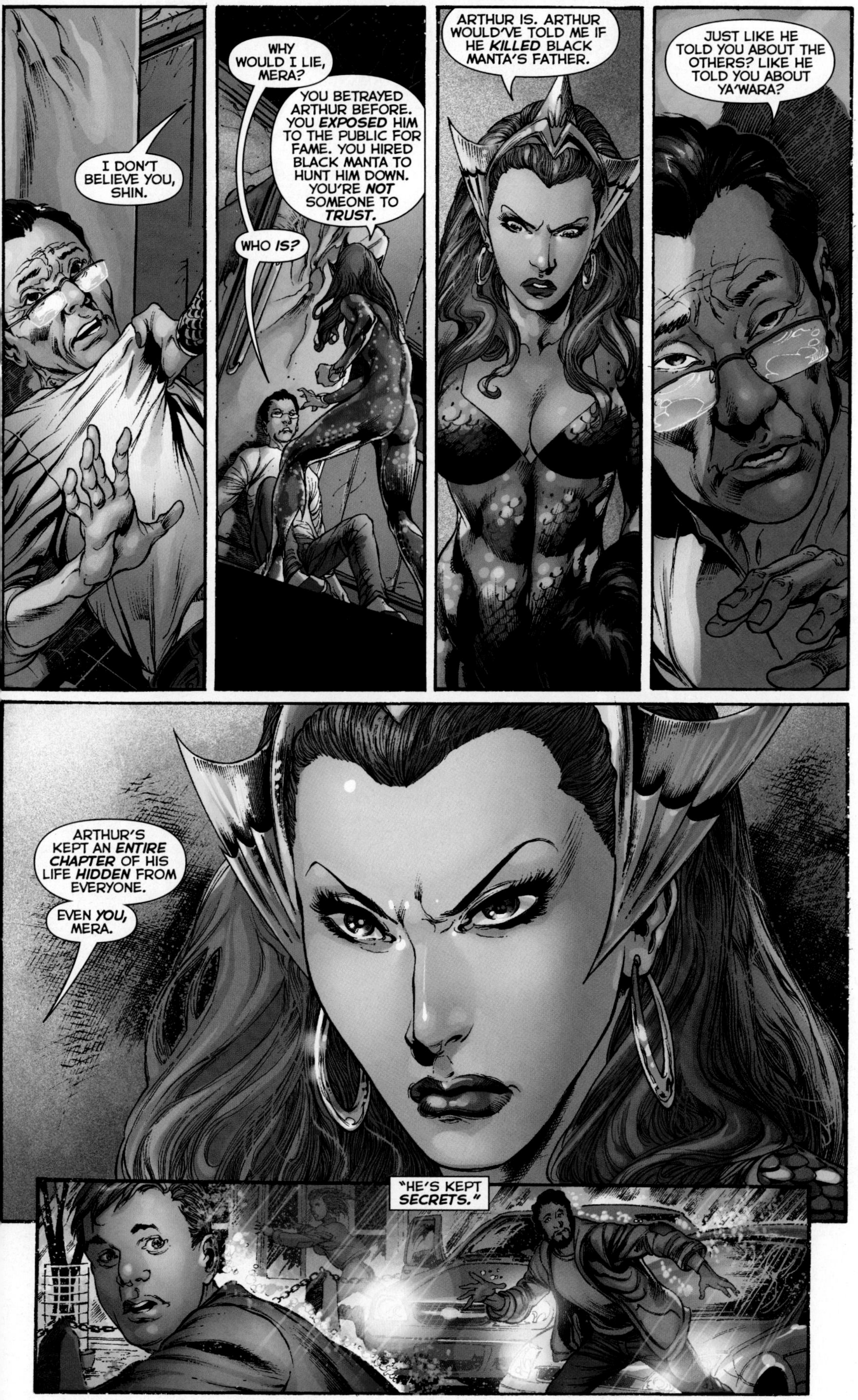

I DON'T BELIEVE YOU, SHIN.
WHY WOULD I LIE, MERA?
YOU BETRAYED ARTHUR BEFORE. YOU EXPOSED HIM TO THE PUBLIC FOR FAME. YOU HIRED BLACK MANTA TO HUNT HIM DOWN. YOU'RE NOT SOMEONE TO TRUST.
WHO IS?
ARTHUR IS. ARTHUR WOULD'VE TOLD ME IF HE KILLED BLACK MANTA'S FATHER.
JUST LIKE HE TOLD YOU ABOUT THE OTHERS? LIKE HE TOLD YOU ABOUT YA'WARA?
ARTHUR'S KEPT AN ENTIRE CHAPTER OF HIS LIFE HIDDEN FROM EVERYONE.
EVEN YOU, MERA.
"HE'S KEPT SECRETS."

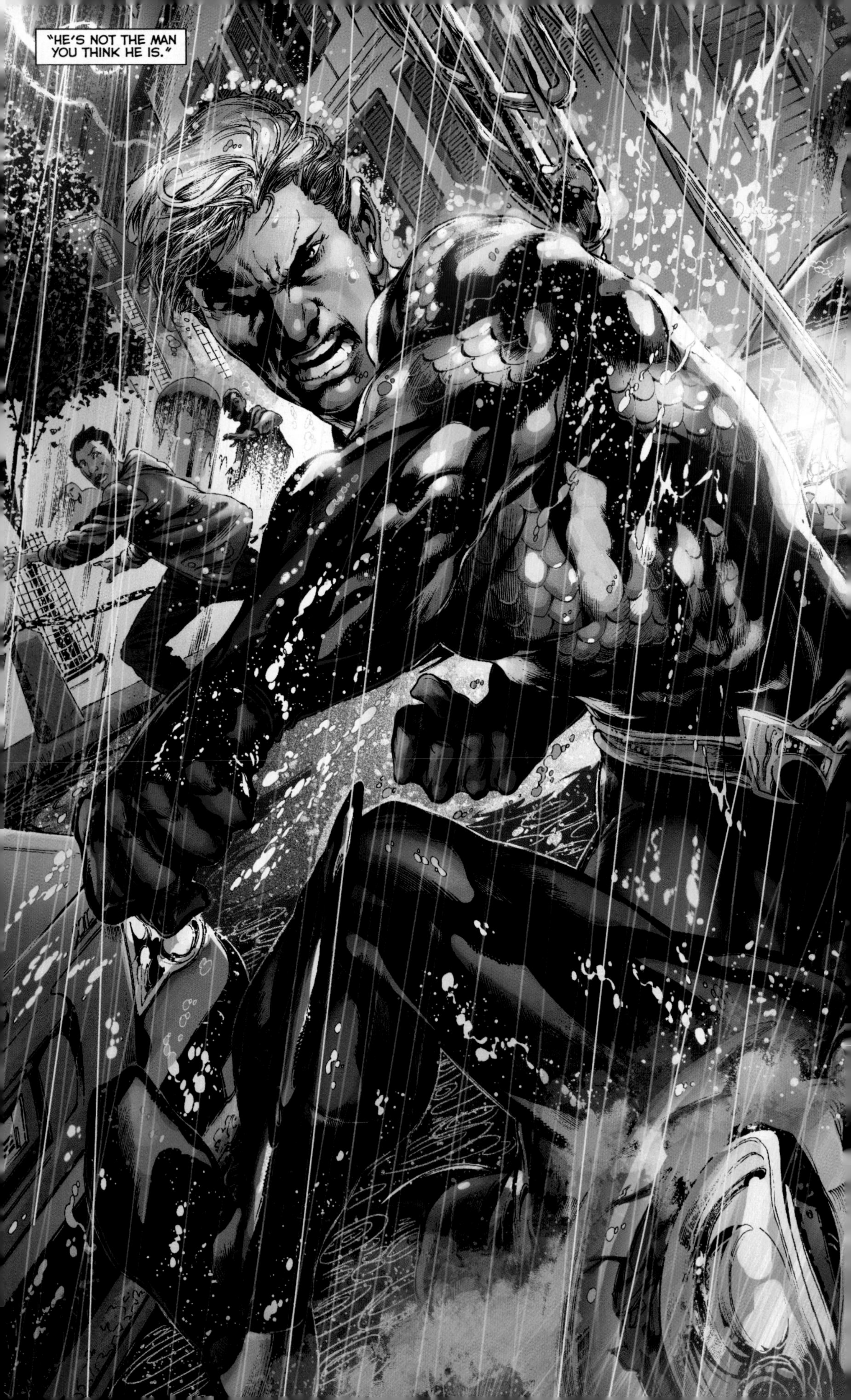
"HE'S NOT THE MAN YOU THINK HE IS."

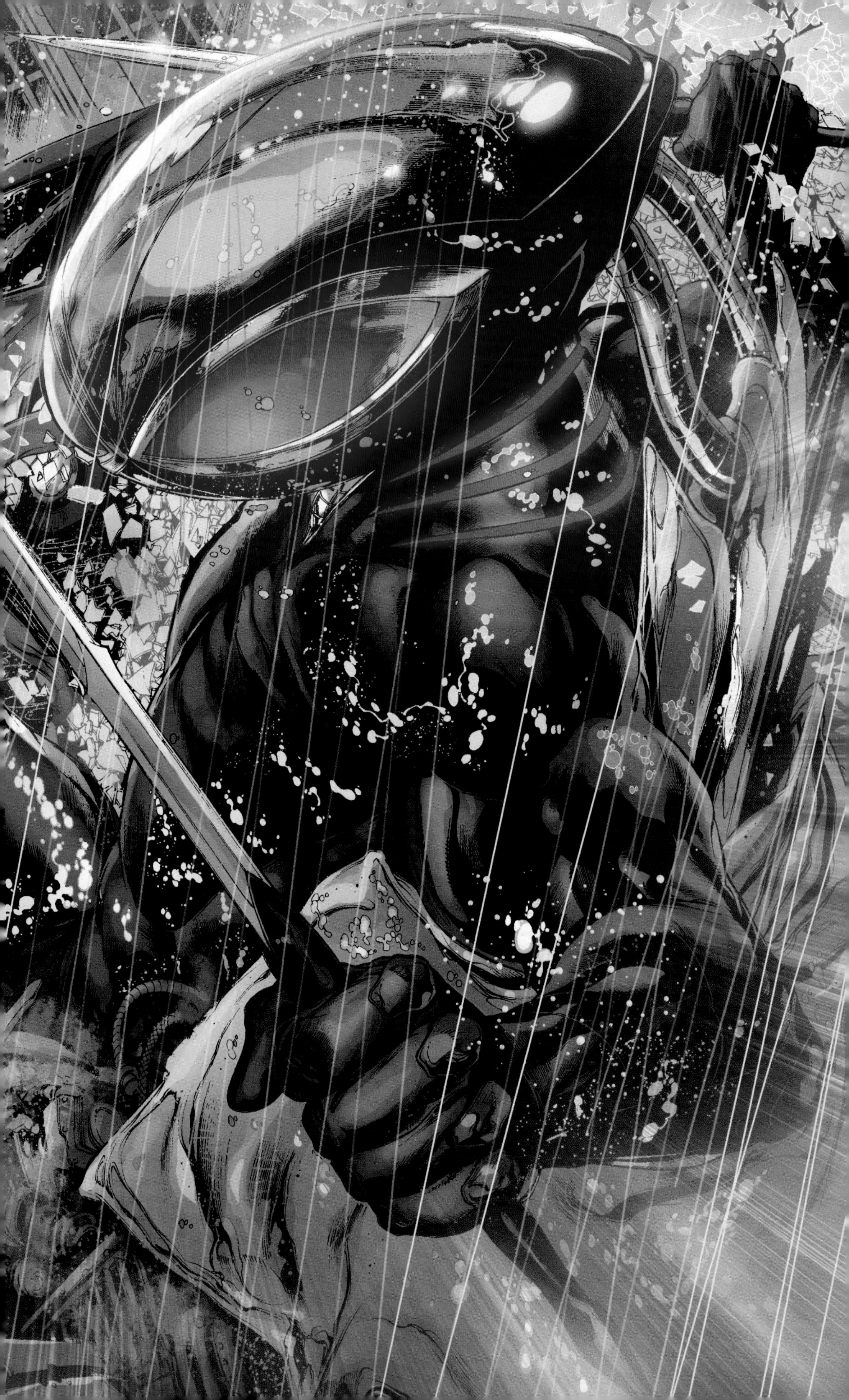

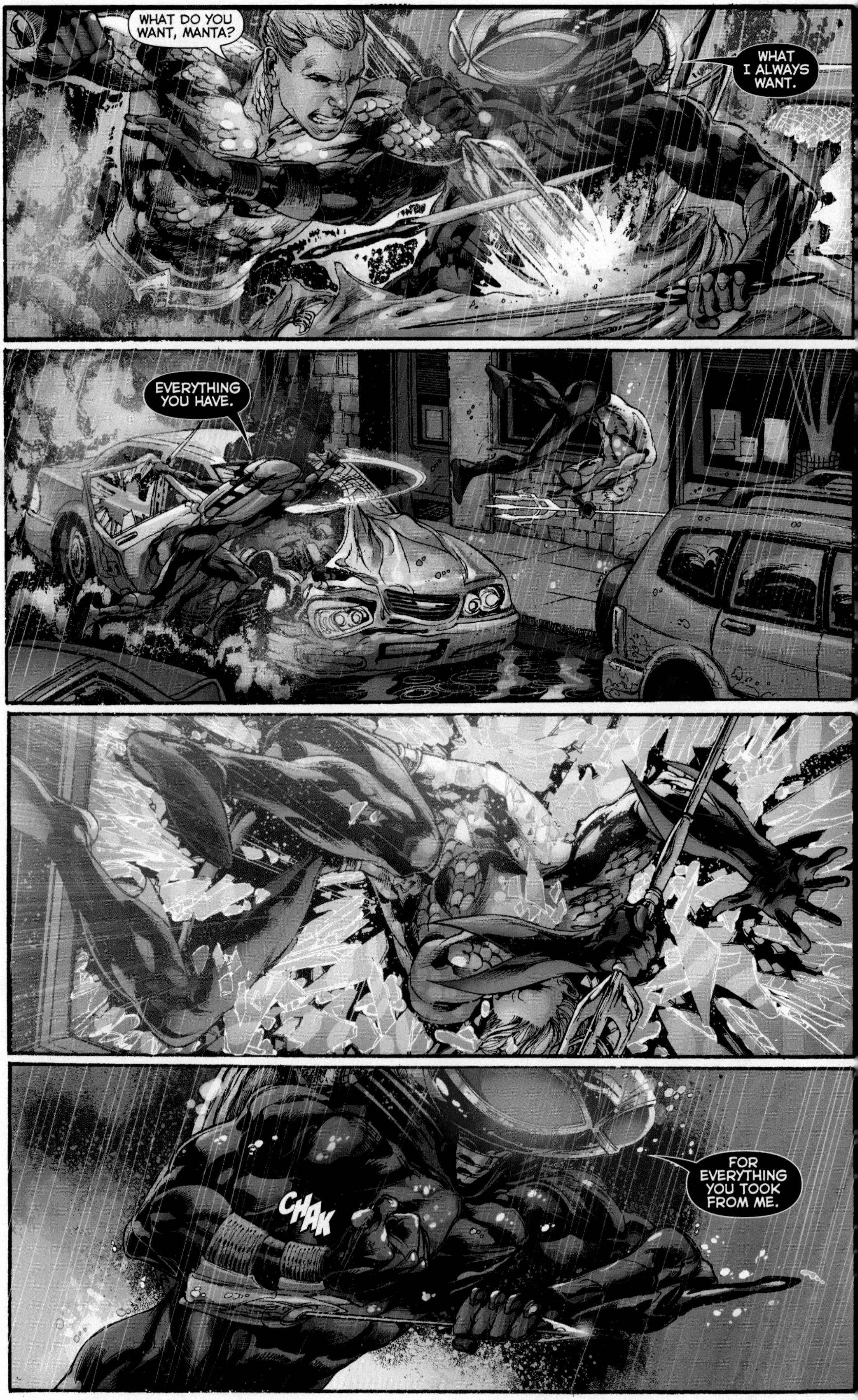
WHAT DO YOU WANT, MANTA?
WHAT I ALWAYS WANT.
EVERYTHING YOU HAVE.
CHAK
FOR EVERYTHING YOU TOOK FROM ME.

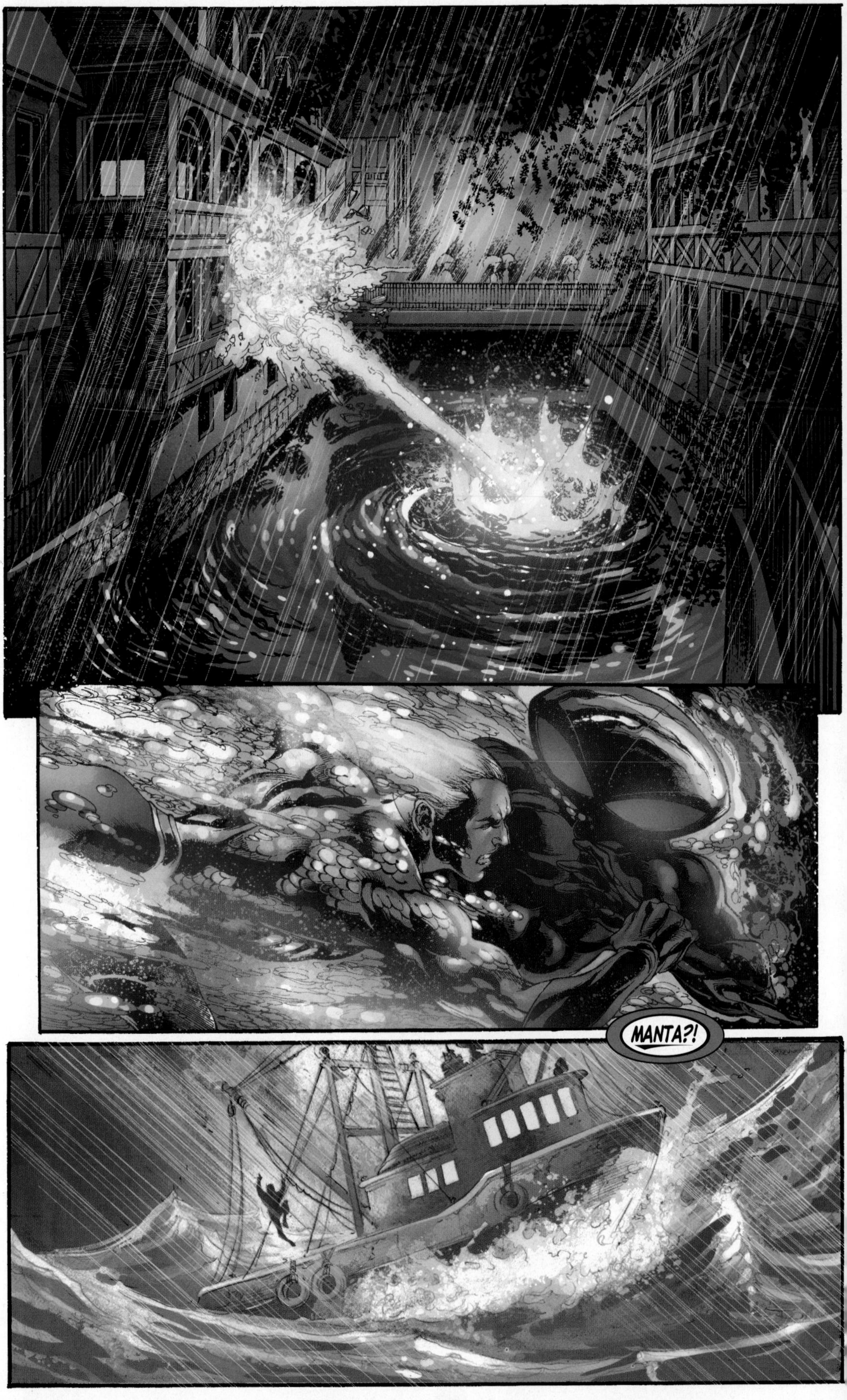
MANTA?!

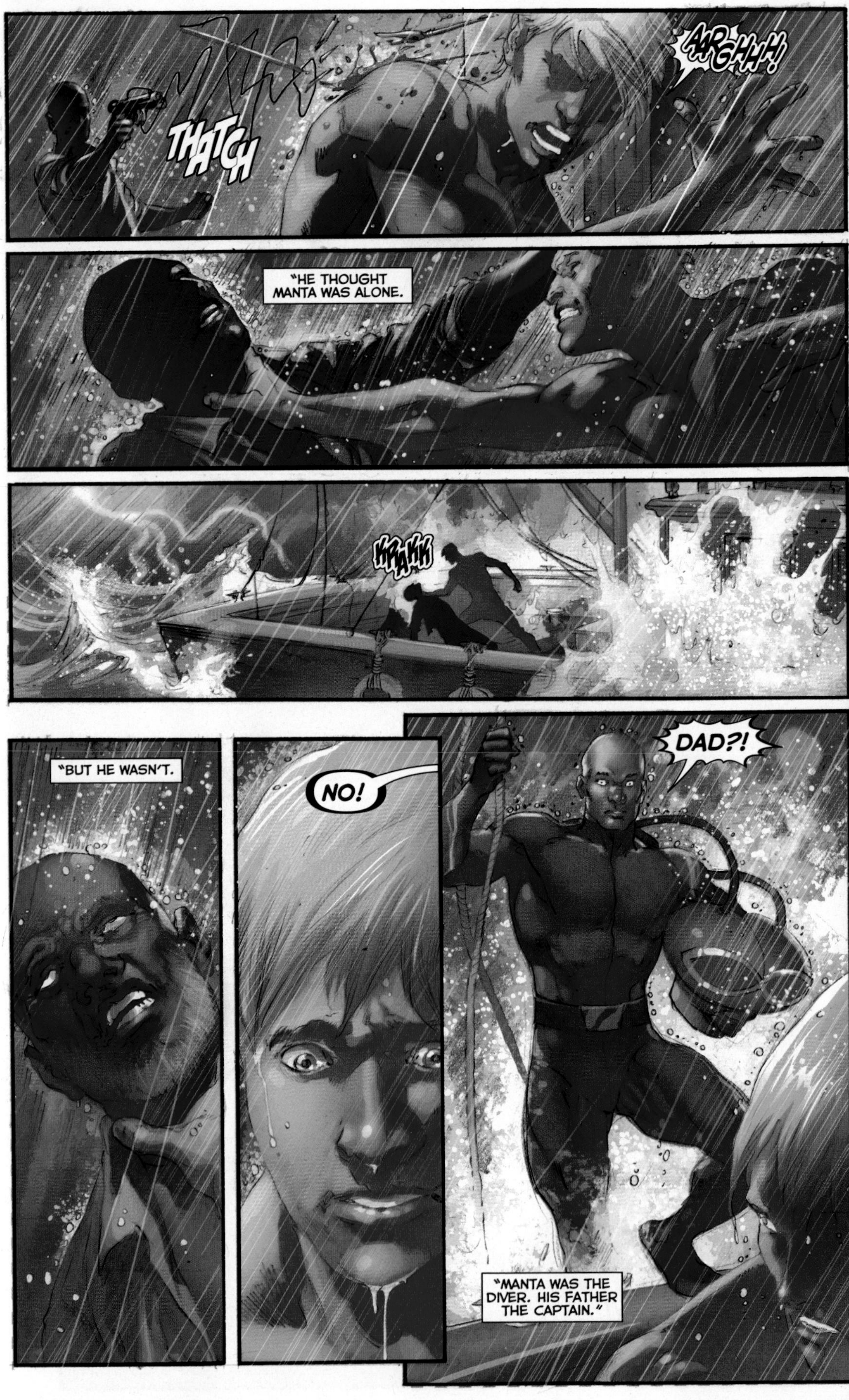
AARGHHH!
THATCH
"HE THOUGHT MANTA WAS ALONE.
KRAKK
"BUT HE WASN'T.
NO!
DAD?!
"MANTA WAS THE DIVER. HIS FATHER THE CAPTAIN."

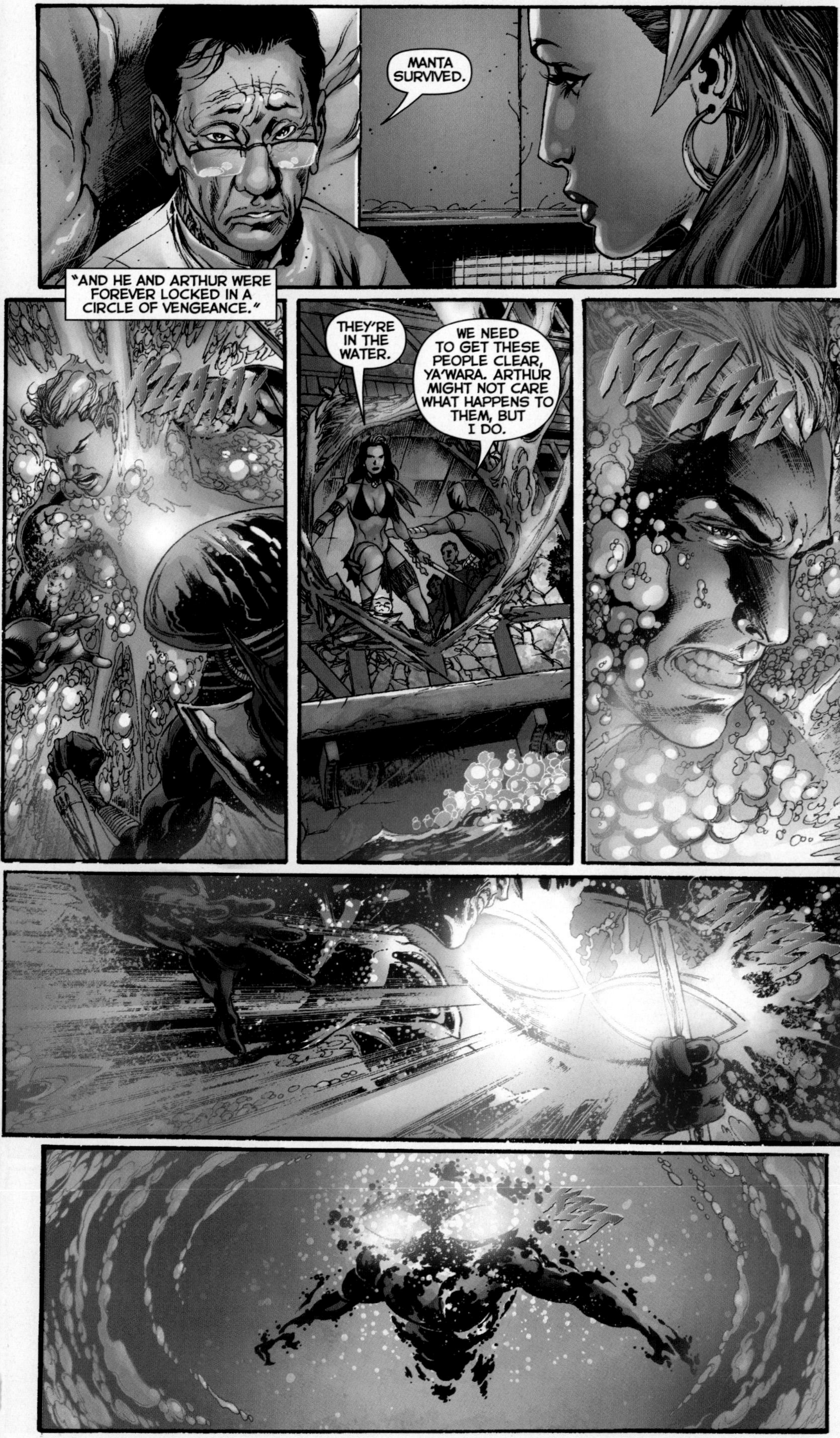
MANTA SURVIVED.
"AND HE AND ARTHUR WERE FOREVER LOCKED IN A CIRCLE OF VENGEANCE."
KZZAAAK
THEY'RE IN THE WATER.
WE NEED TO GET THESE PEOPLE CLEAR, YA'WARA. ARTHUR MIGHT NOT CARE WHAT HAPPENS TO THEM, BUT I DO.
KZZZZZZZ

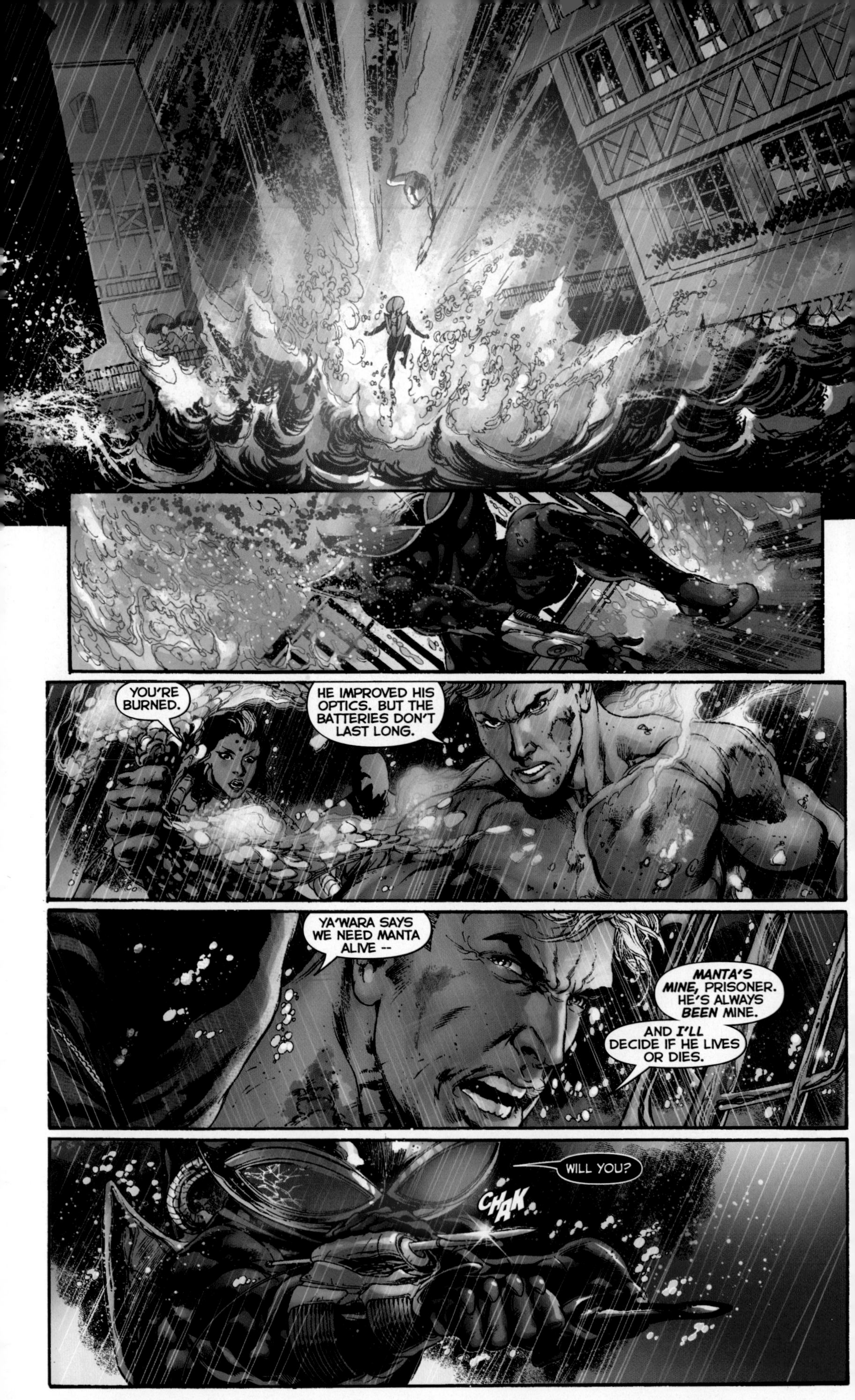
YOU'RE BURNED.
HE IMPROVED HIS OPTICS. BUT THE BATTERIES DON'T LAST LONG.
YA'WARA SAYS WE NEED MANTA ALIVE --
MANTA'S MINE, PRISONER. HE'S ALWAYS *BEEN* MINE.
AND *I'LL* DECIDE IF HE LIVES OR DIES.
WILL YOU?
CHAK

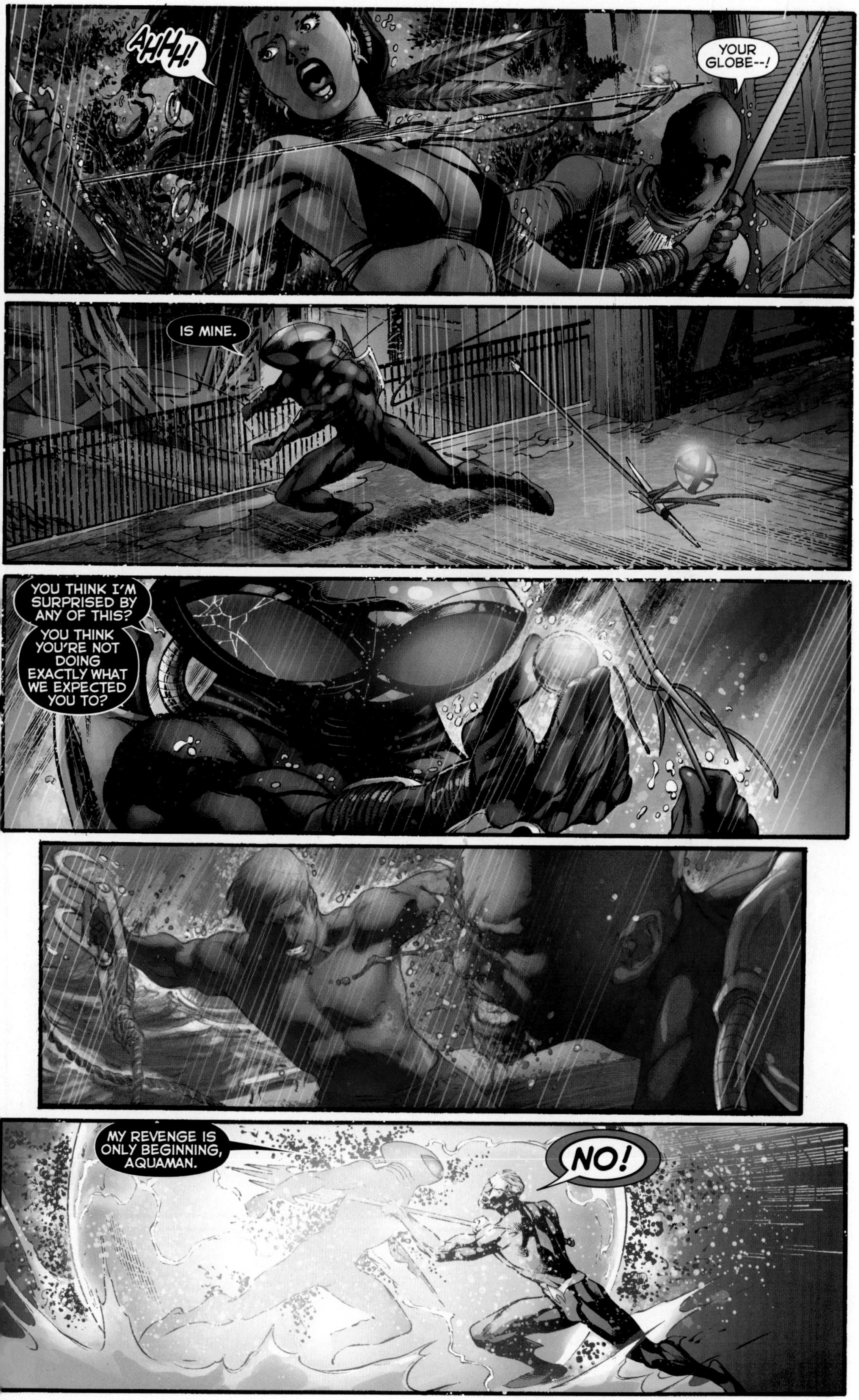

AHHH!
YOUR GLOBE--!
IS MINE.
YOU THINK I'M SURPRISED BY ANY OF THIS?
YOU THINK YOU'RE NOT DOING EXACTLY WHAT WE EXPECTED YOU TO?
MY REVENGE IS ONLY BEGINNING, AQUAMAN.
NO!

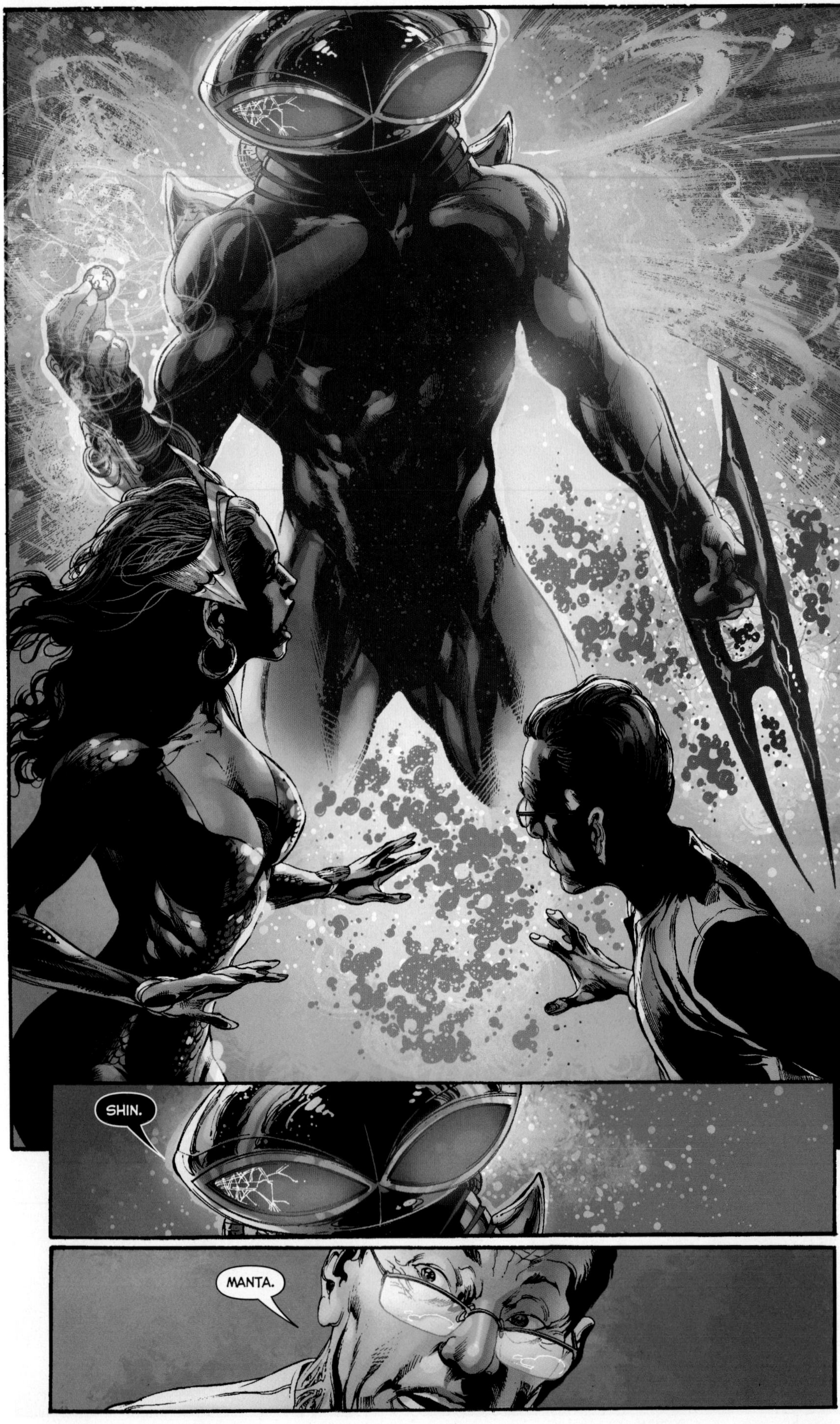
SHIN.
MANTA.

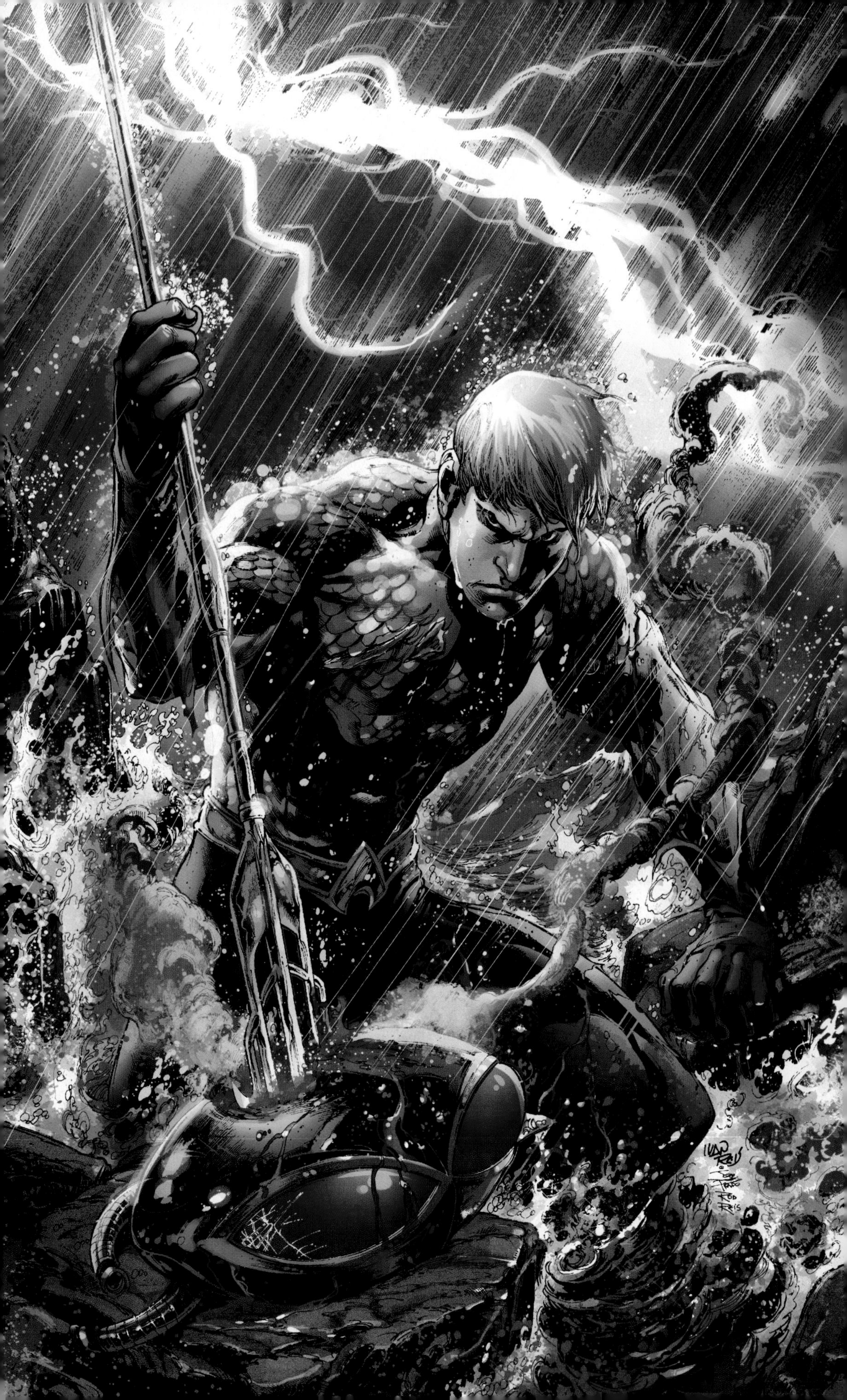

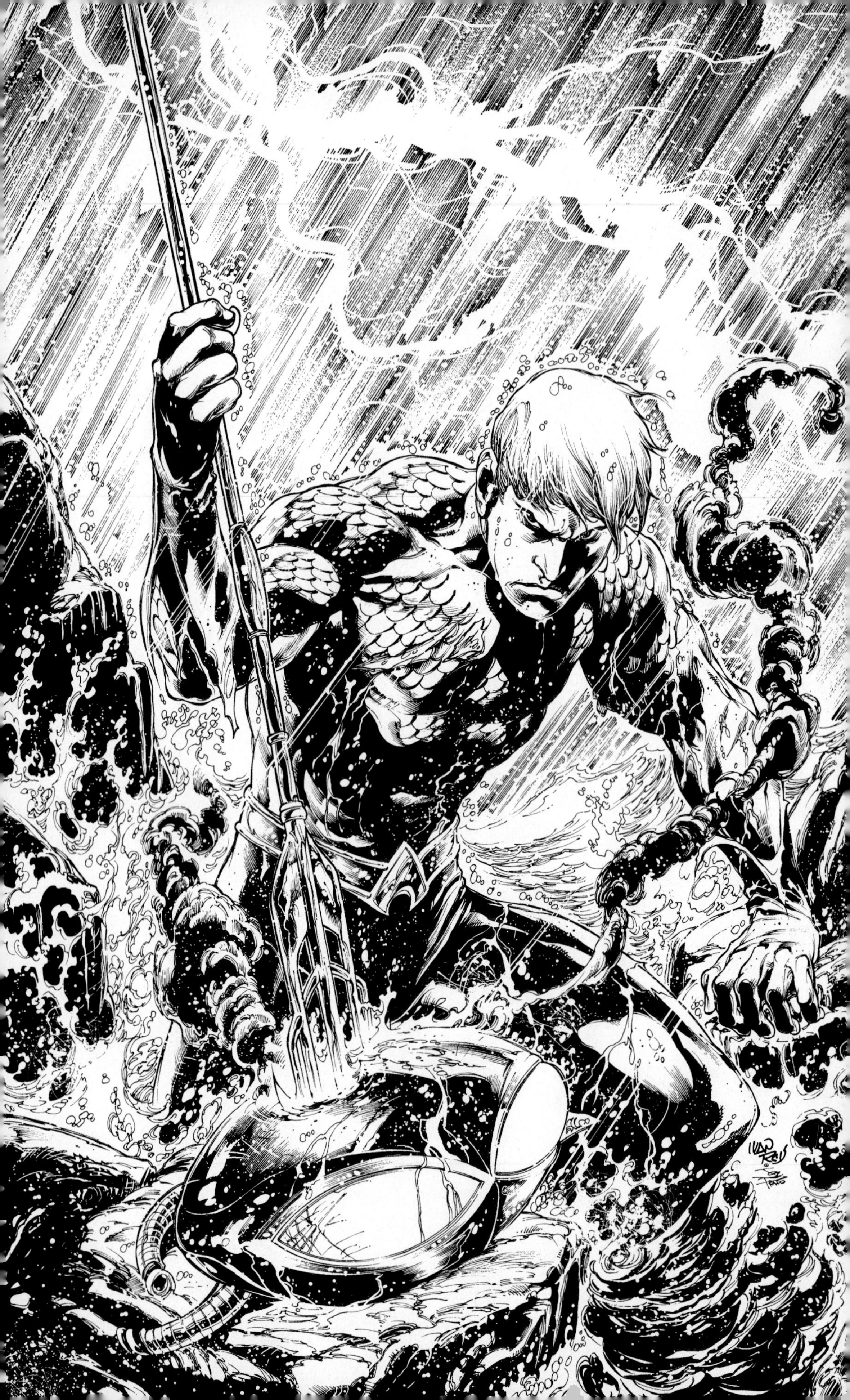

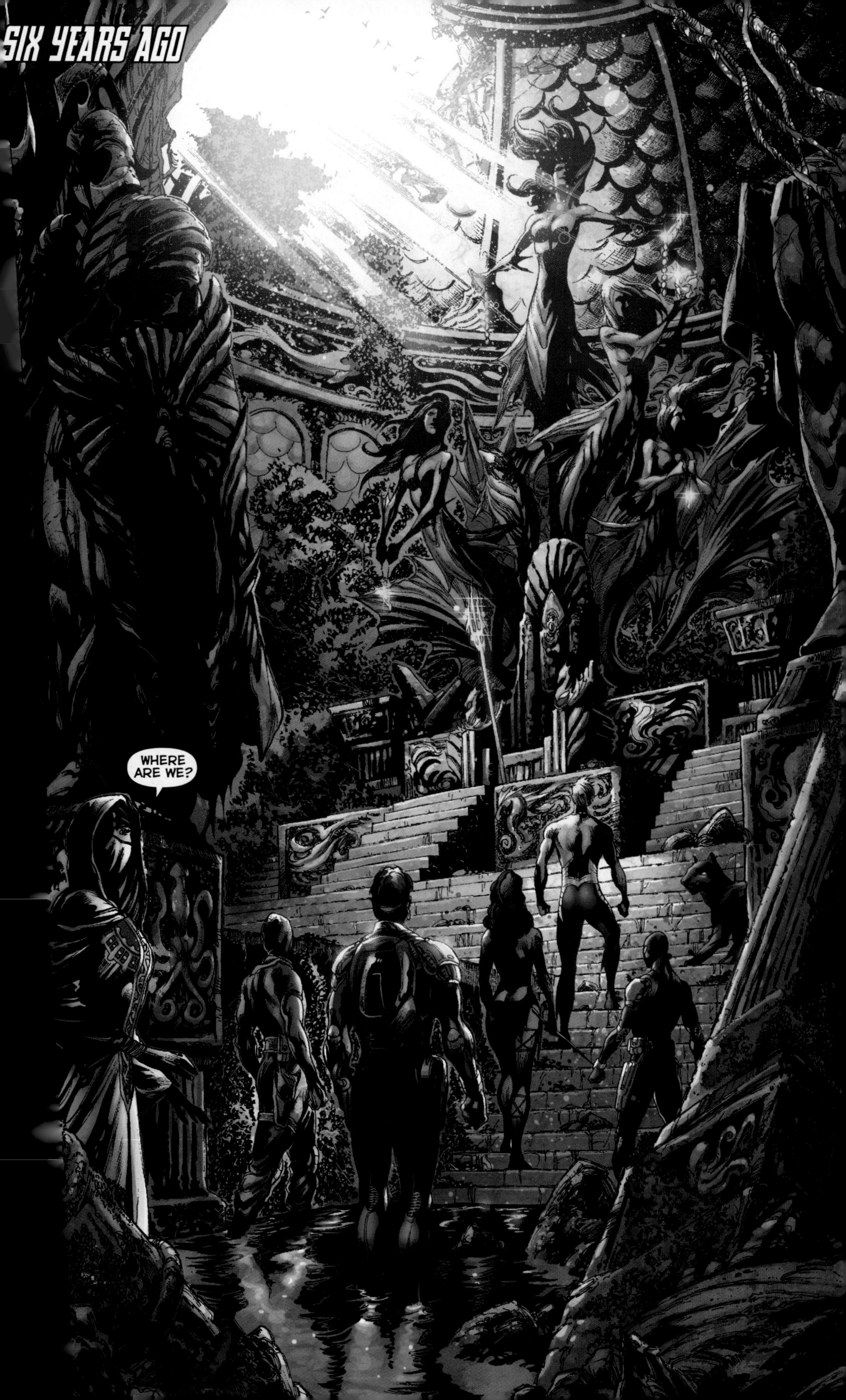
SIX YEARS AGO
WHERE ARE WE?

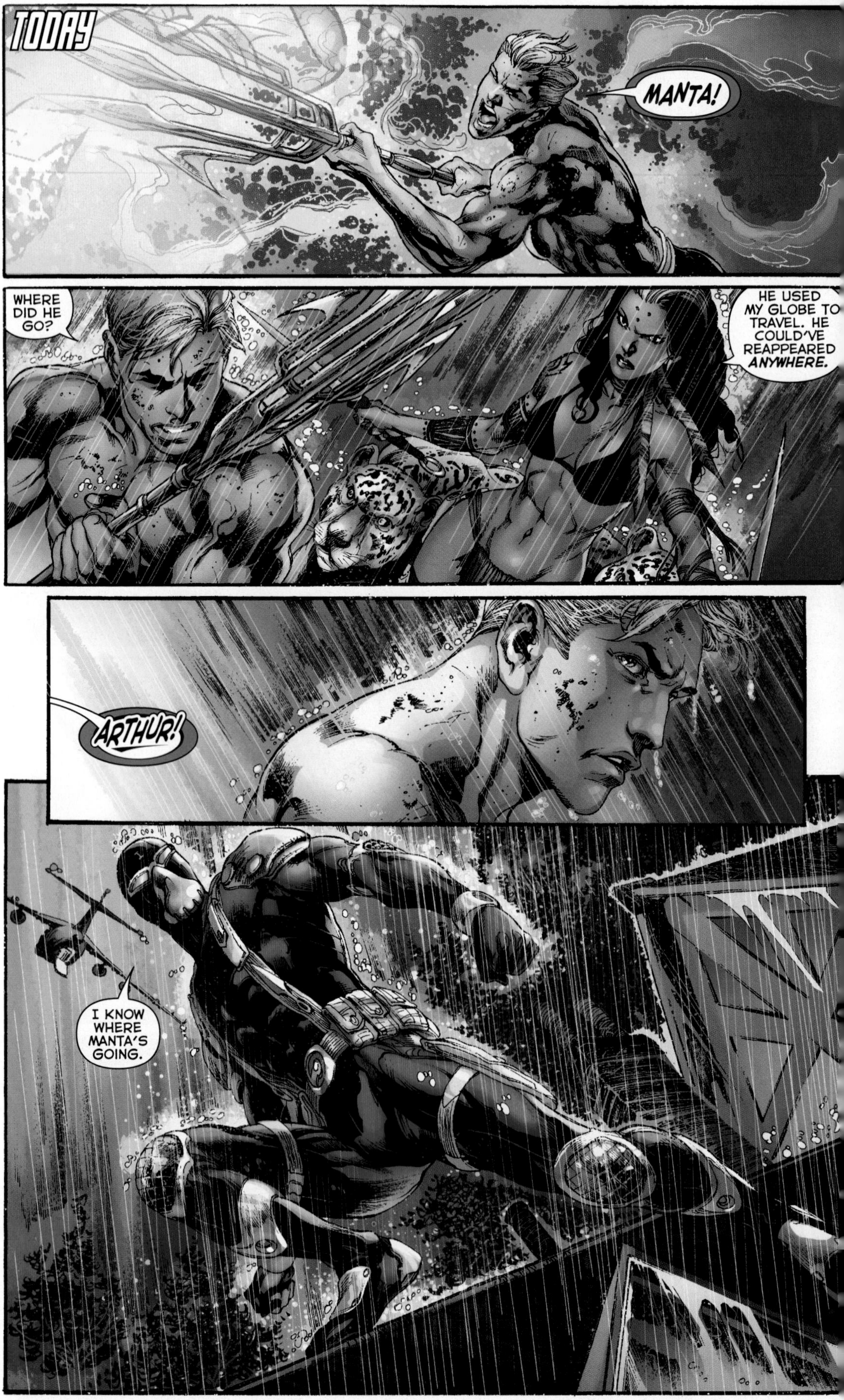
TODAY
MANTA!
WHERE DID HE GO?
HE USED MY GLOBE TO TRAVEL. HE COULD'VE REAPPEARED ANYWHERE.
ARTHUR!
I KNOW WHERE MANTA'S GOING.

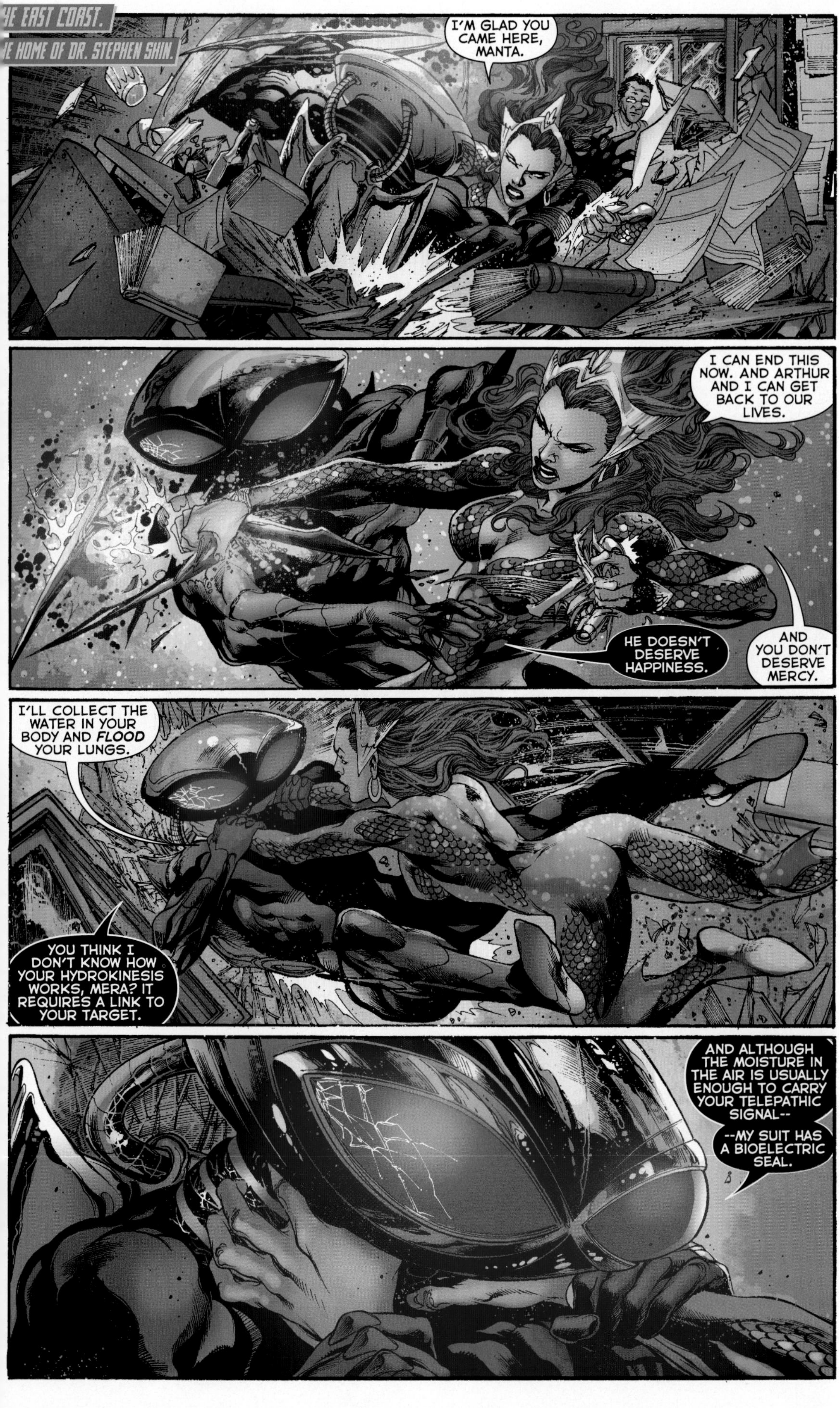
HE EAST COAST.
HE HOME OF DR. STEPHEN SHIN.
I'M GLAD YOU CAME HERE, MANTA.
I CAN END THIS NOW. AND ARTHUR AND I CAN GET BACK TO OUR LIVES.
HE DOESN'T DESERVE HAPPINESS.
AND YOU DON'T DESERVE MERCY.
I'LL COLLECT THE WATER IN YOUR BODY AND FLOOD YOUR LUNGS.
YOU THINK I DON'T KNOW HOW YOUR HYDROKINESIS WORKS, MERA? IT REQUIRES A LINK TO YOUR TARGET.
AND ALTHOUGH THE MOISTURE IN THE AIR IS USUALLY ENOUGH TO CARRY YOUR TELEPATHIC SIGNAL--
--MY SUIT HAS A BIOELECTRIC SEAL.

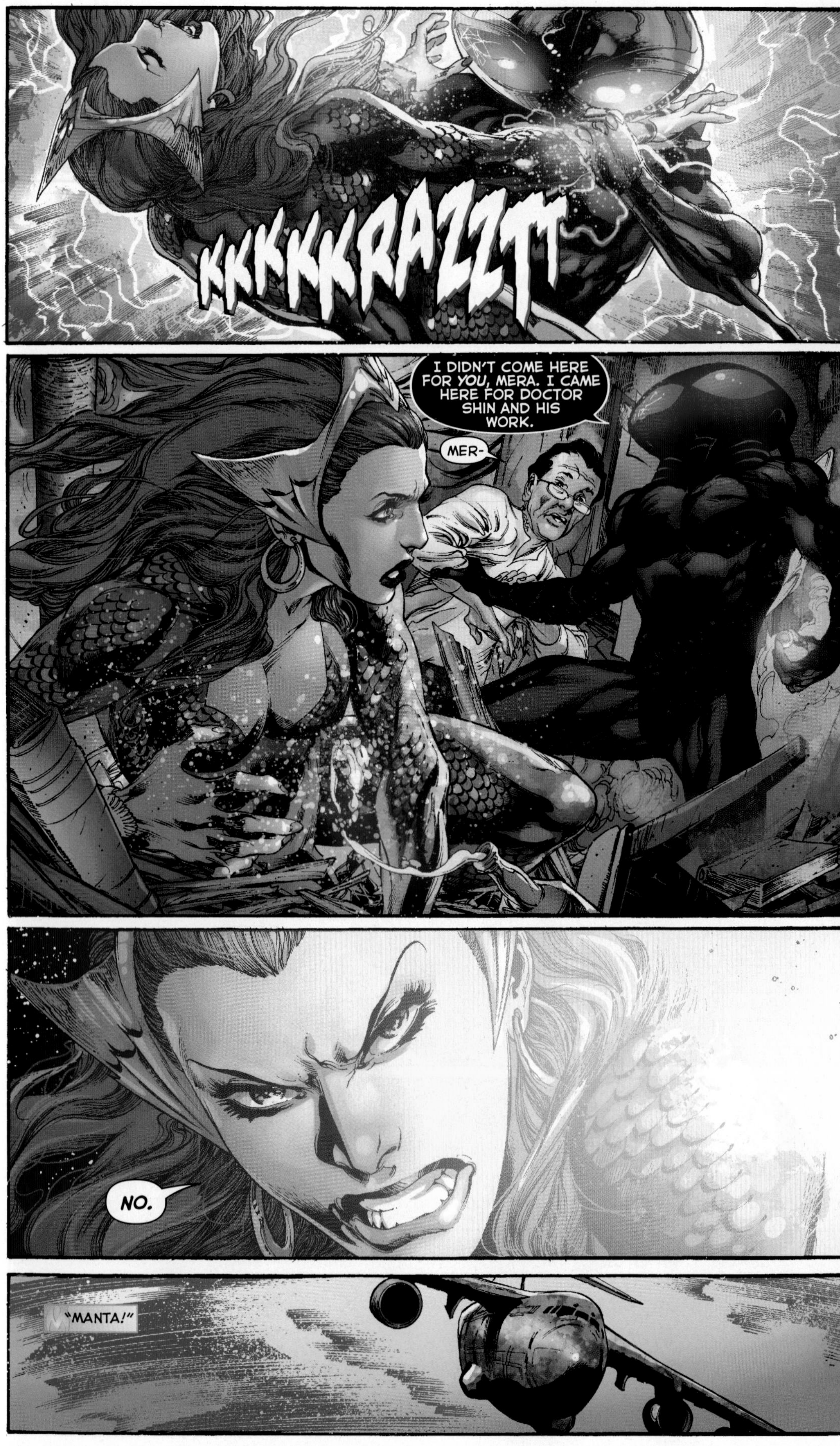
KKKKKRAZZTT
I DIDN'T COME HERE FOR YOU, MERA. I CAME HERE FOR DOCTOR SHIN AND HIS WORK.
MER-
NO.
"MANTA!"

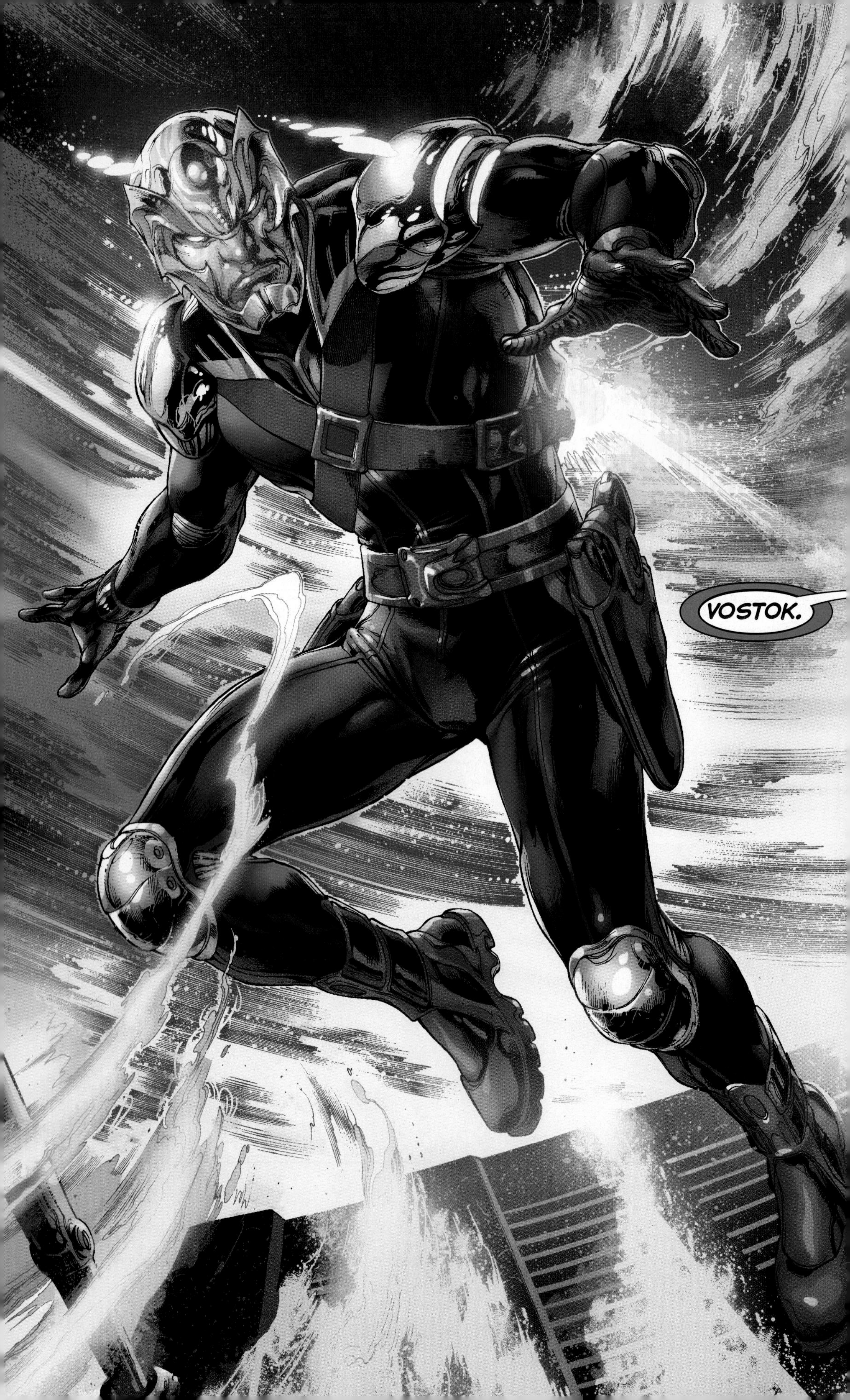
VOSTOK.

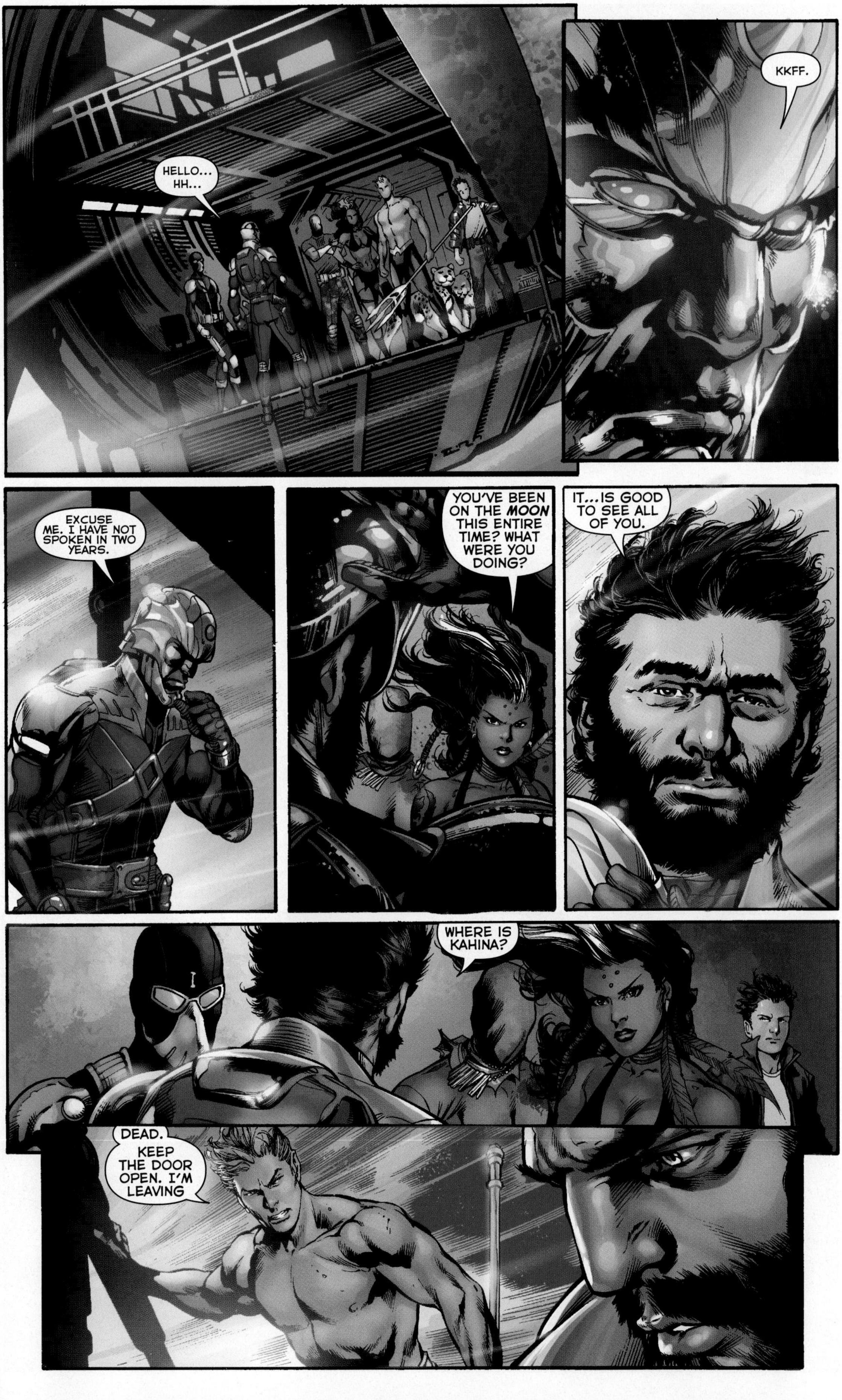
HELLO... HH...
KKFF.
EXCUSE ME. I HAVE NOT SPOKEN IN TWO YEARS.
YOU'VE BEEN ON THE MOON THIS ENTIRE TIME? WHAT WERE YOU DOING?
IT...IS GOOD TO SEE ALL OF YOU.
WHERE IS KAHINA?
DEAD.
KEEP THE DOOR OPEN. I'M LEAVING

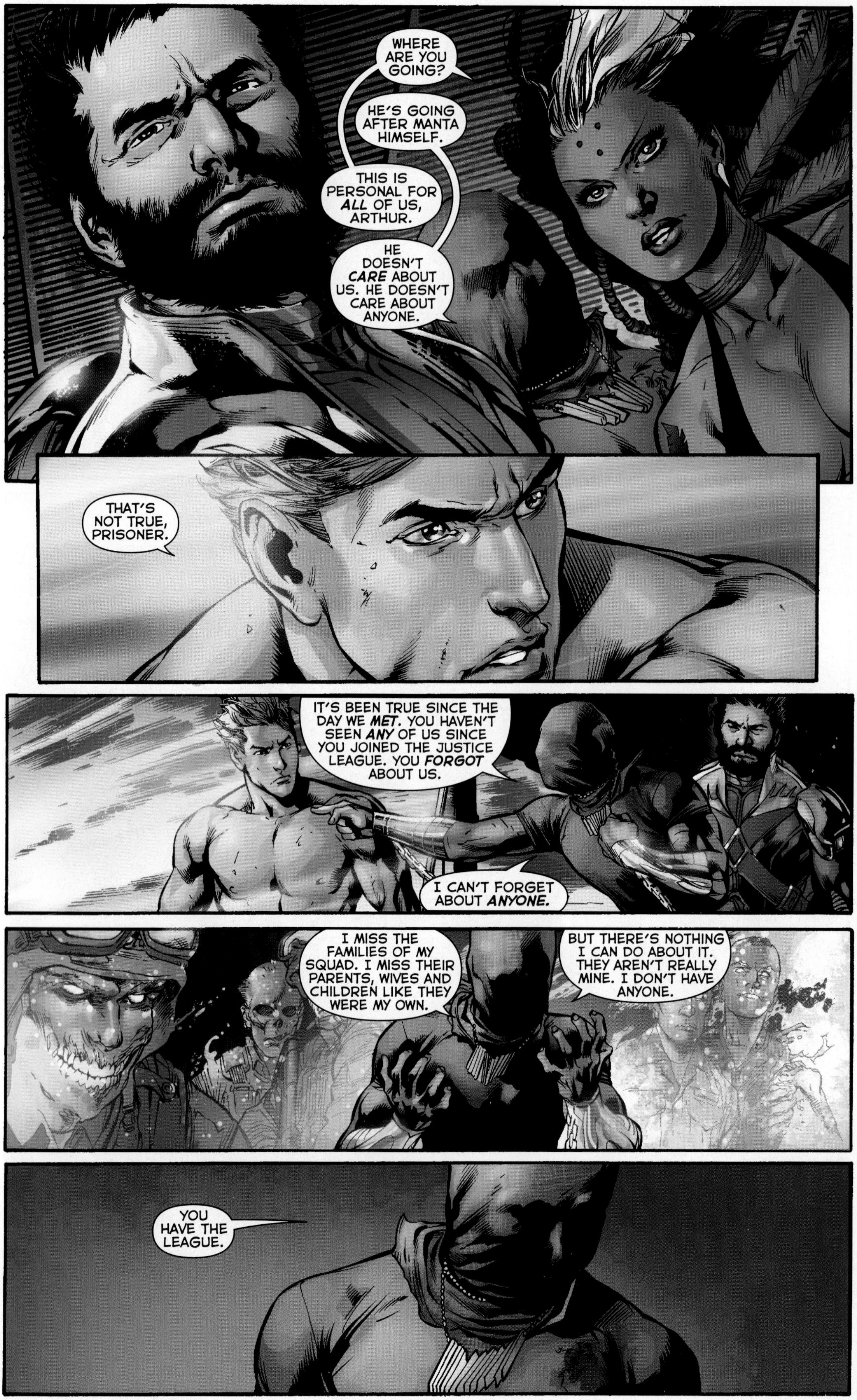
WHERE ARE YOU GOING?
HE'S GOING AFTER MANTA HIMSELF.
THIS IS PERSONAL FOR ALL OF US, ARTHUR.
HE DOESN'T CARE ABOUT US. HE DOESN'T CARE ABOUT ANYONE.
THAT'S NOT TRUE, PRISONER.
IT'S BEEN TRUE SINCE THE DAY WE MET. YOU HAVEN'T SEEN ANY OF US SINCE YOU JOINED THE JUSTICE LEAGUE. YOU FORGOT ABOUT US.
I CAN'T FORGET ABOUT ANYONE.
I MISS THE FAMILIES OF MY SQUAD. I MISS THEIR PARENTS, WIVES AND CHILDREN LIKE THEY WERE MY OWN.
BUT THERE'S NOTHING I CAN DO ABOUT IT. THEY AREN'T REALLY MINE. I DON'T HAVE ANYONE.
YOU HAVE THE LEAGUE.

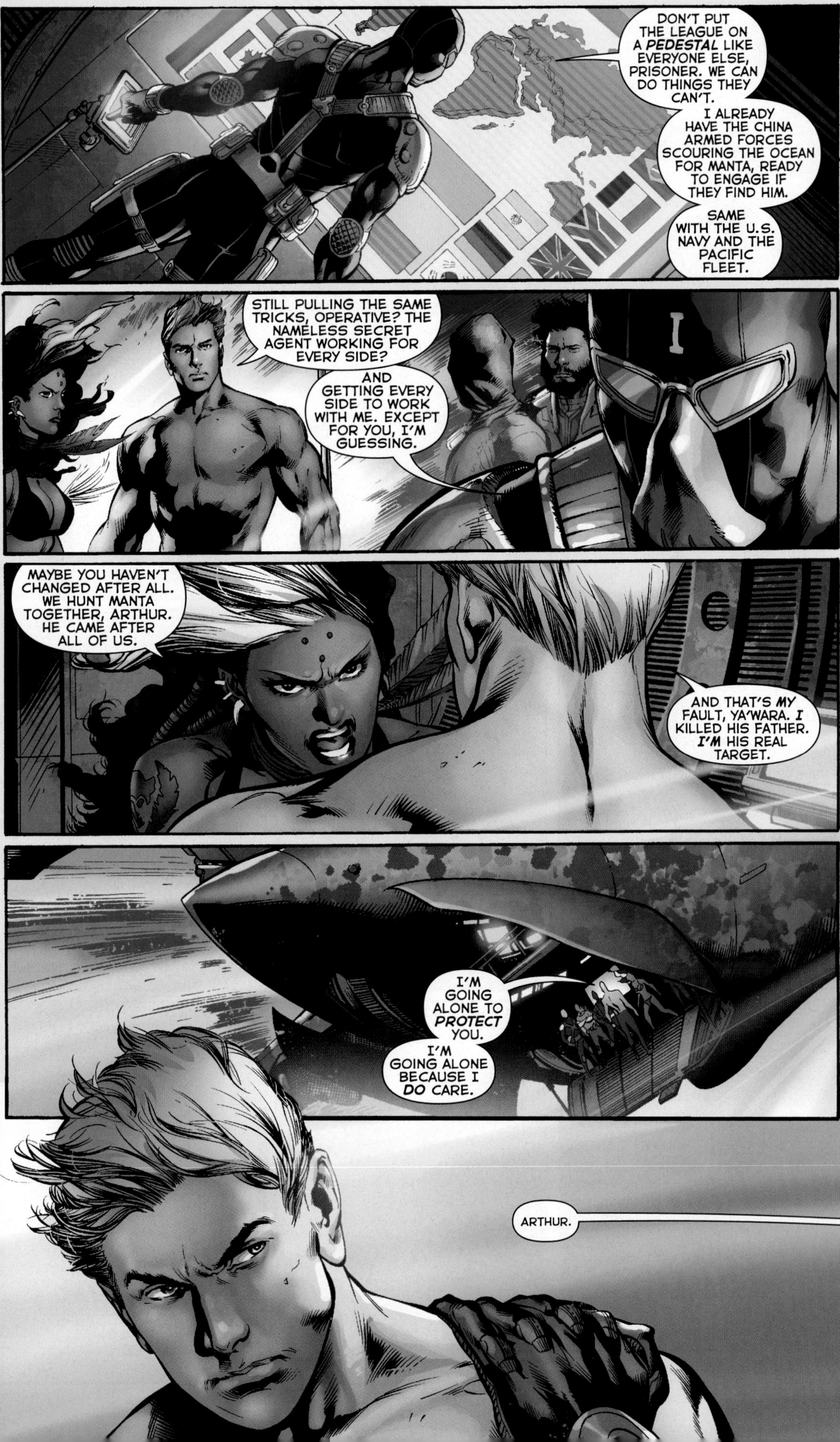
DON'T PUT THE LEAGUE ON A *PEDESTAL* LIKE EVERYONE ELSE, PRISONER. WE CAN DO THINGS THEY CAN'T.
I ALREADY HAVE THE CHINA ARMED FORCES SCOURING THE OCEAN FOR MANTA, READY TO ENGAGE IF THEY FIND HIM.
SAME WITH THE U.S. NAVY AND THE PACIFIC FLEET.
STILL PULLING THE SAME TRICKS, OPERATIVE? THE NAMELESS SECRET AGENT WORKING FOR EVERY SIDE?
AND GETTING EVERY SIDE TO WORK WITH ME. EXCEPT FOR YOU, I'M GUESSING.
MAYBE YOU HAVEN'T CHANGED AFTER ALL. WE HUNT MANTA TOGETHER, ARTHUR. HE CAME AFTER ALL OF US.
AND THAT'S *MY* FAULT, YA'WARA. *I* KILLED HIS FATHER. *I'M* HIS REAL TARGET.
I'M GOING ALONE TO *PROTECT* YOU.
I'M GOING ALONE BECAUSE I *DO* CARE.
ARTHUR.

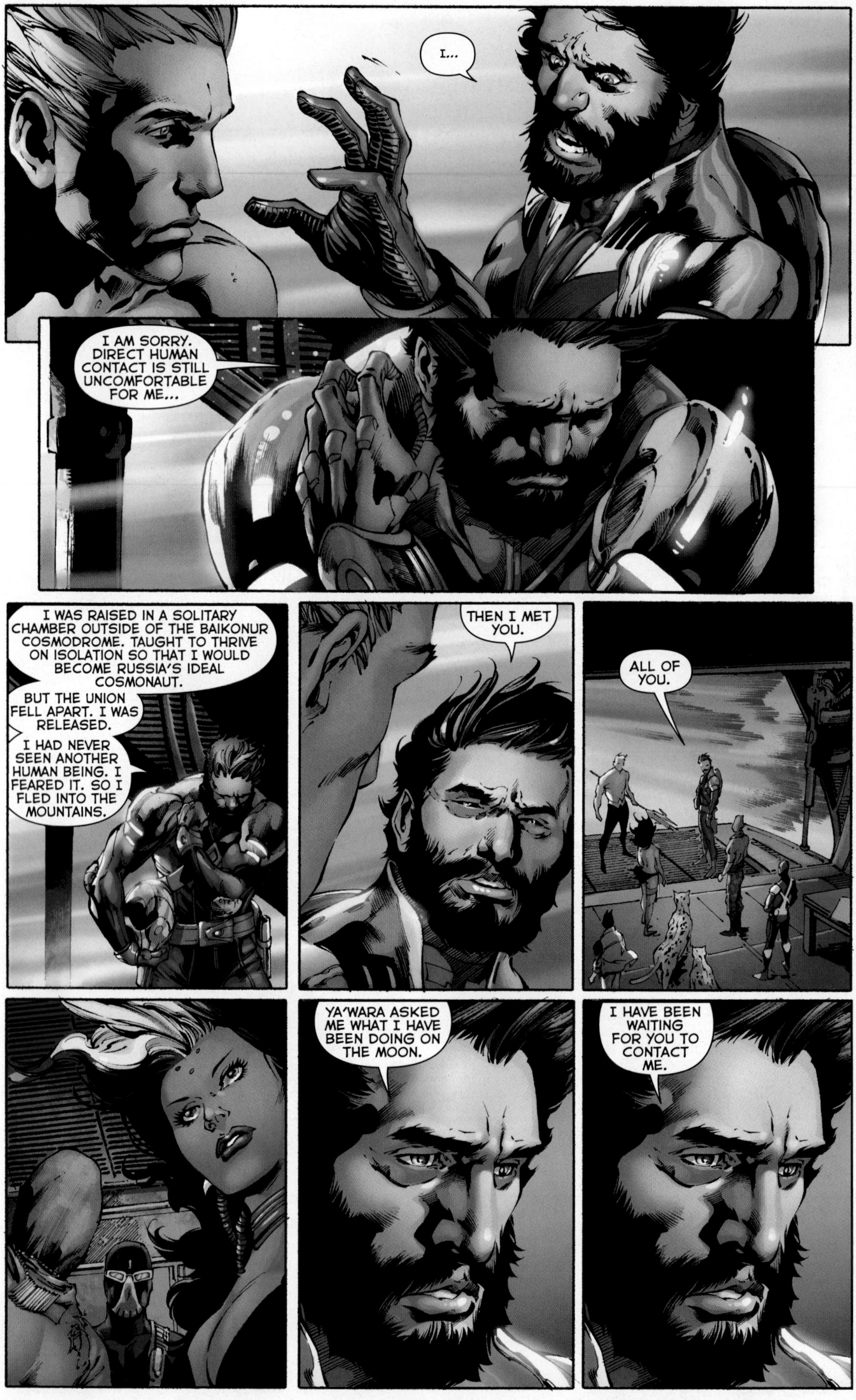
I...
I AM SORRY. DIRECT HUMAN CONTACT IS STILL UNCOMFORTABLE FOR ME...
I WAS RAISED IN A SOLITARY CHAMBER OUTSIDE OF THE BAIKONUR COSMODROME. TAUGHT TO THRIVE ON ISOLATION SO THAT I WOULD BECOME RUSSIA'S IDEAL COSMONAUT.
BUT THE UNION FELL APART. I WAS RELEASED.
I HAD NEVER SEEN ANOTHER HUMAN BEING. I FEARED IT. SO I FLED INTO THE MOUNTAINS.
THEN I MET YOU.
ALL OF YOU.
YA'WARA ASKED ME WHAT I HAVE BEEN DOING ON THE MOON.
I HAVE BEEN WAITING FOR YOU TO CONTACT ME.

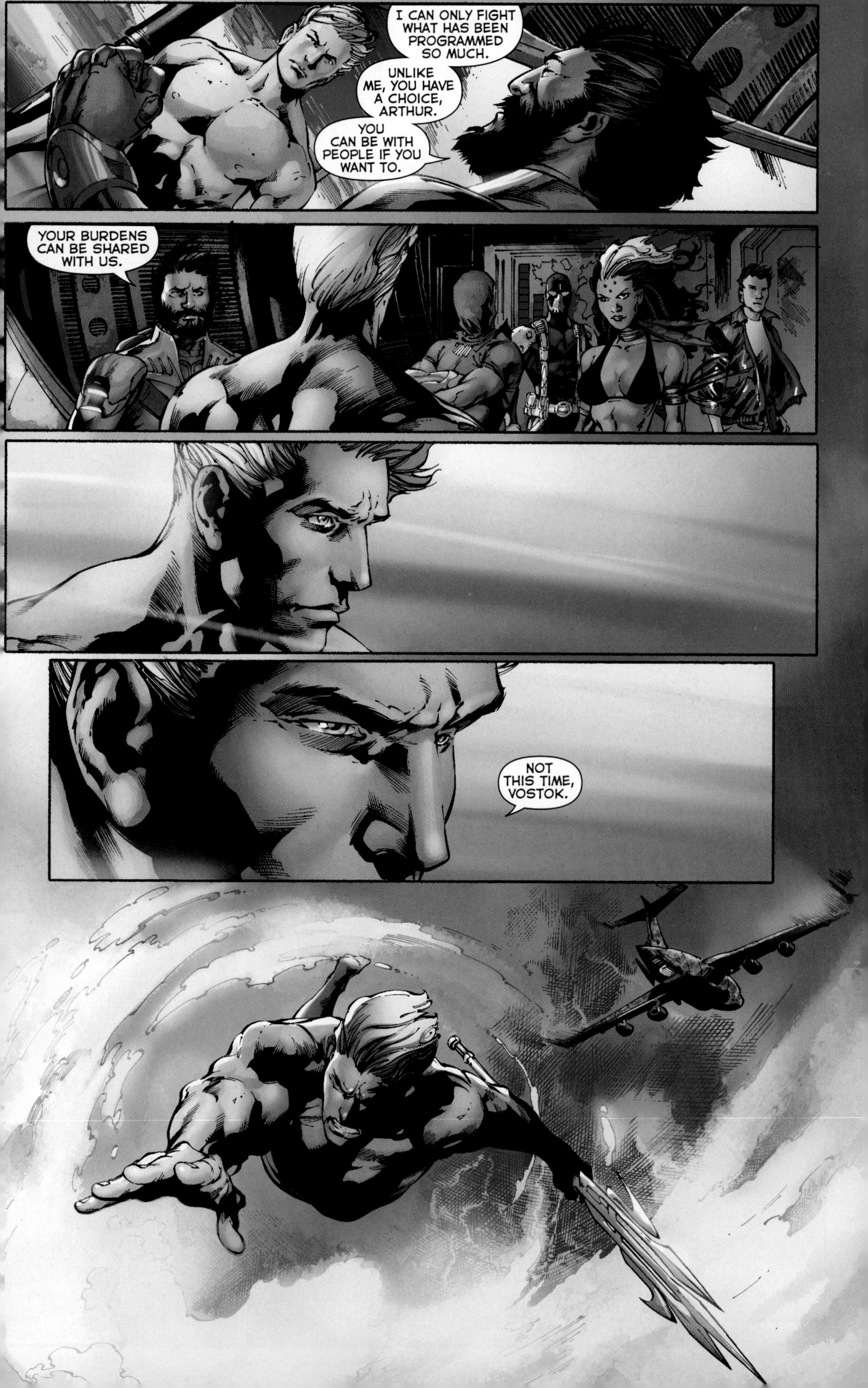
I CAN ONLY FIGHT WHAT HAS BEEN PROGRAMMED SO MUCH.
UNLIKE ME, YOU HAVE A CHOICE, ARTHUR.
YOU CAN BE WITH PEOPLE IF YOU WANT TO.
YOUR BURDENS CAN BE SHARED WITH US.
NOT THIS TIME, VOSTOK.

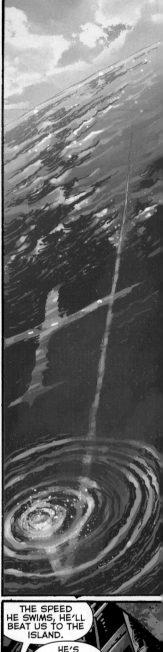

THE SPEED HE SWIMS, HE'LL BEAT US TO THE ISLAND.

HE'S NOT GOING TO LISTEN TO ANY OF US ANYWAY. HE NEVER HAS BEFORE.

I KNOW SOMEONE HE'LL LISTEN TO, PRISONER.

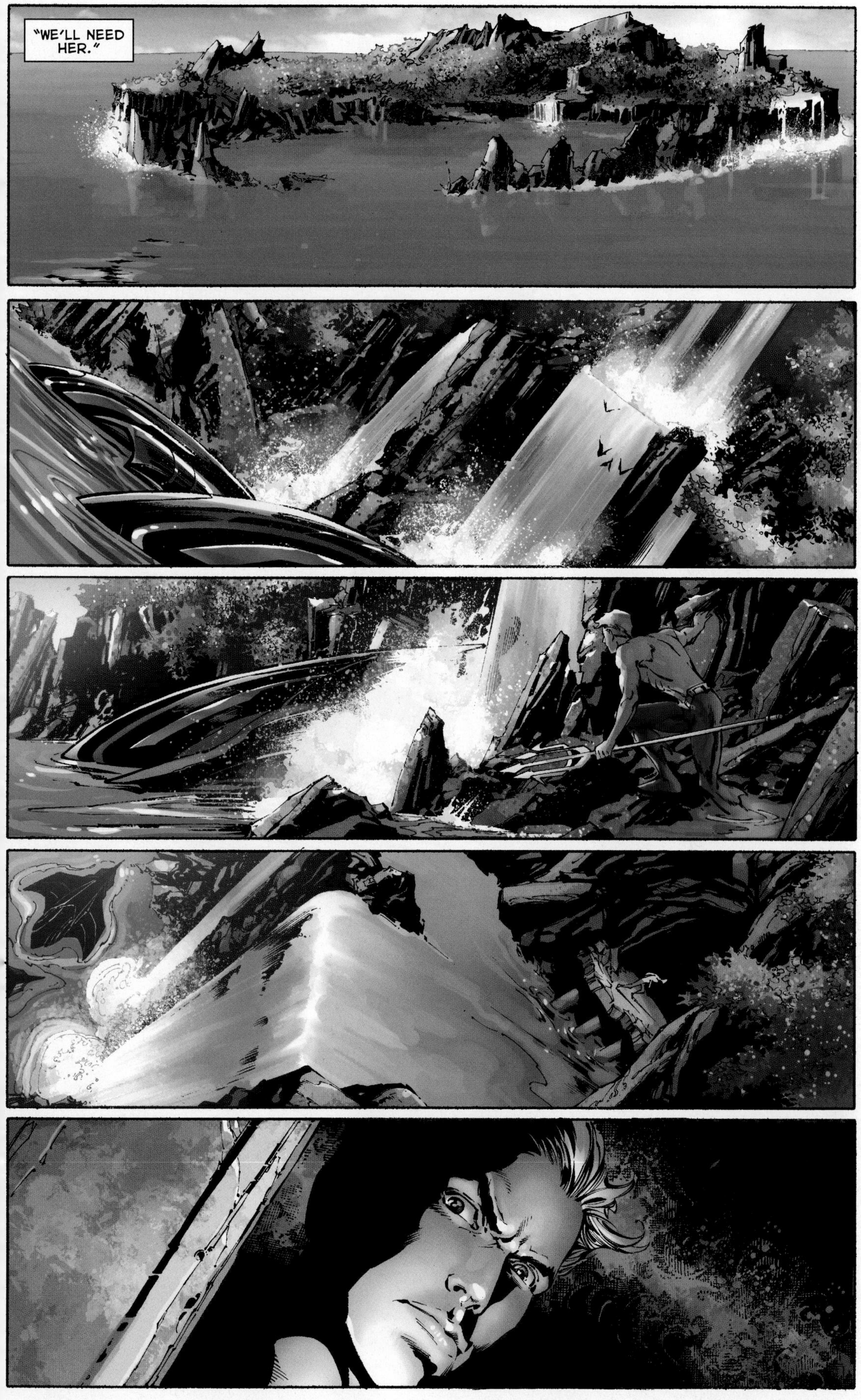
"WE'LL NEED HER."

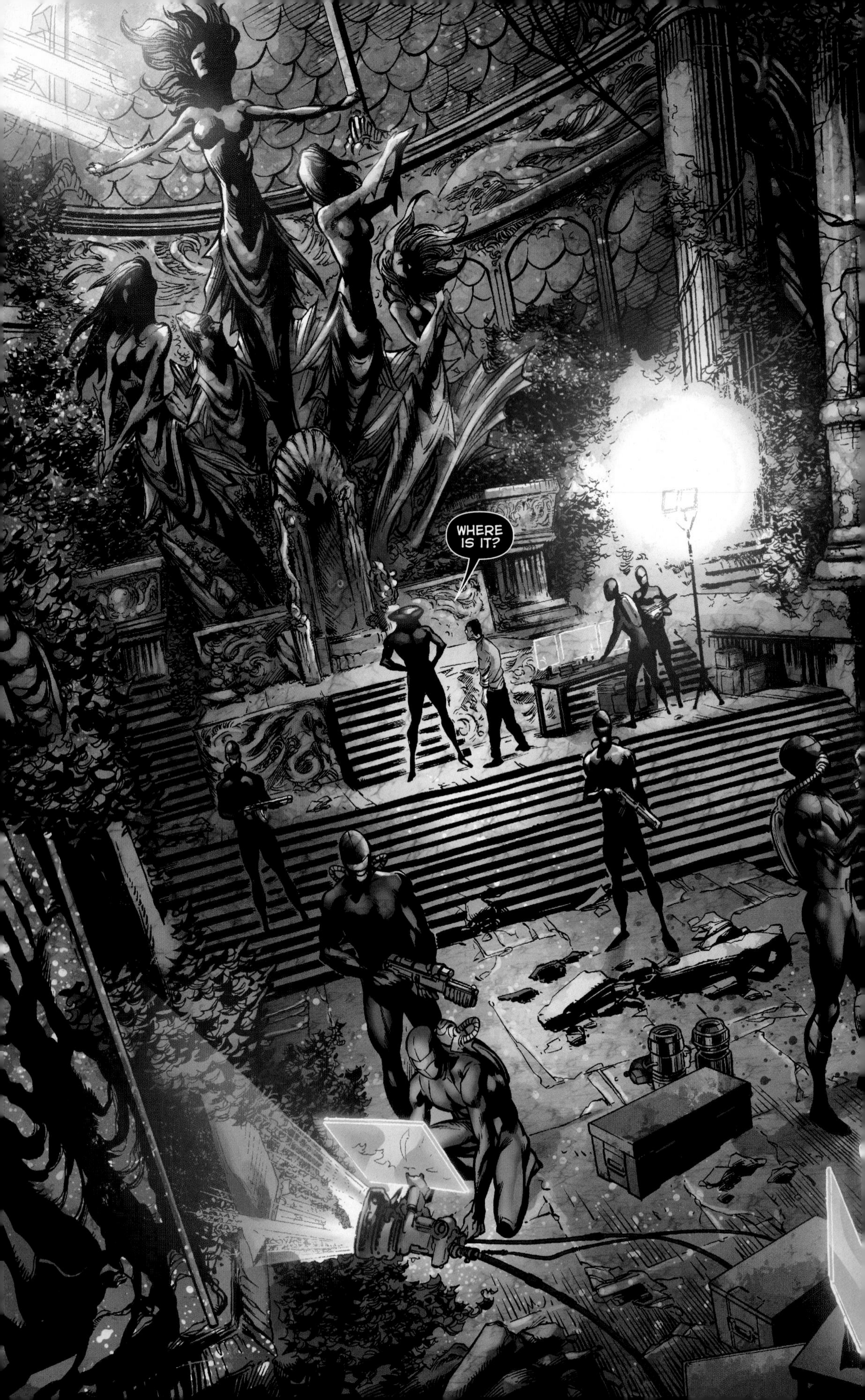
WHERE IS IT?

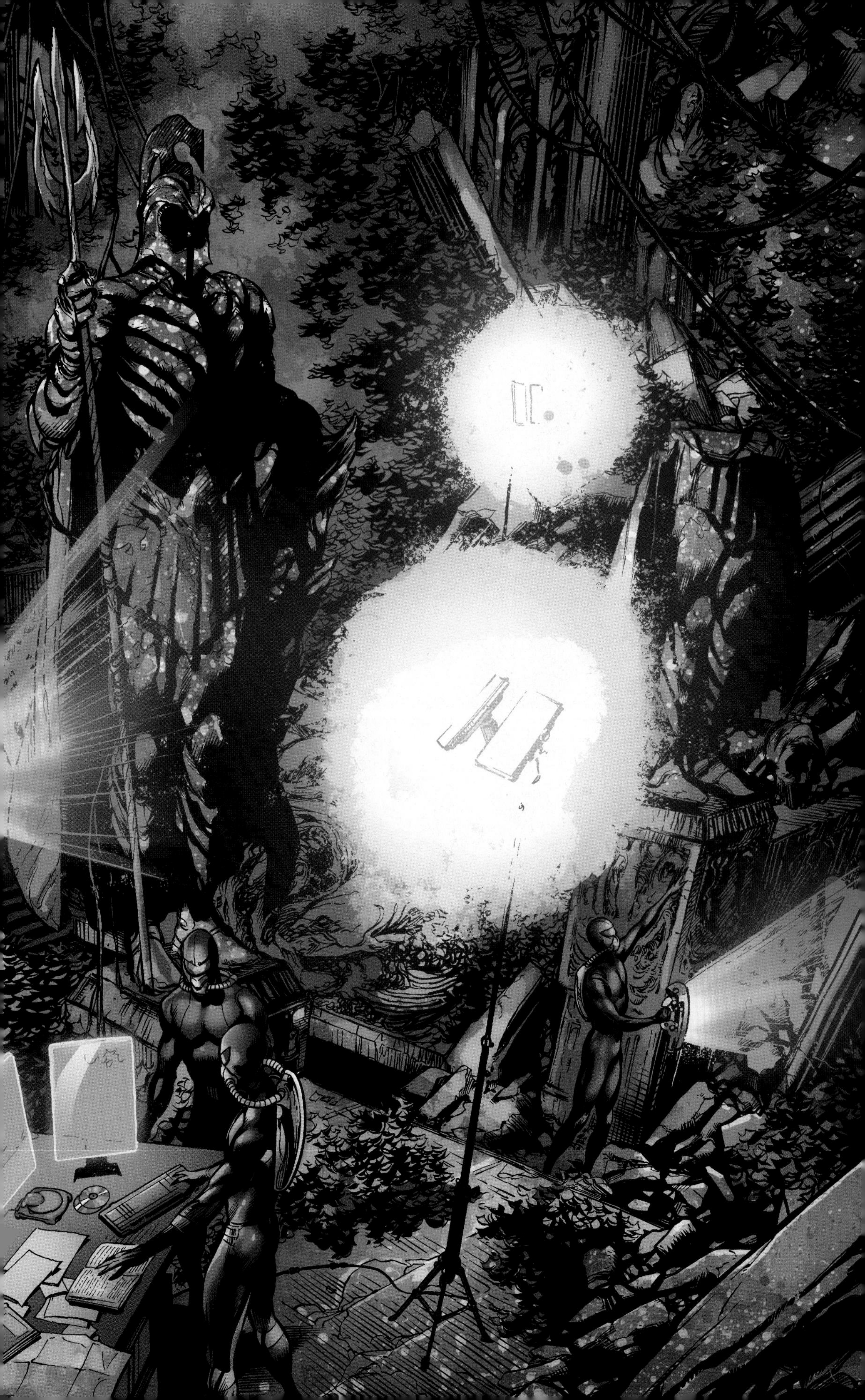

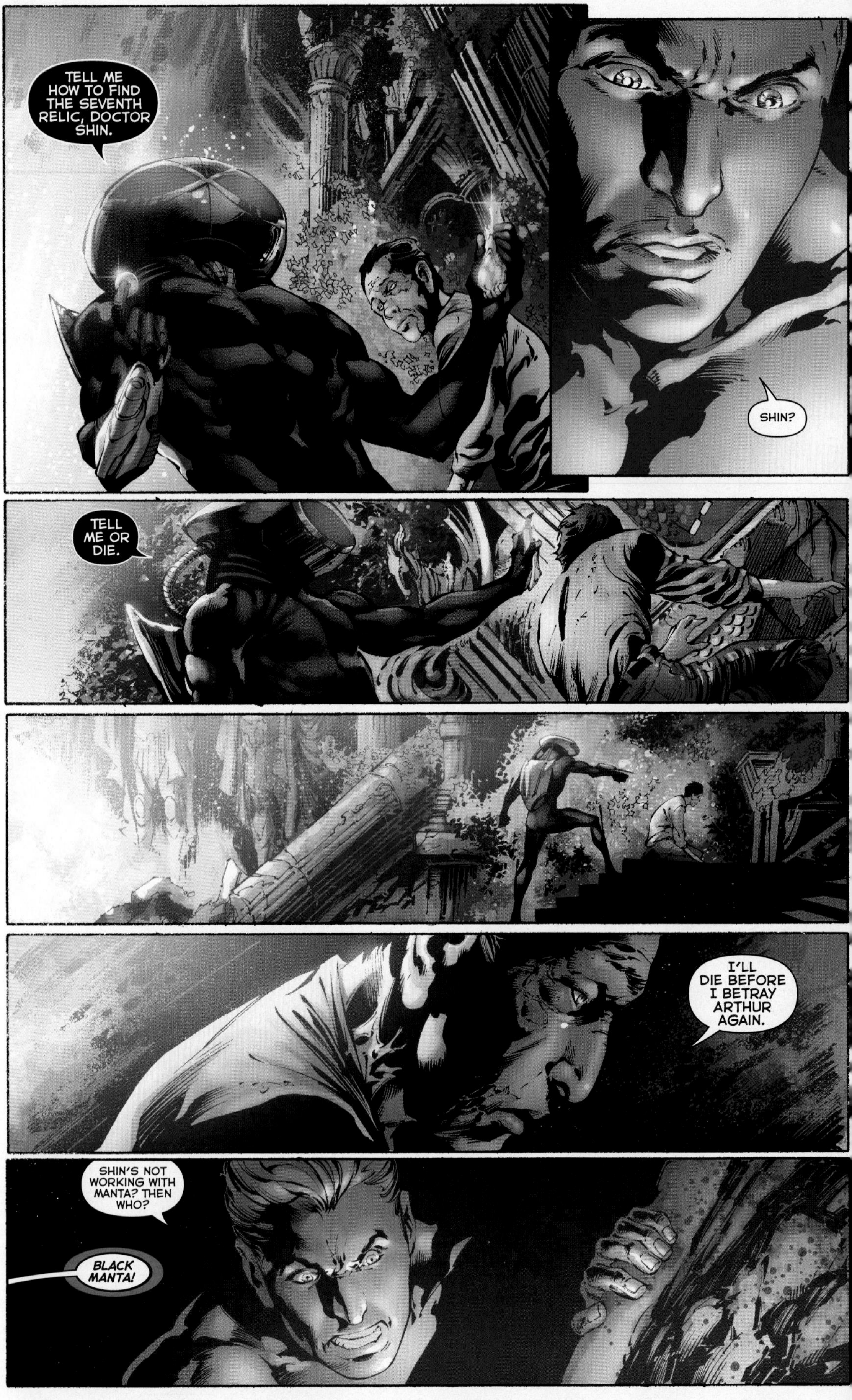
TELL ME HOW TO FIND THE SEVENTH RELIC, DOCTOR SHIN.
SHIN?
TELL ME OR DIE.
I'LL DIE BEFORE I BETRAY ARTHUR AGAIN.
SHIN'S NOT WORKING WITH MANTA? THEN WHO?
BLACK MANTA!

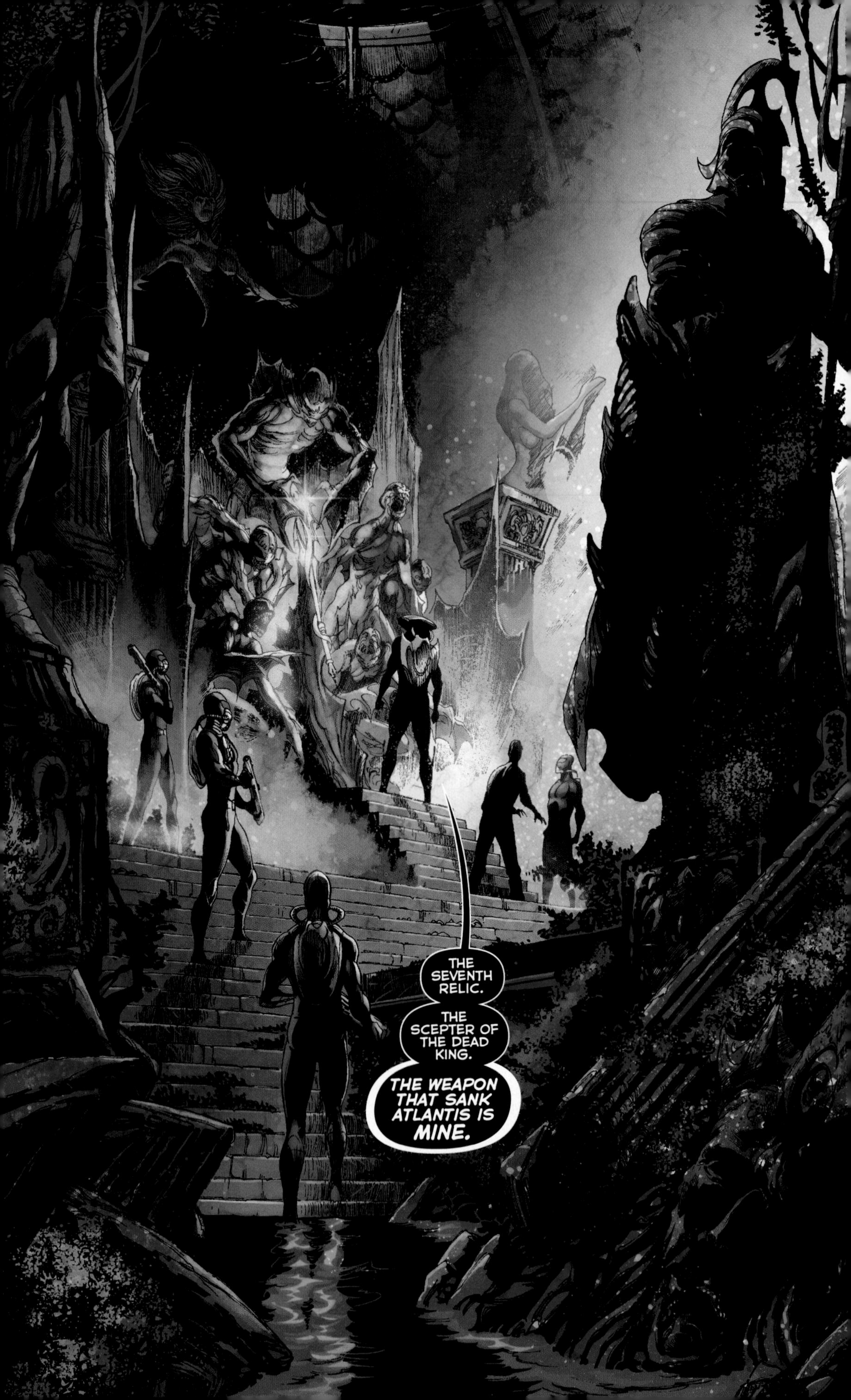

THE SEVENTH RELIC.
THE SCEPTER OF THE DEAD KING.
THE WEAPON THAT SANK ATLANTIS IS MINE.

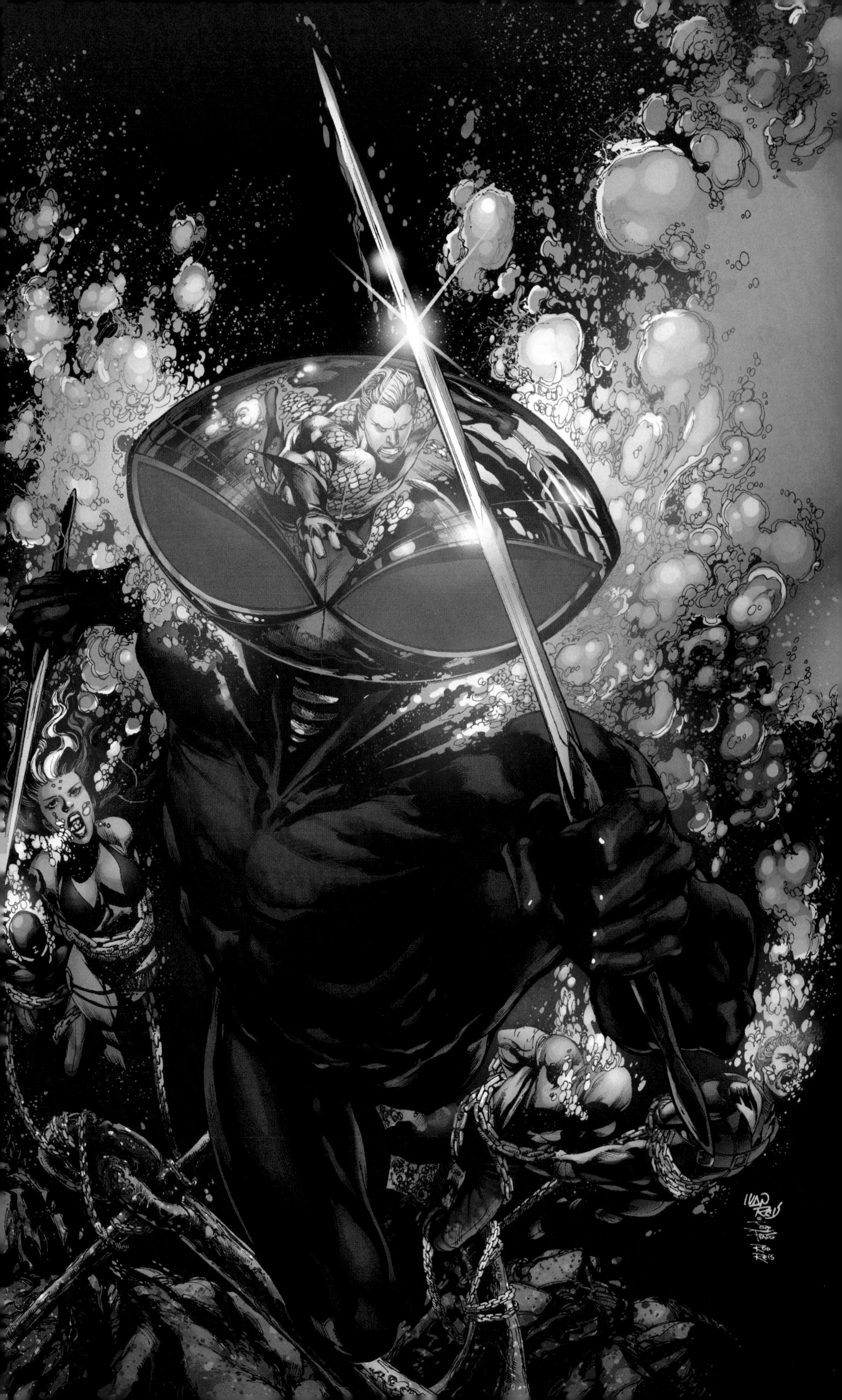

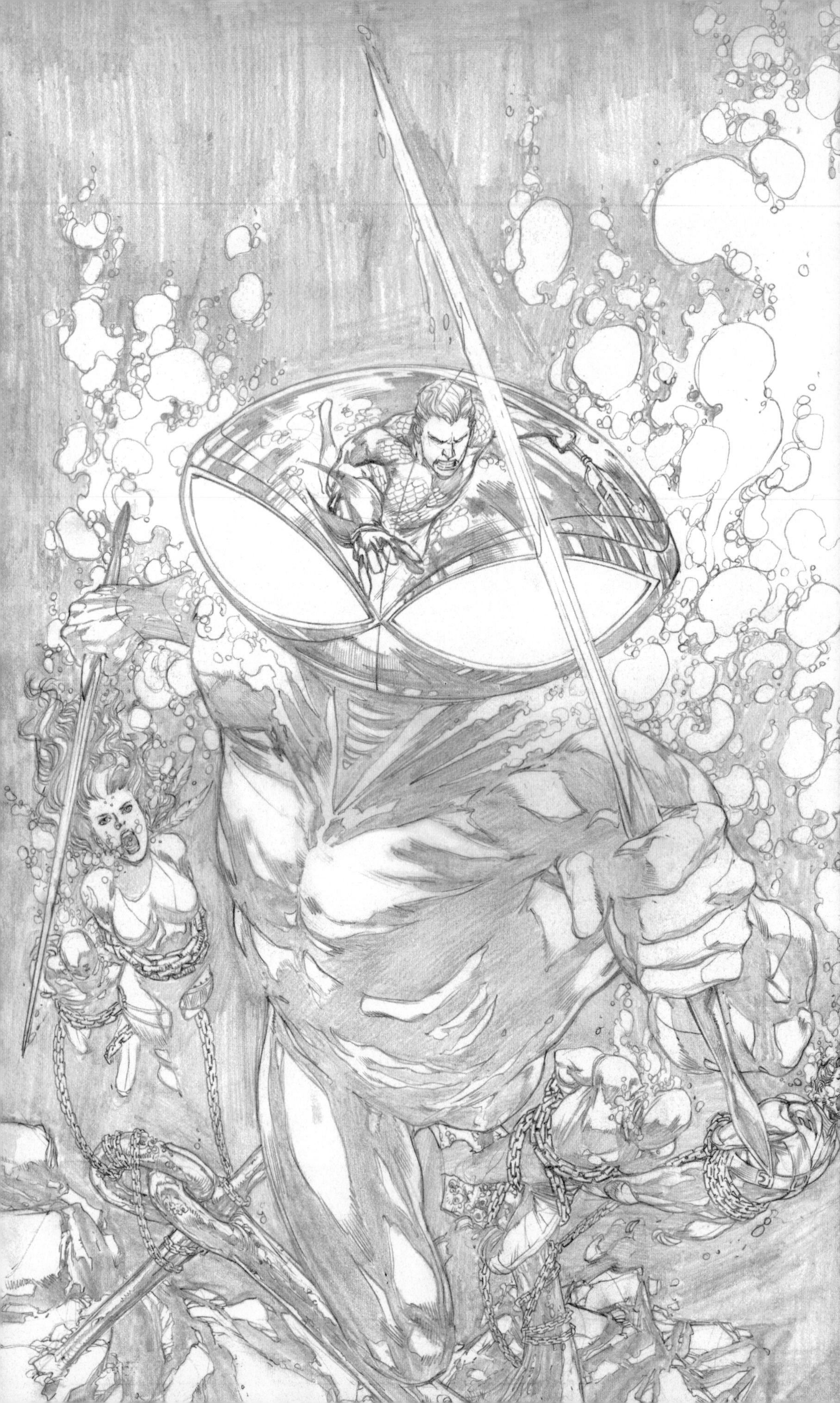

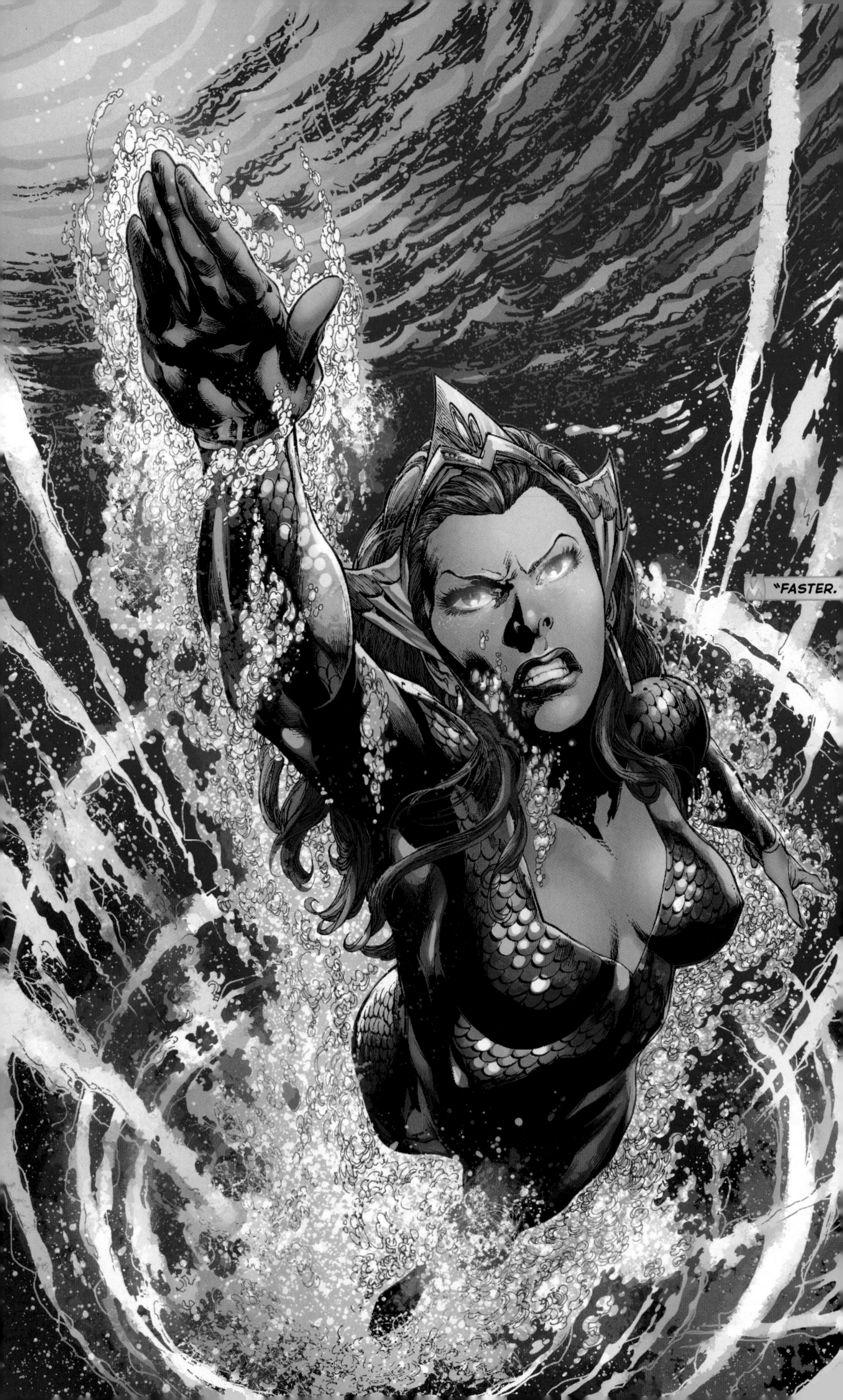
"FASTER.

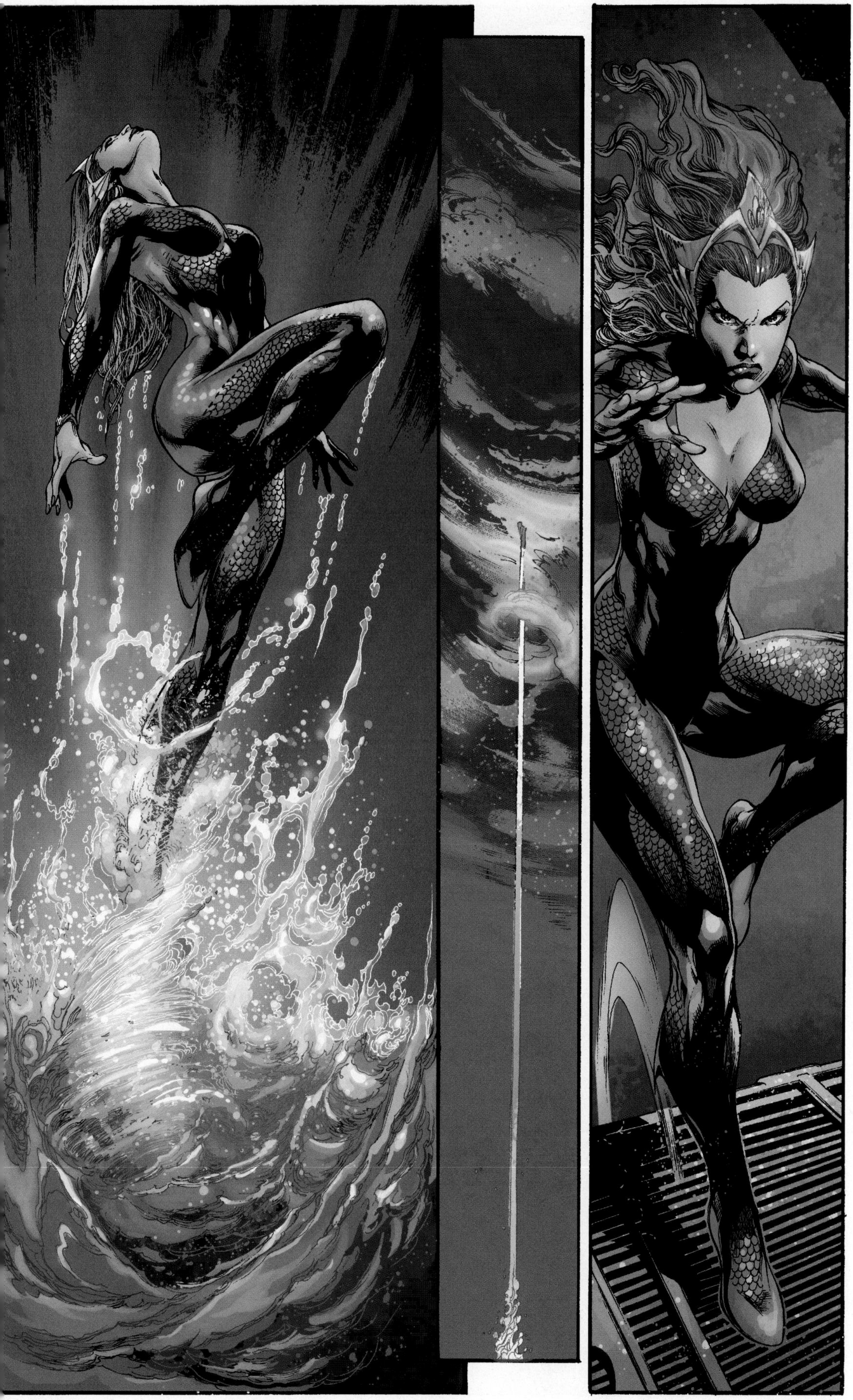

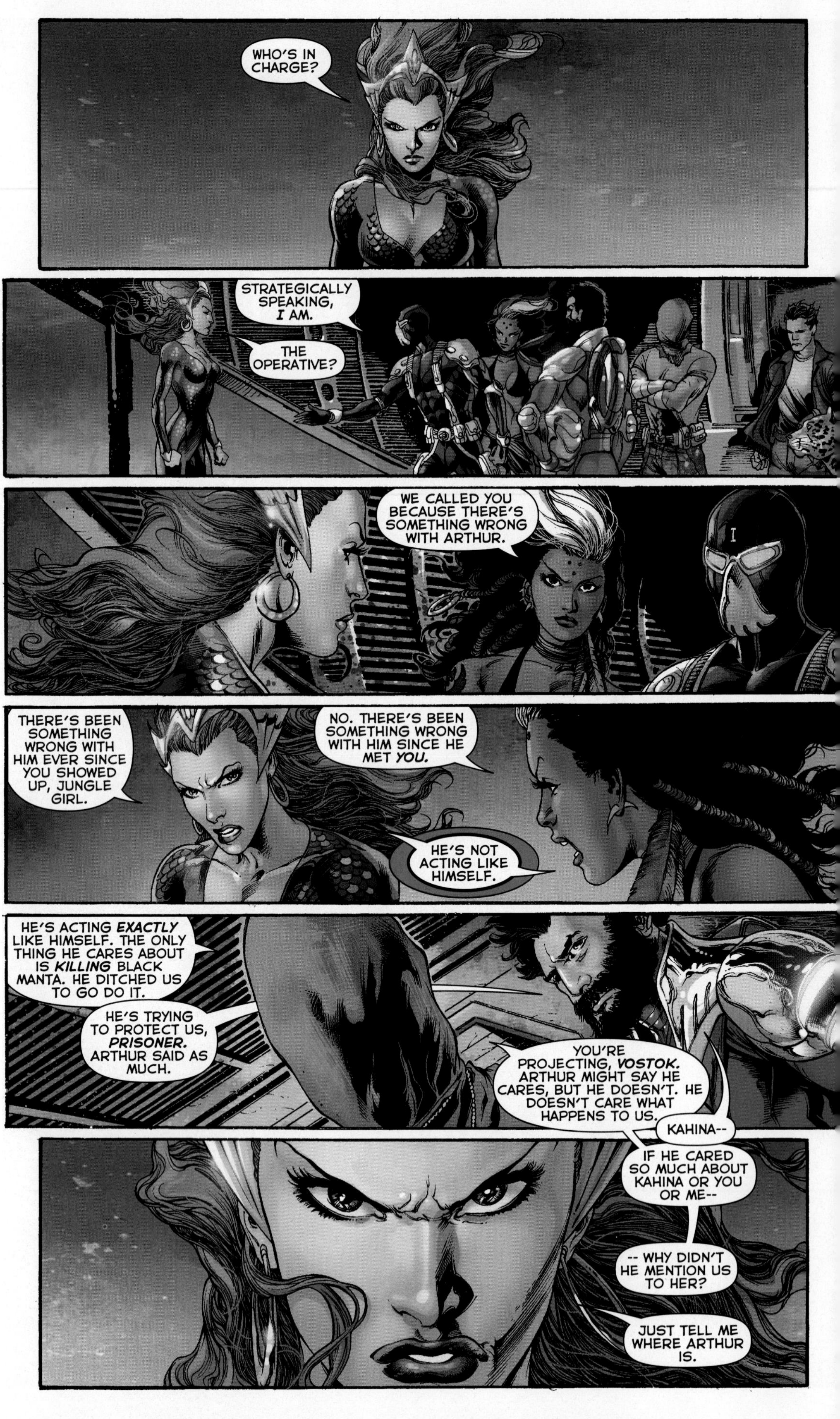
WHO'S IN CHARGE?
STRATEGICALLY SPEAKING, I AM.
THE OPERATIVE?
WE CALLED YOU BECAUSE THERE'S SOMETHING WRONG WITH ARTHUR.
THERE'S BEEN SOMETHING WRONG WITH HIM EVER SINCE YOU SHOWED UP, JUNGLE GIRL.
NO. THERE'S BEEN SOMETHING WRONG WITH HIM SINCE HE MET YOU.
HE'S NOT ACTING LIKE HIMSELF.
HE'S ACTING EXACTLY LIKE HIMSELF. THE ONLY THING HE CARES ABOUT IS KILLING BLACK MANTA. HE DITCHED US TO GO DO IT.
HE'S TRYING TO PROTECT US, PRISONER. ARTHUR SAID AS MUCH.
YOU'RE PROJECTING, VOSTOK. ARTHUR MIGHT SAY HE CARES, BUT HE DOESN'T. HE DOESN'T CARE WHAT HAPPENS TO US.
KAHINA--
IF HE CARED SO MUCH ABOUT KAHINA OR YOU OR ME--
-- WHY DIDN'T HE MENTION US TO HER?
JUST TELL ME WHERE ARTHUR IS.

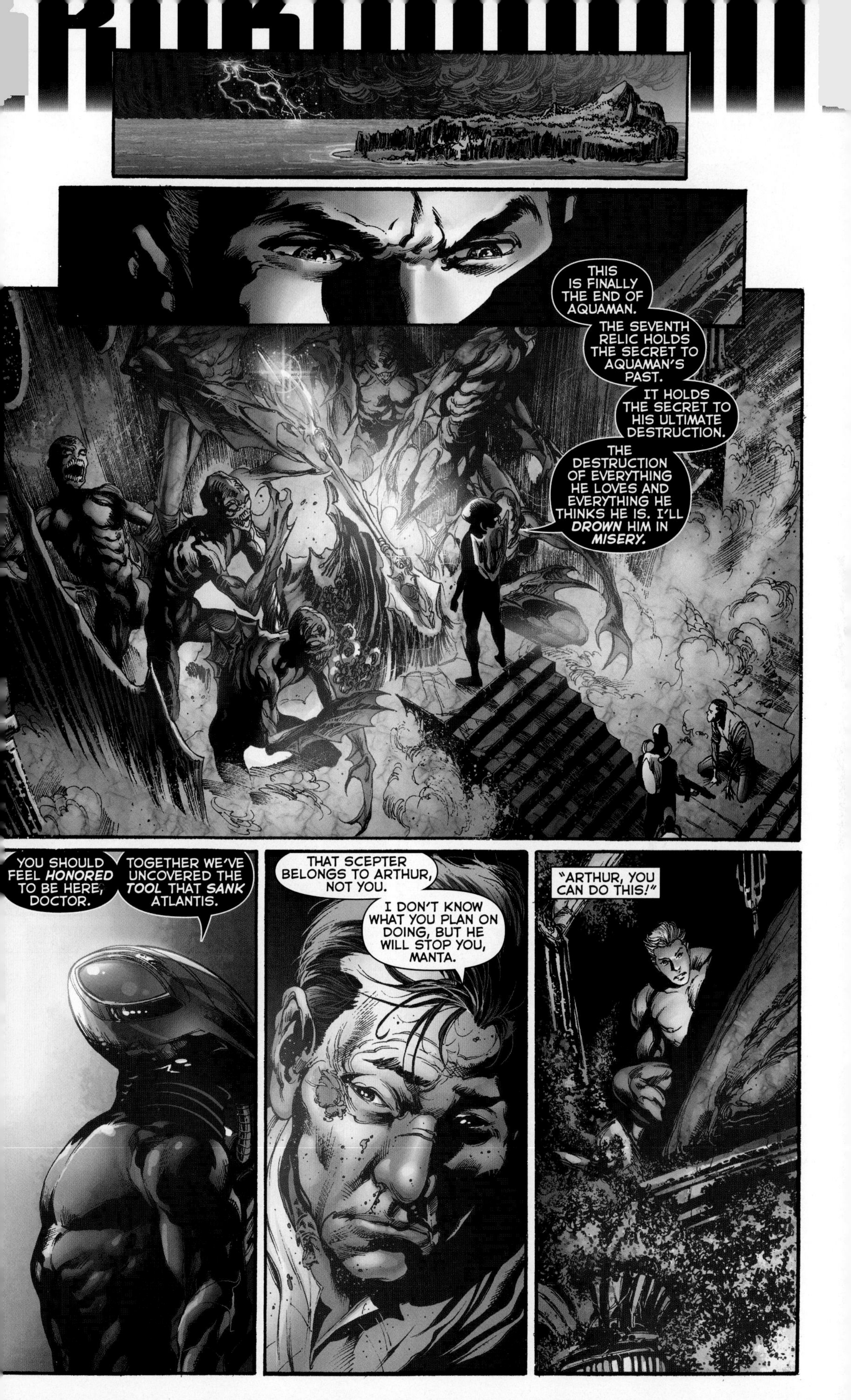
THIS IS FINALLY THE END OF AQUAMAN.
THE SEVENTH RELIC HOLDS THE SECRET TO AQUAMAN'S PAST.
IT HOLDS THE SECRET TO HIS ULTIMATE DESTRUCTION.
THE DESTRUCTION OF EVERYTHING HE LOVES AND EVERYTHING HE THINKS HE IS. I'LL ***DROWN*** HIM IN ***MISERY.***
YOU SHOULD FEEL ***HONORED*** TO BE HERE, DOCTOR.
TOGETHER WE'VE UNCOVERED THE ***TOOL*** THAT ***SANK*** ATLANTIS.
THAT SCEPTER BELONGS TO ARTHUR, NOT YOU.
I DON'T KNOW WHAT YOU PLAN ON DOING, BUT HE WILL STOP YOU, MANTA.
"ARTHUR, YOU CAN DO THIS!"

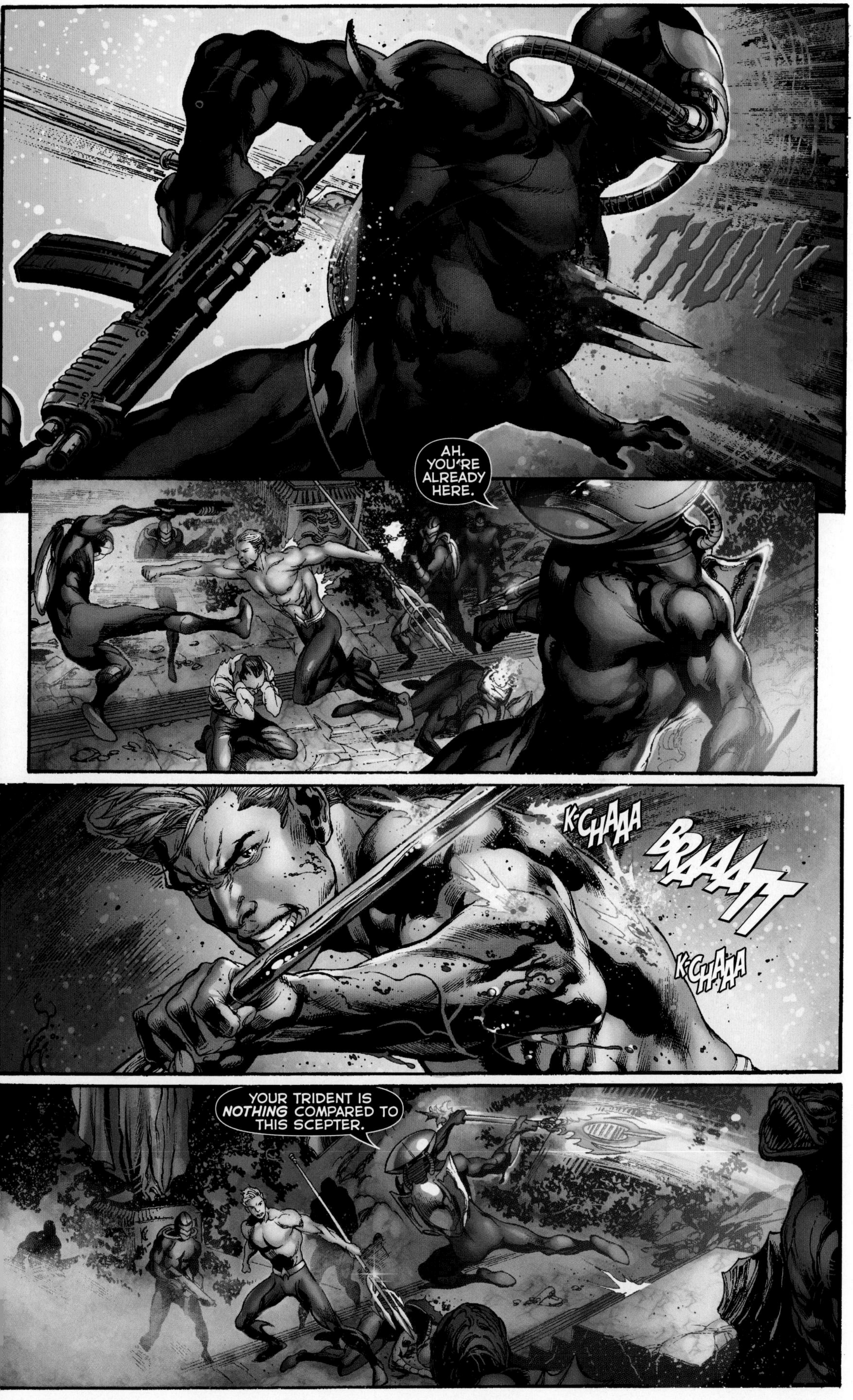
THUNK
AH. YOU'RE ALREADY HERE.
K-CHAAA
BRAAATT
K-CHAAA
YOUR TRIDENT IS NOTHING COMPARED TO THIS SCEPTER.

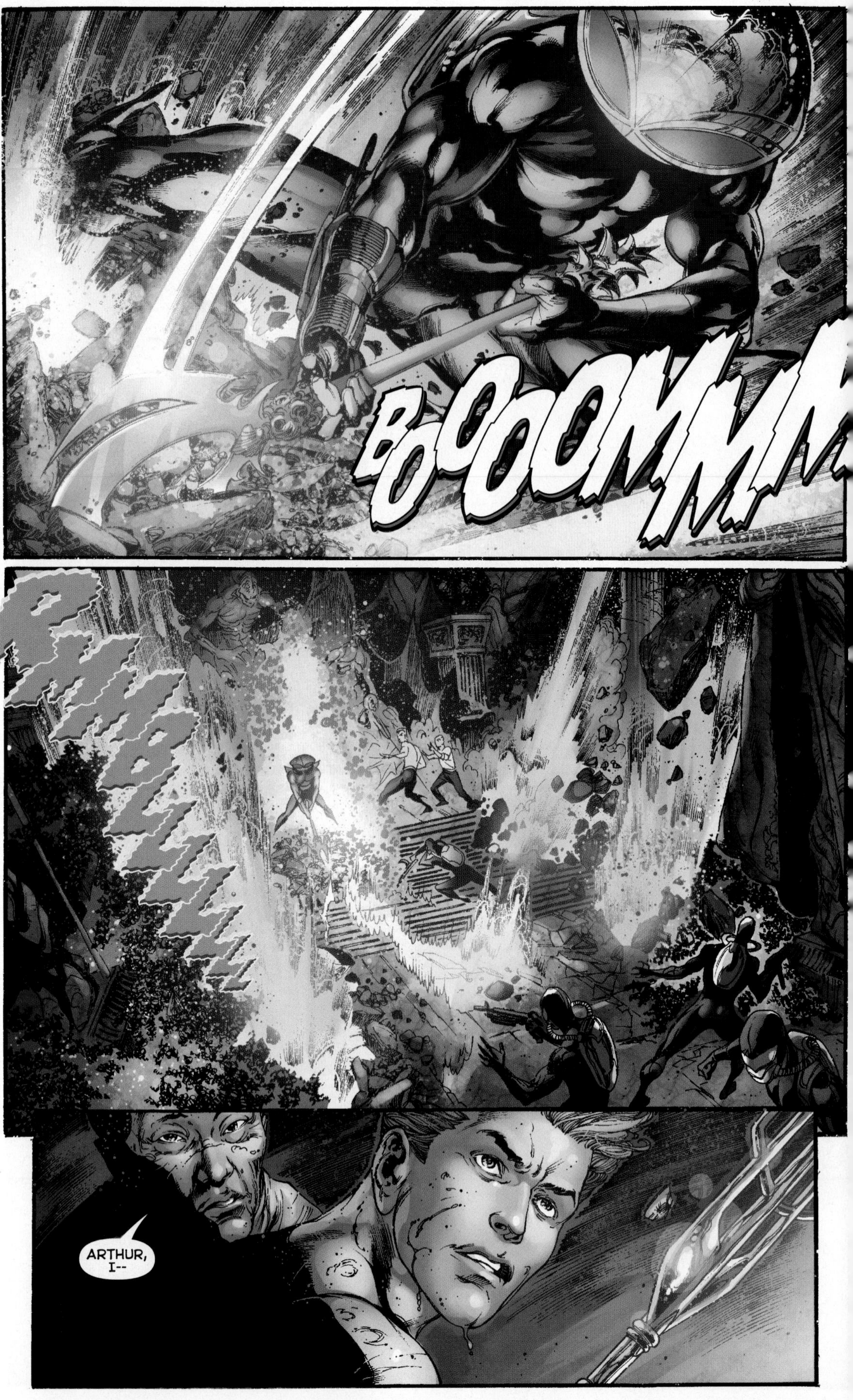
BOOOOMMMM
ARTHUR, I--

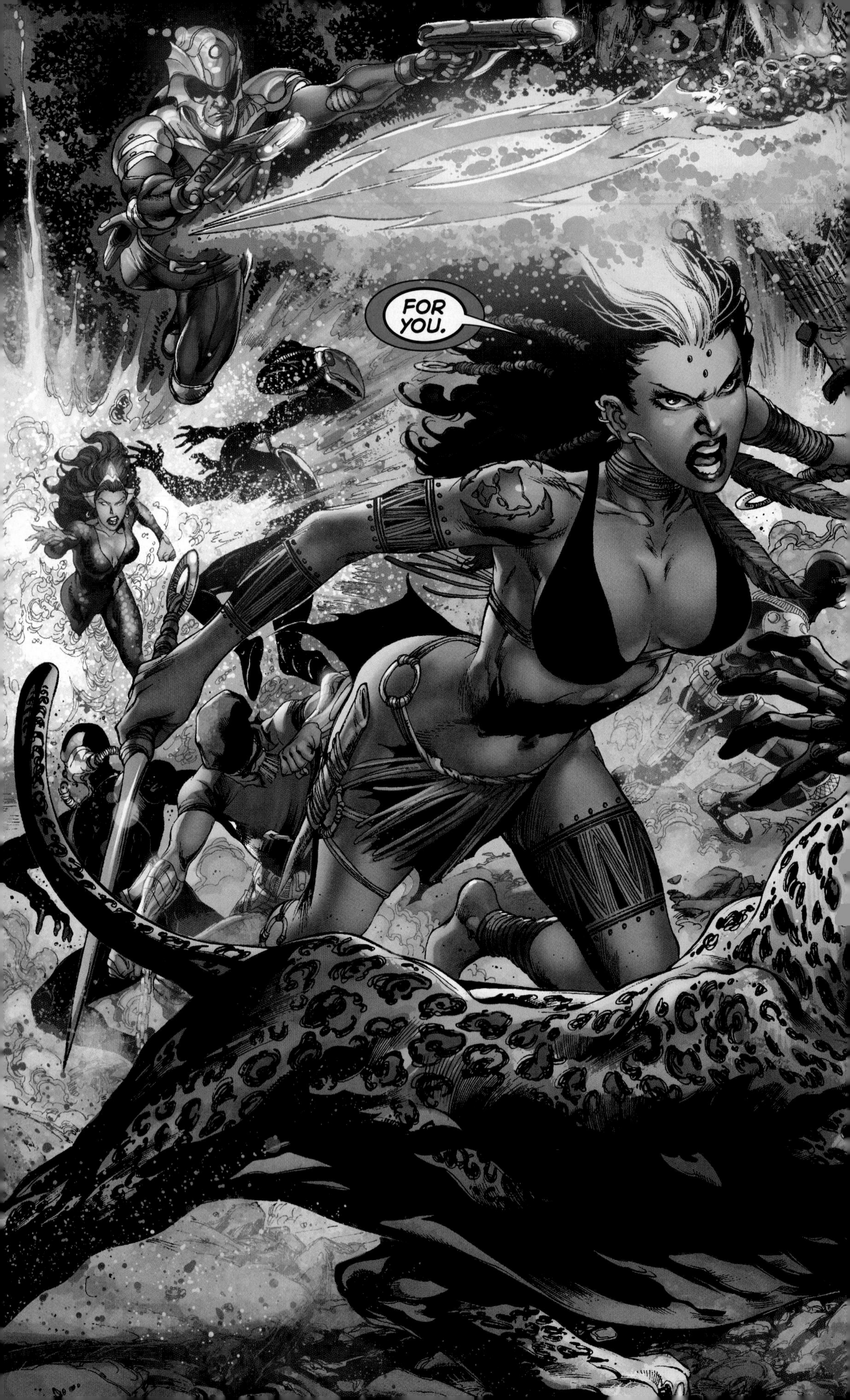
FOR YOU.

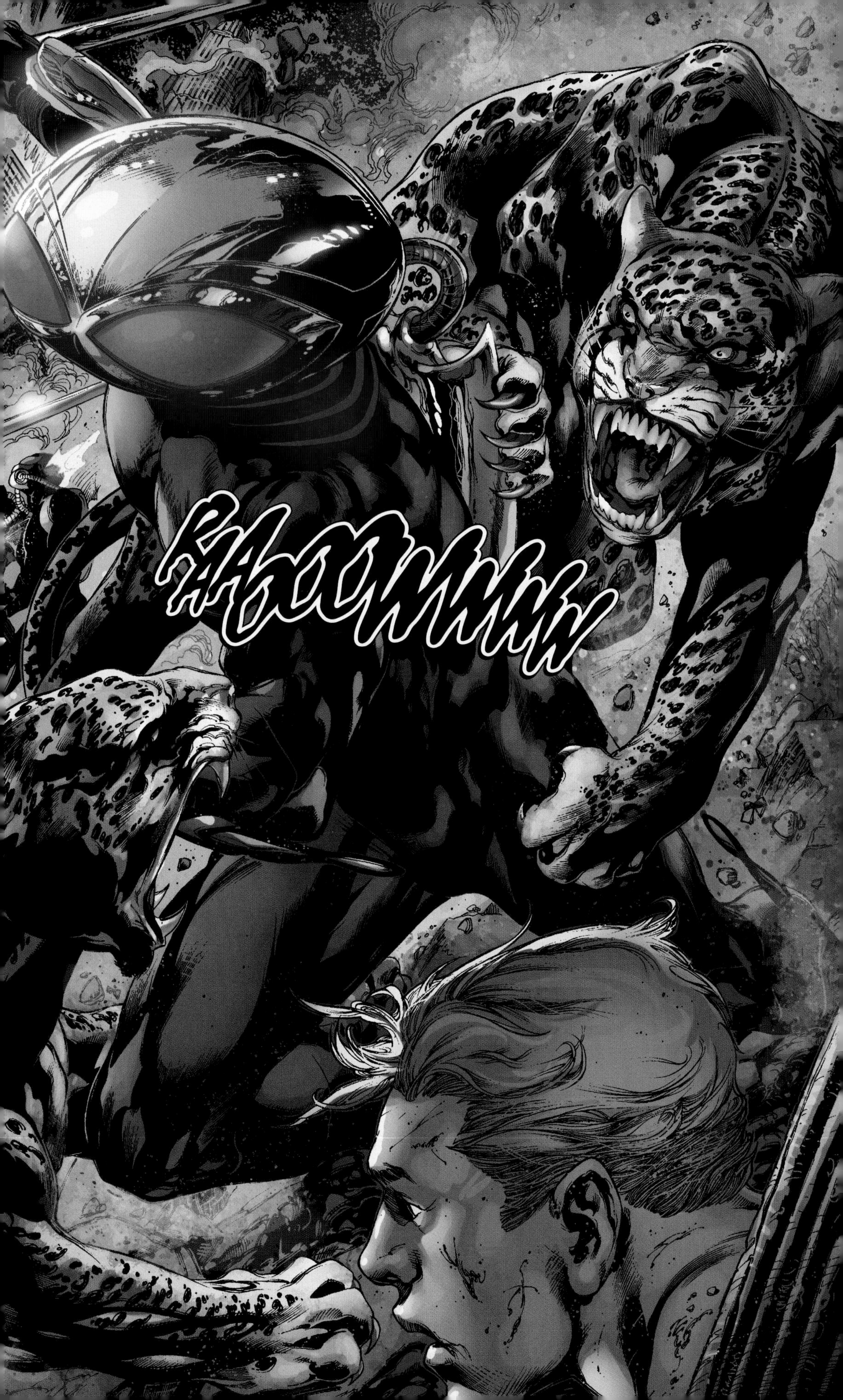

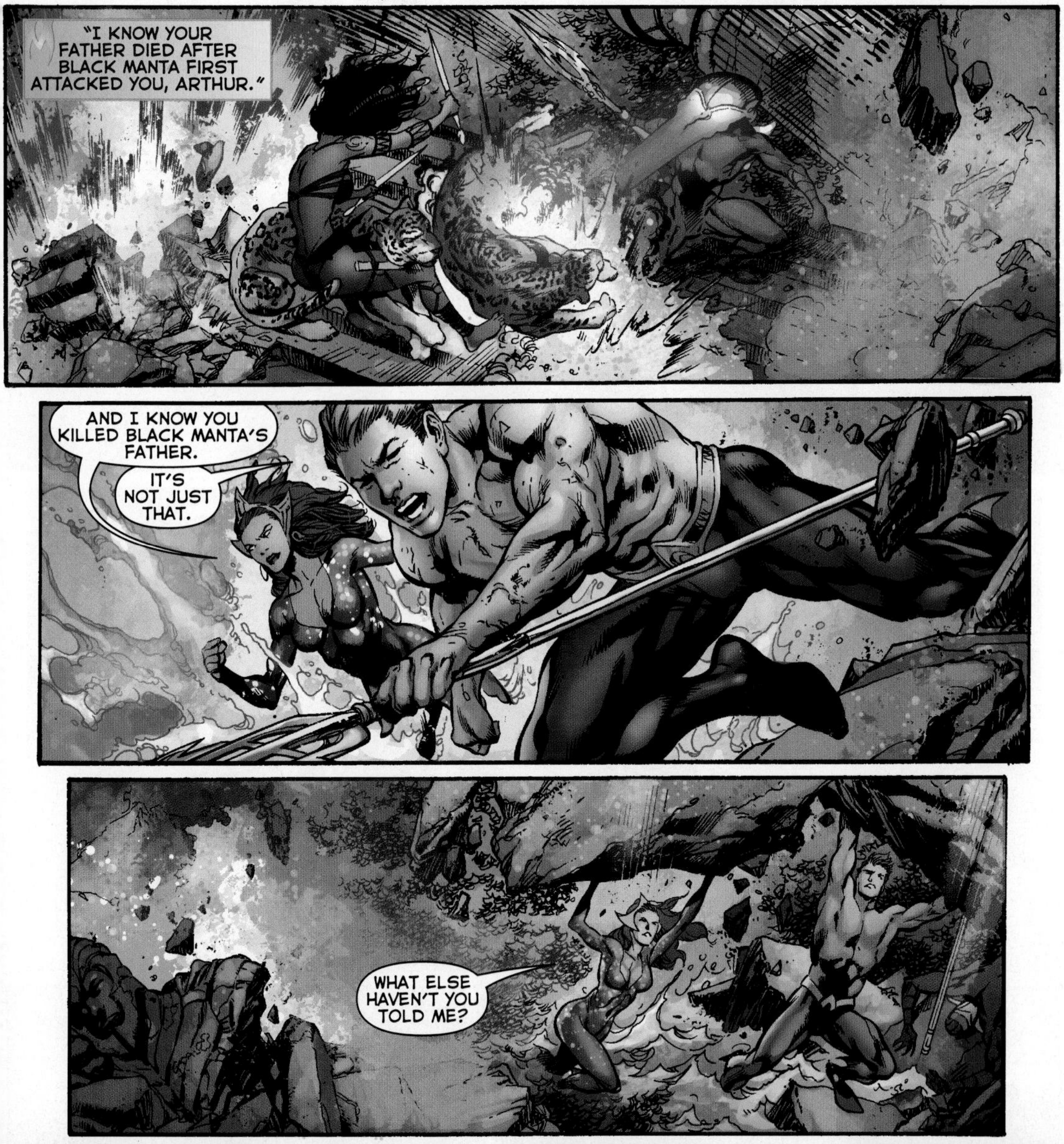
"I KNOW YOUR FATHER DIED AFTER BLACK MANTA FIRST ATTACKED YOU, ARTHUR."
AND I KNOW YOU KILLED BLACK MANTA'S FATHER.
IT'S NOT JUST THAT.
WHAT ELSE HAVEN'T YOU TOLD ME?
SHIN?
WHERE DO YOU THINK YOU'RE GOING?
IT'S CLEAR YOU WERE INVOLVED IN THIS.
THE JAGUARS FEED THIS TIME.

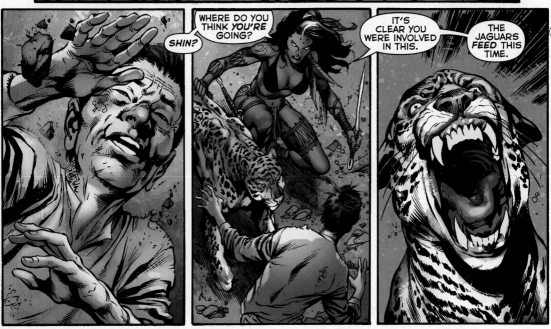

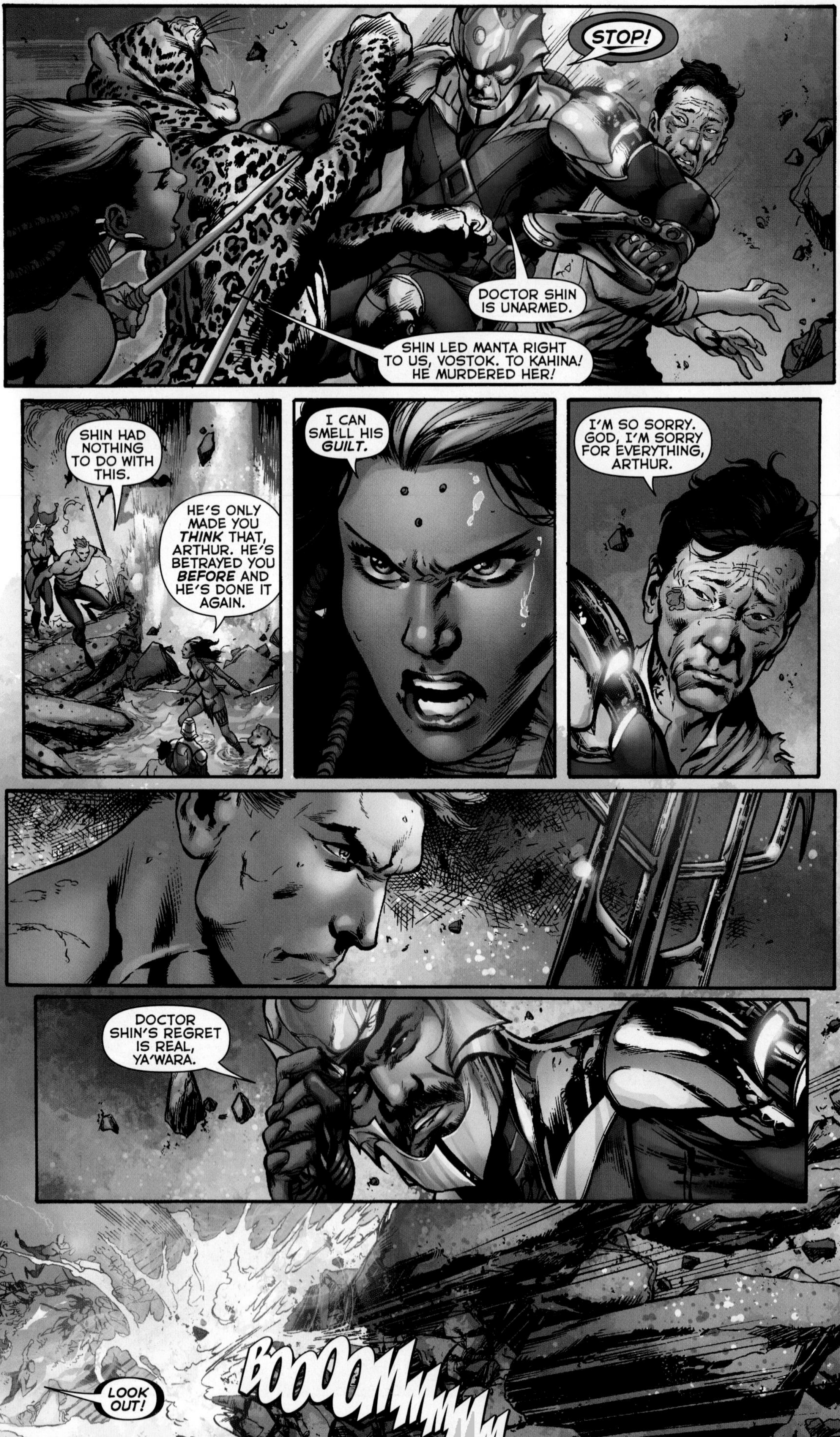
STOP!
DOCTOR SHIN IS UNARMED.
SHIN LED MANTA RIGHT TO US, VOSTOK. TO KAHINA! HE MURDERED HER!
SHIN HAD NOTHING TO DO WITH THIS.
HE'S ONLY MADE YOU *THINK* THAT, ARTHUR. HE'S BETRAYED YOU *BEFORE* AND HE'S DONE IT AGAIN.
I CAN SMELL HIS *GUILT*.
I'M SO SORRY. GOD, I'M SORRY FOR EVERYTHING, ARTHUR.
DOCTOR SHIN'S REGRET IS REAL, YA'WARA.
LOOK OUT!
BOOOOMMMMM

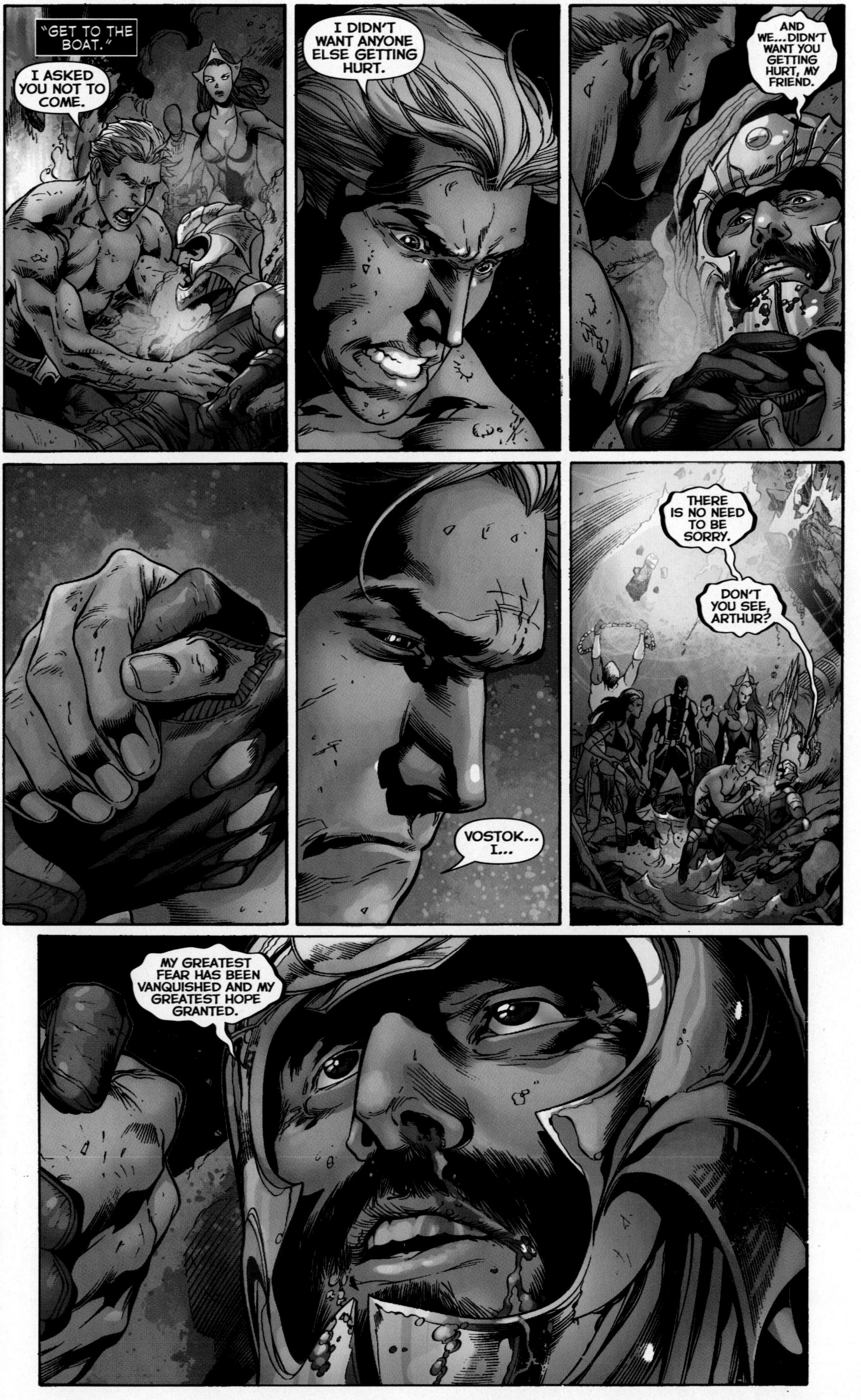
"GET TO THE BOAT."
I ASKED YOU NOT TO COME.
I DIDN'T WANT ANYONE ELSE GETTING HURT.
AND WE...DIDN'T WANT YOU GETTING HURT, MY FRIEND.
VOSTOK... I...
THERE IS NO NEED TO BE SORRY.
DON'T YOU SEE, ARTHUR?
MY GREATEST FEAR HAS BEEN VANQUISHED AND MY GREATEST HOPE GRANTED.

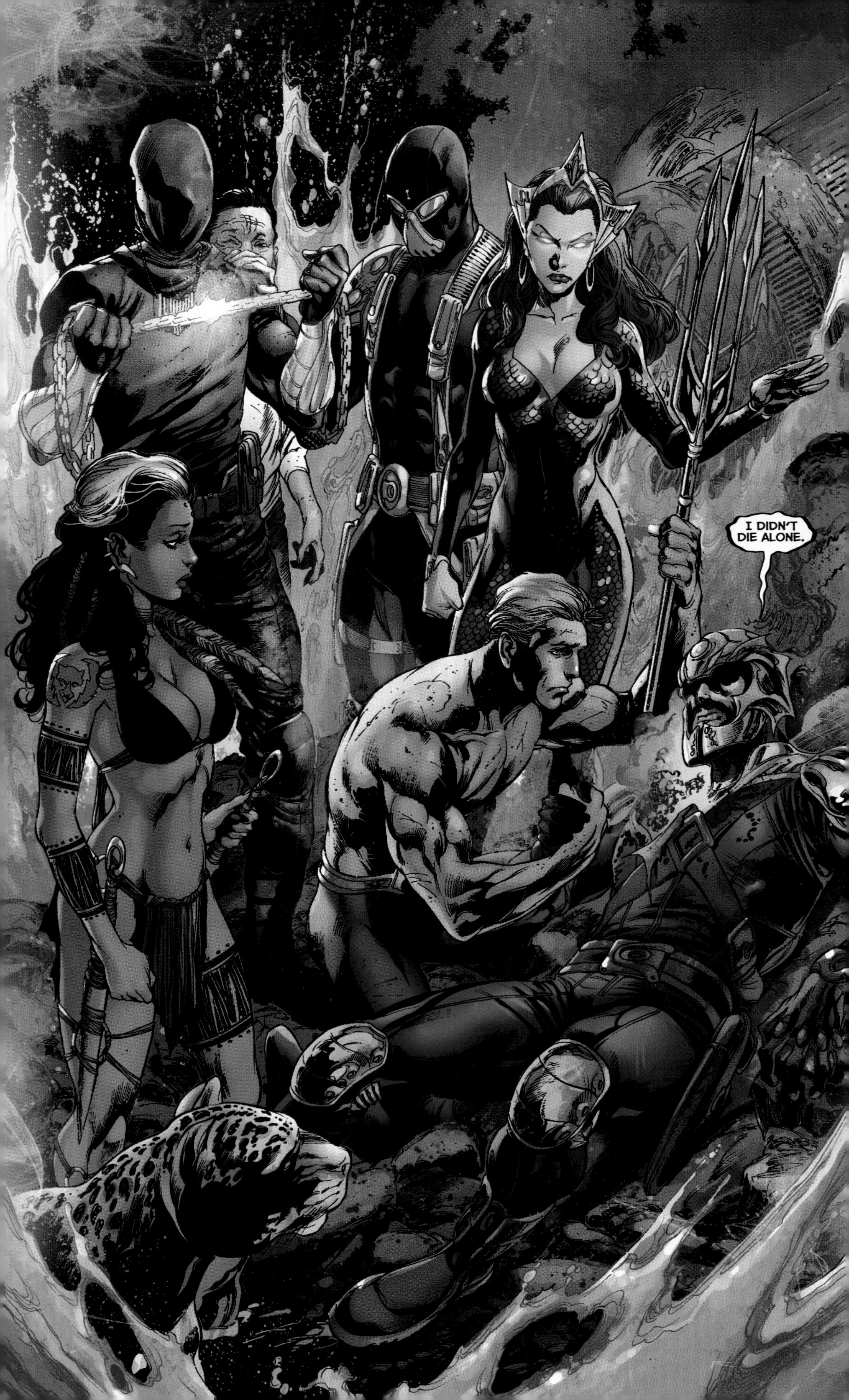
I DIDN'T DIE ALONE.

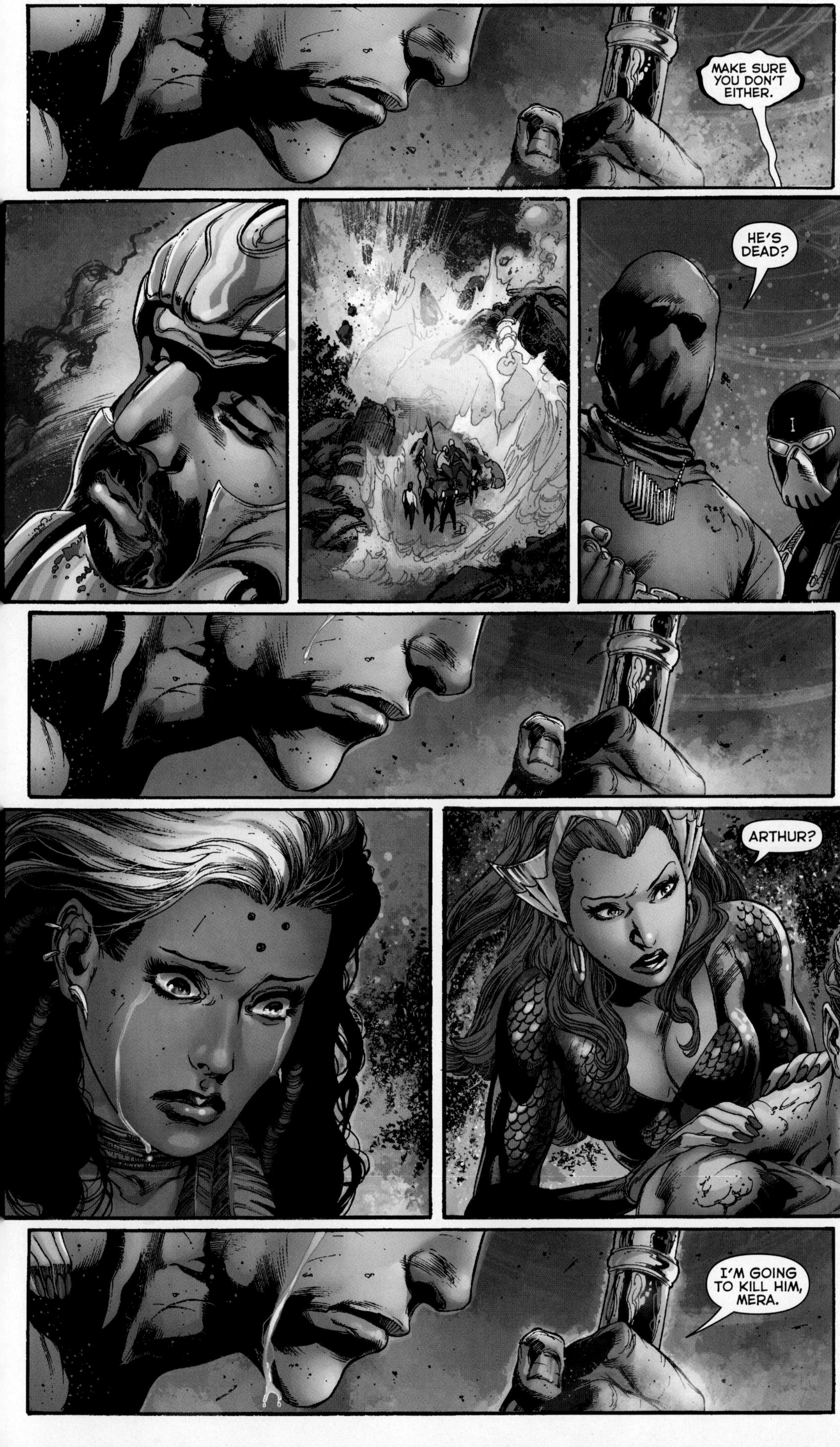

MAKE SURE YOU DON'T EITHER.
HE'S DEAD?
ARTHUR?
I'M GOING TO KILL HIM, MERA.

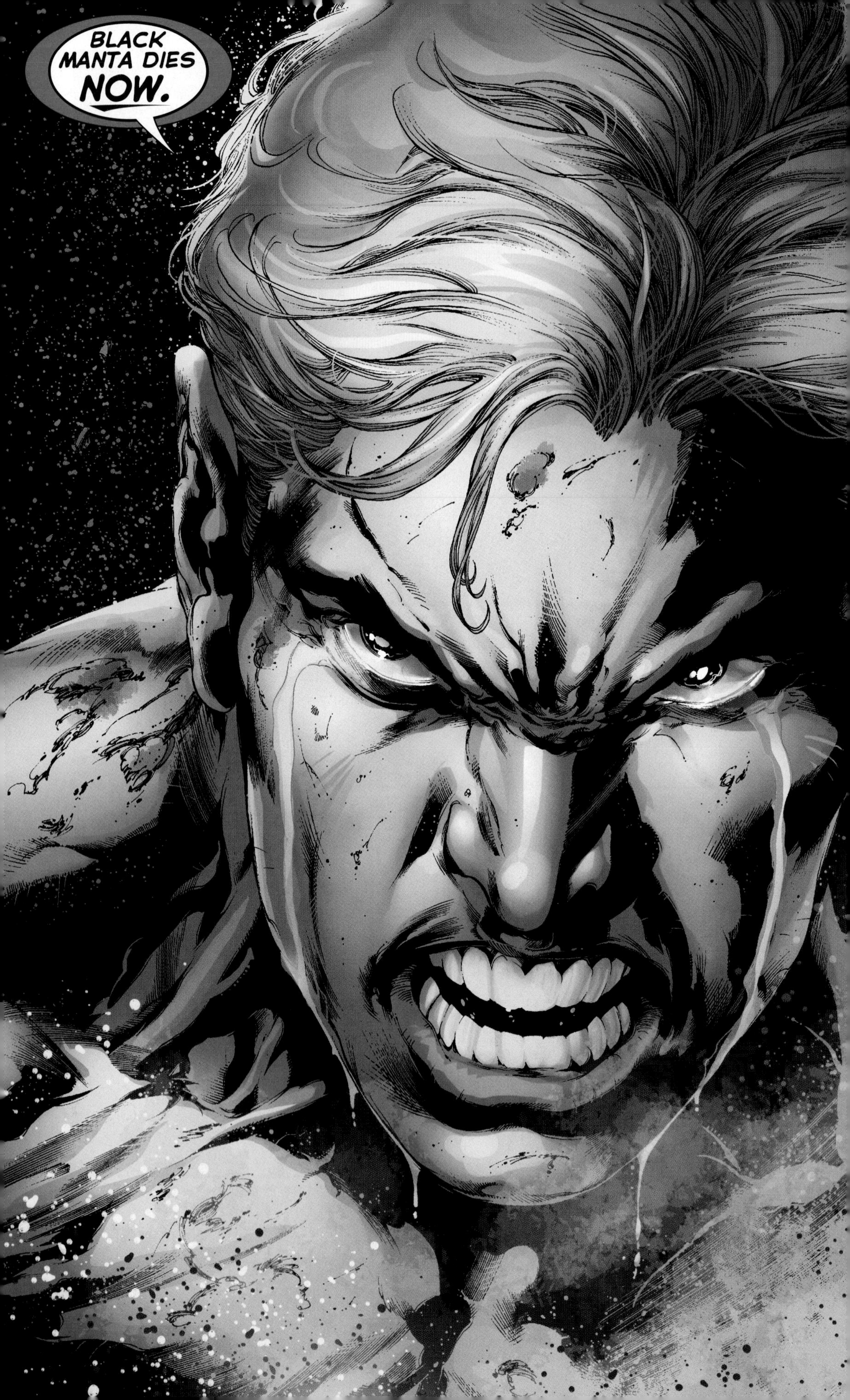
BLACK MANTA DIES NOW.

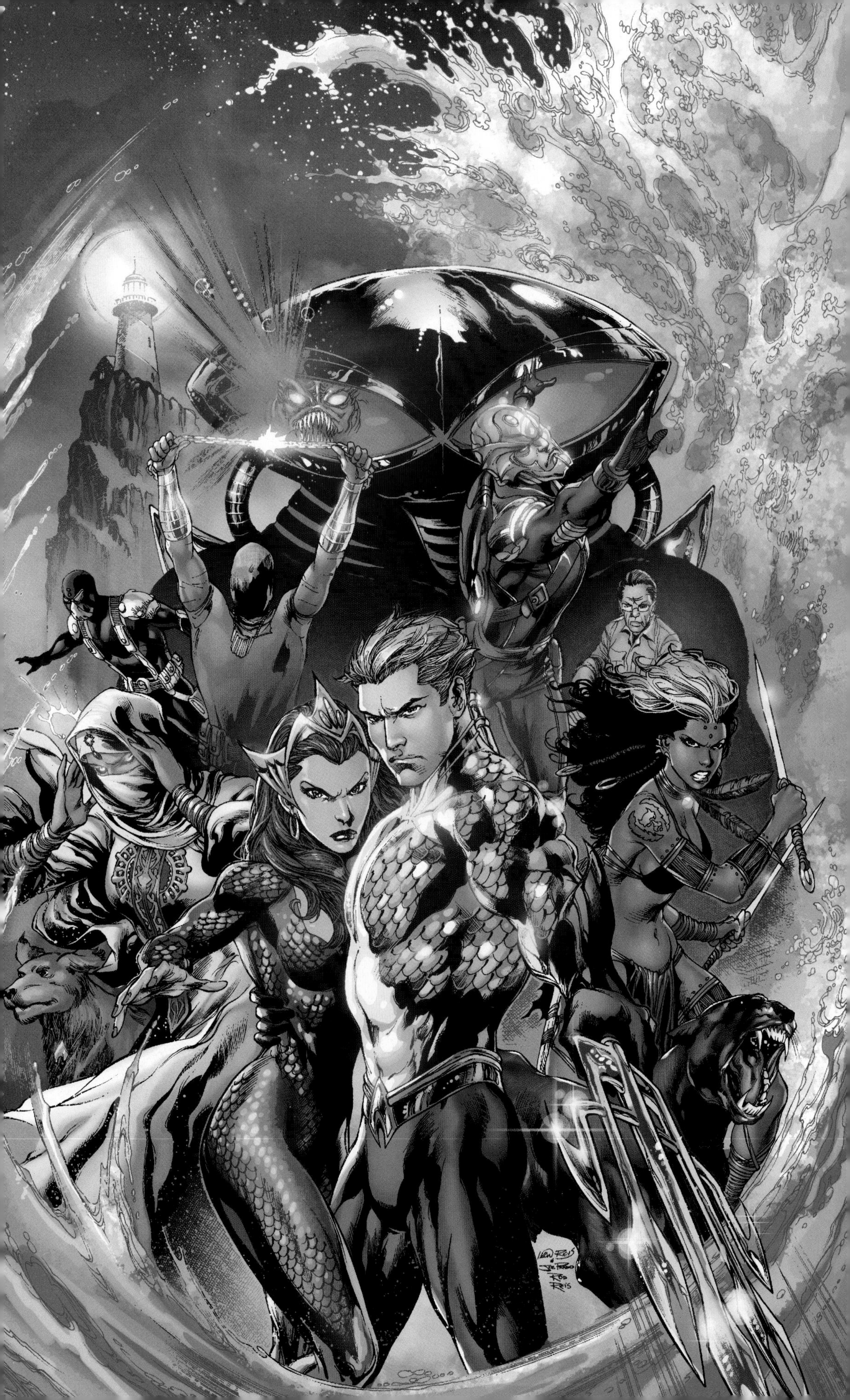

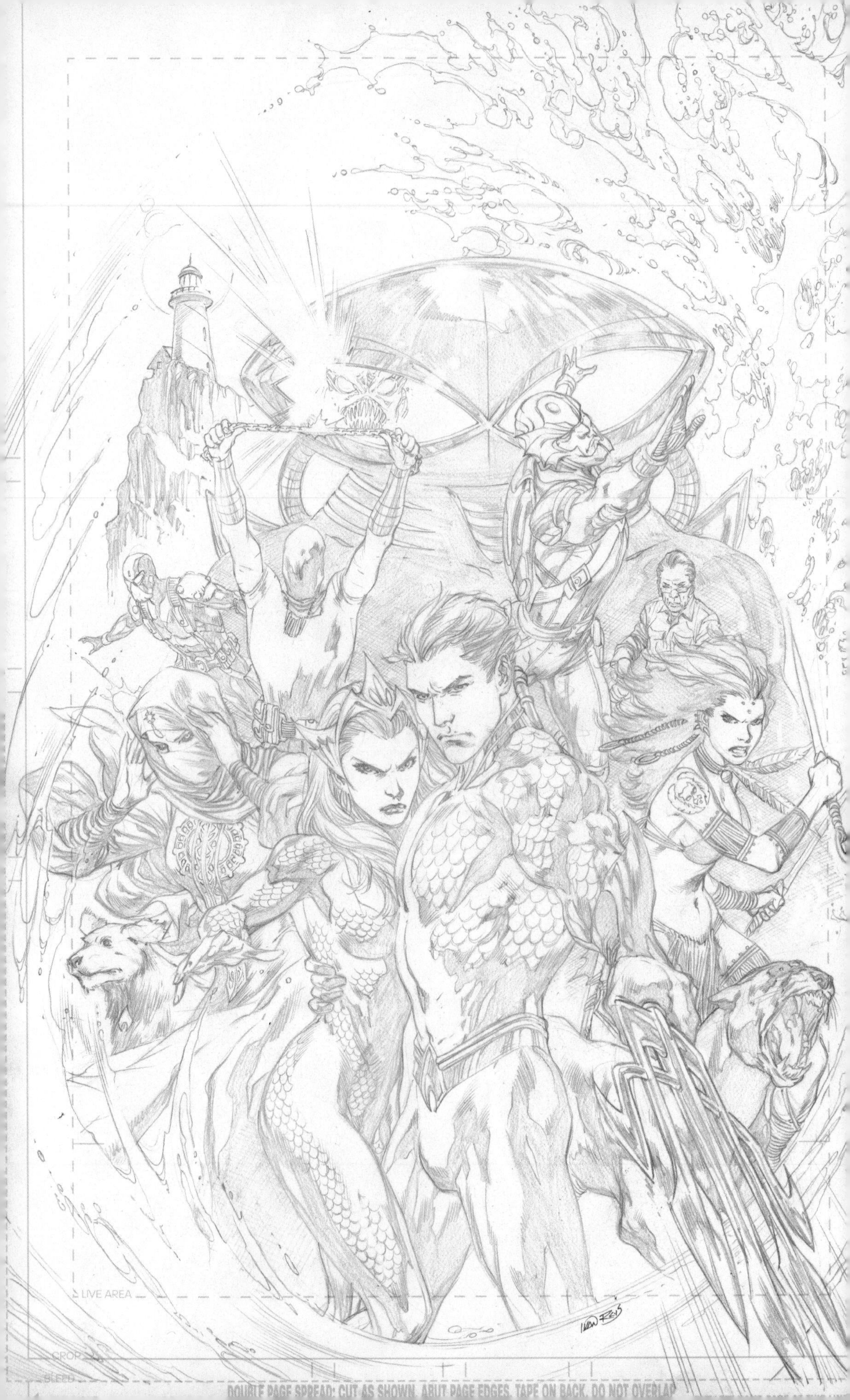
LIVE AREA
CROP
BLEED
DOUBLE PAGE SPREAD: CUT AS SHOWN. ABUT PAGE EDGES. TAPE ON BACK. DO NOT OVERLAP

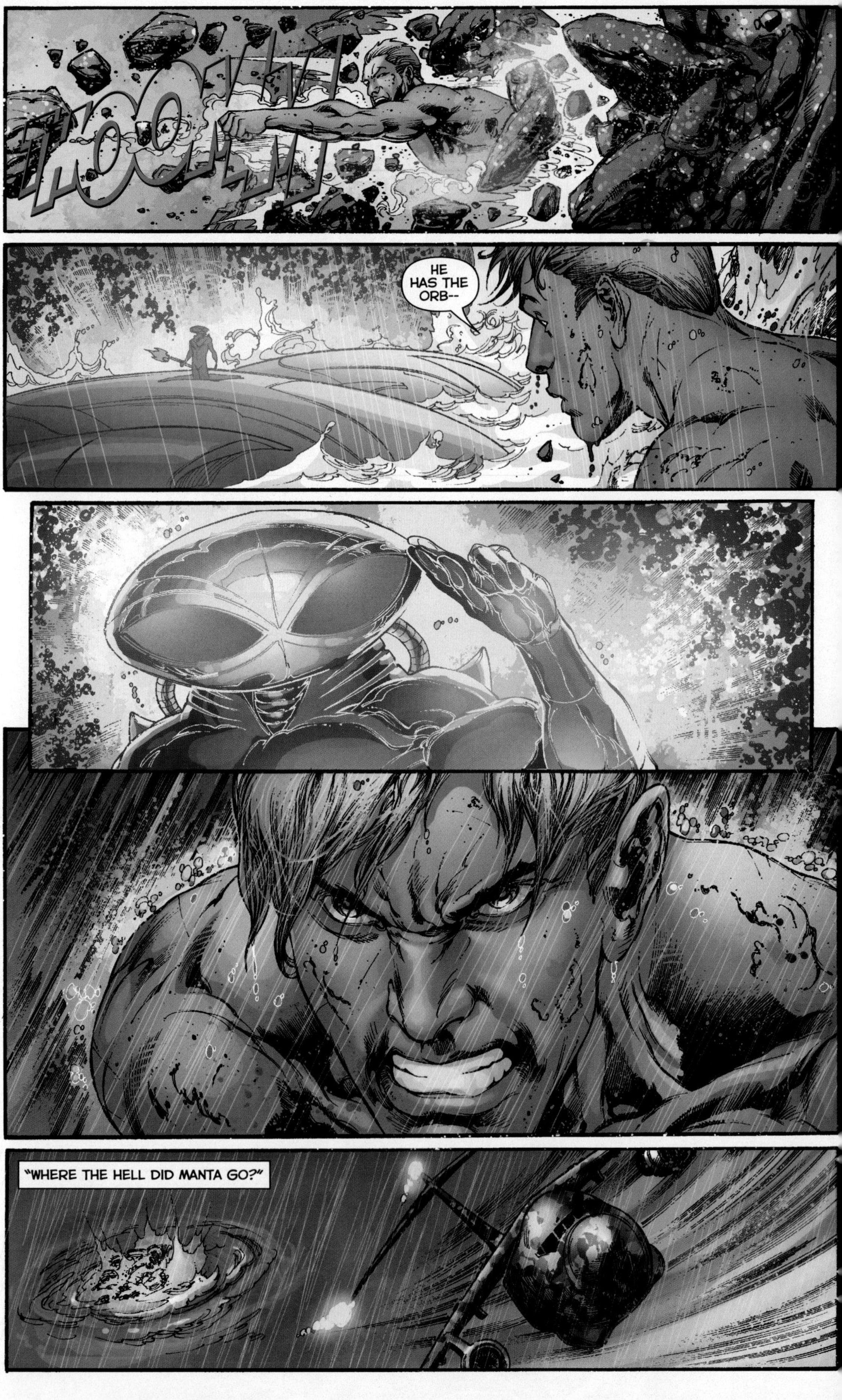
THOOM!
HE HAS THE ORB--
"WHERE THE HELL DID MANTA GO?"

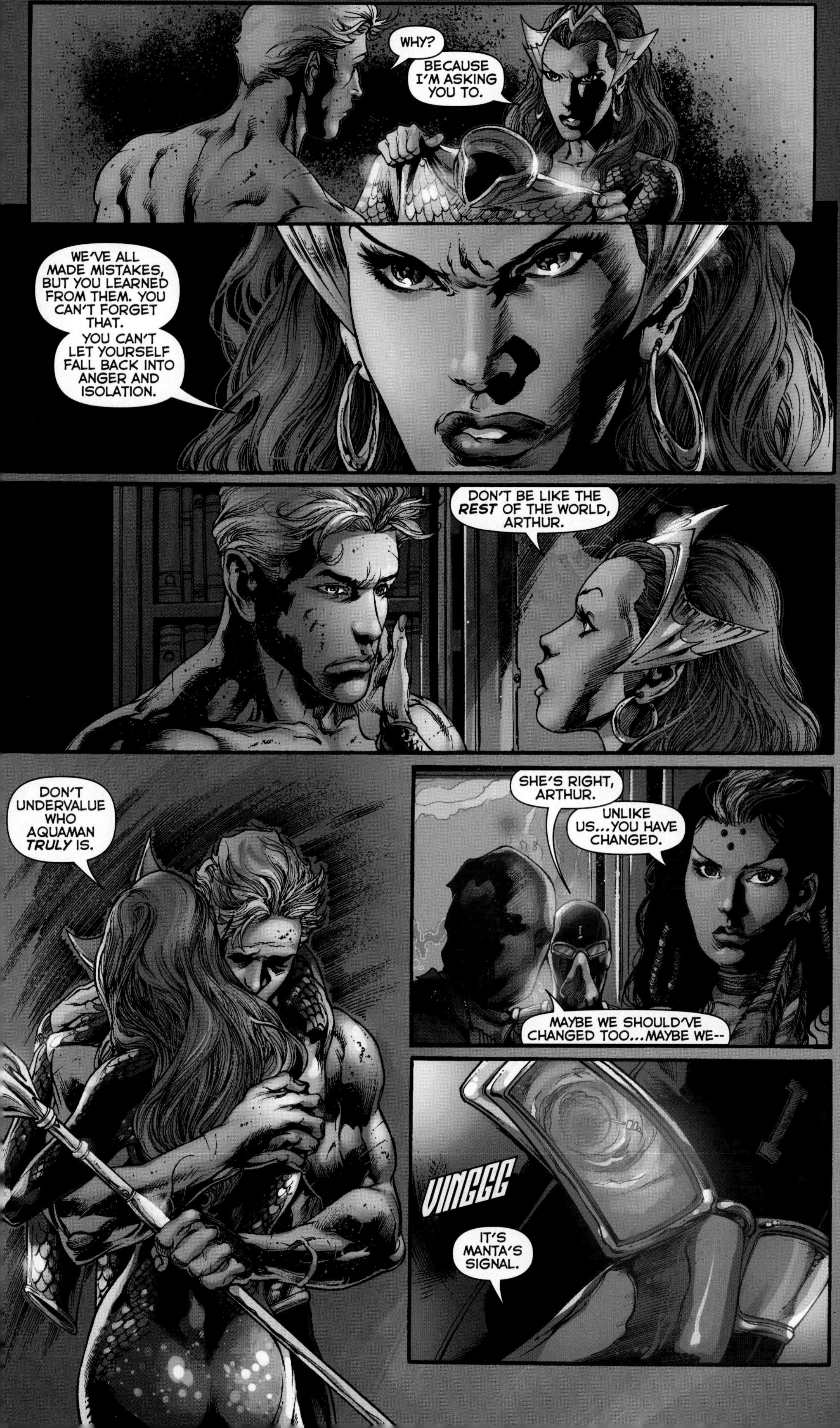
WHY?
BECAUSE I'M ASKING YOU TO.
WE'VE ALL MADE MISTAKES, BUT YOU LEARNED FROM THEM. YOU CAN'T FORGET THAT.
YOU CAN'T LET YOURSELF FALL BACK INTO ANGER AND ISOLATION.
DON'T BE LIKE THE *REST* OF THE WORLD, ARTHUR.
DON'T UNDERVALUE WHO AQUAMAN *TRULY* IS.
SHE'S RIGHT, ARTHUR.
UNLIKE US...YOU HAVE CHANGED.
MAYBE WE SHOULD'VE CHANGED TOO...MAYBE WE--
VINGGG
IT'S MANTA'S SIGNAL.

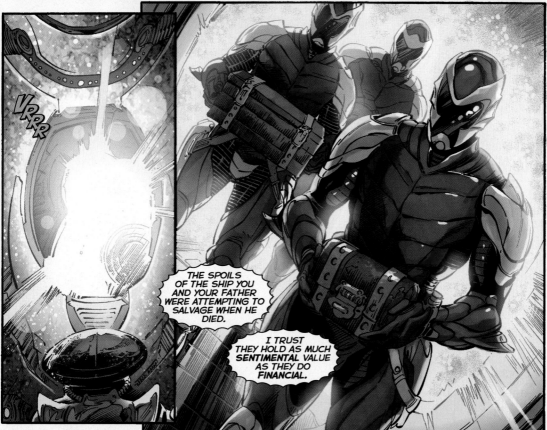

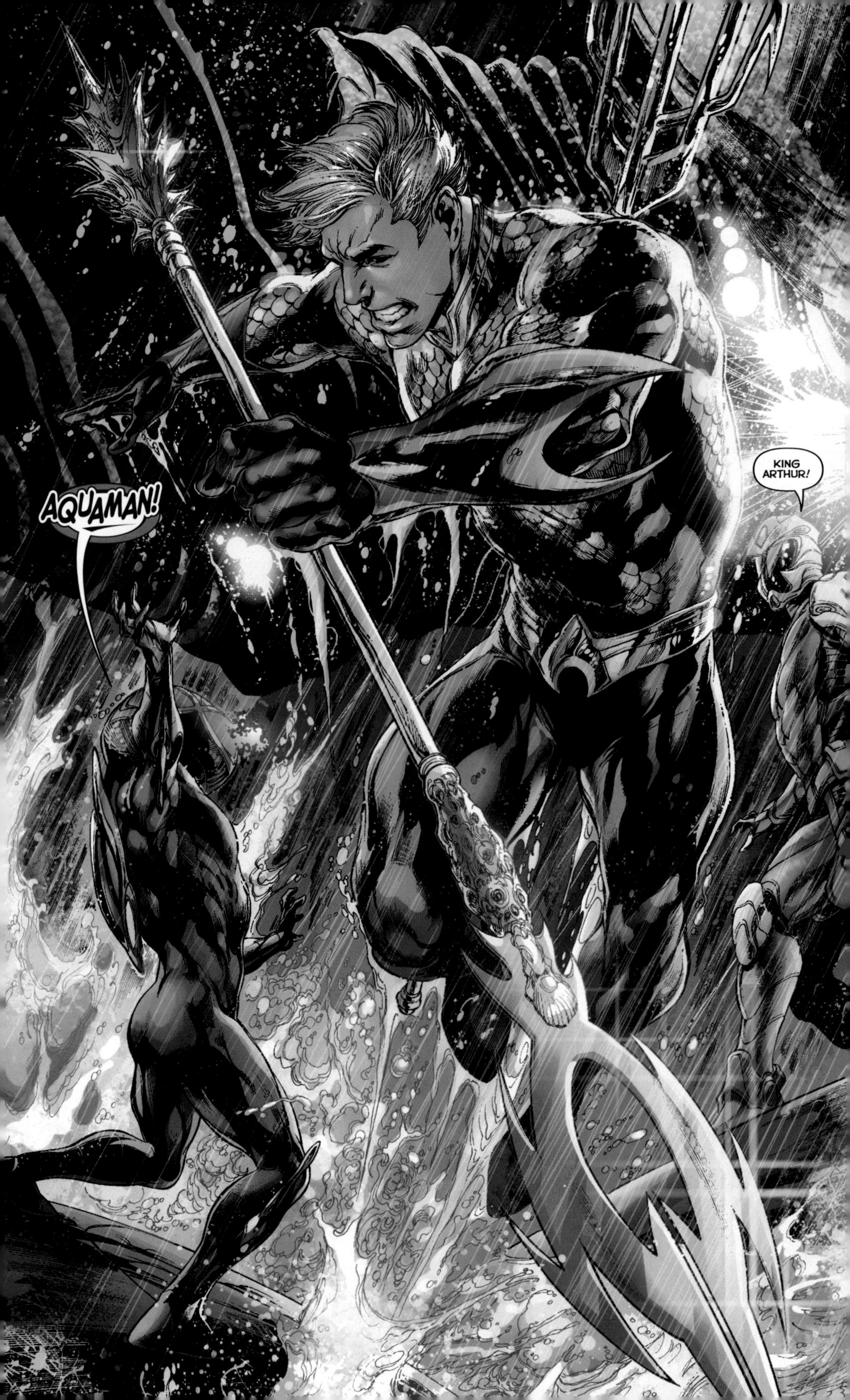
AQUAMAN!
KING ARTHUR!

Robot Chicken: DC Comics Special variant cover to AQUAMAN #12

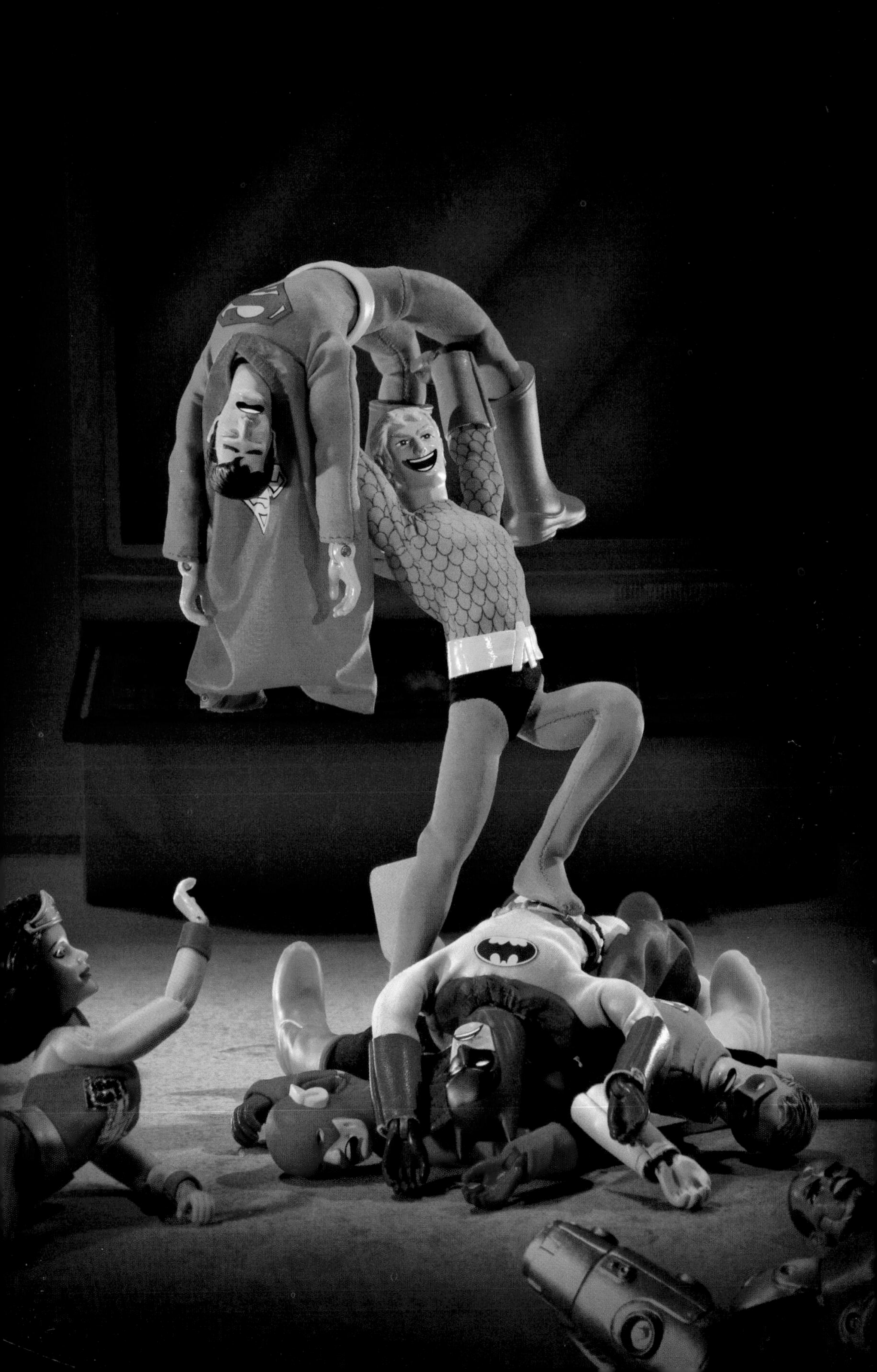

DC COMICS™

START AT THE BEGINNING!
JUSTICE LEAGUE
VOLUME 1: ORIGIN

AQUAMAN VOLUME 1: THE TRENCH

THE SAVAGE HAWKMAN VOLUME 1: DARKNESS RISING

GREEN ARROW VOLUME 1: THE MIDAS TOUCH

GEOFF **JOHNS** JIM **LEE** SCOTT **WILLIAMS**